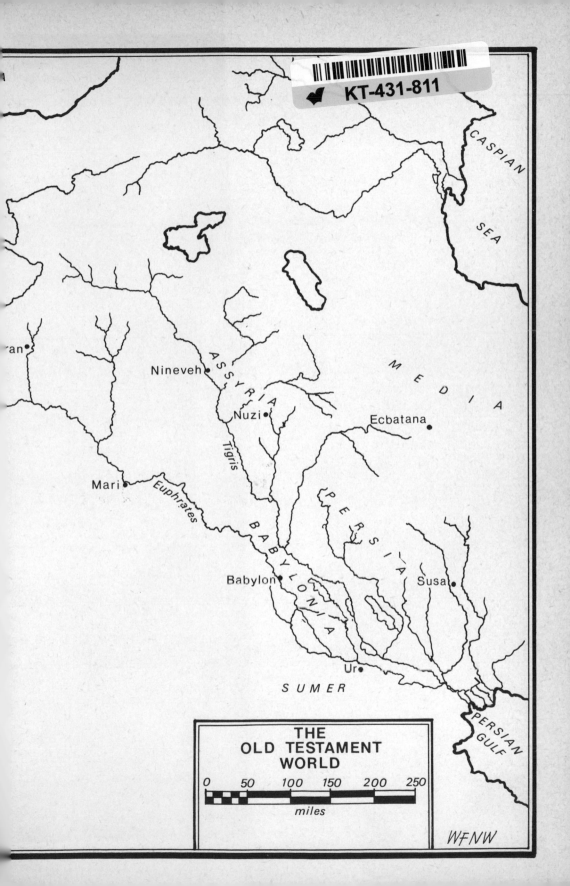

CASPIAN

SEA

Nineveh

ASSYRIA

MEDIA

Nuzi

Ecbatana

Tigris

Mari

Euphrates

BABYLONIA

PERSIA

Babylon

Susa

Ur

SUMER

PERSIAN GULF

THE OLD TESTAMENT WORLD

0   50   100   150   200   250

miles

WFNW

WHO'S WHO IN THE BIBLE

To the people of
St Mathew's, Brixton,
with deep gratitude

Who's Who
in
The Bible

Richard Coggins

B.T. Batsford Ltd
London

First published 1981
Reprinted 1982
Reprinted 1983
© Richard Coggins 1981
ISBN 0 7134 0144 3

Maps by Lt. Colonel W.F.N. Watson

Typeset by Tek-Art Ltd
London S.E.20
Printed in Great Britain by The Anchor Press Ltd
and bound by Wm Brendon & Son Ltd
both of Tiptree, Essex
for the publishers
B.T. Batsford Ltd,
4 Fitzhardinge Street,
London W1H 0AH

Contents

Acknowledgment

I wish to express my gratitude to my colleagues — too numerous to name individually — who have helped me in the gathering of information and the formation of judgements contained in this book; but the responsibility for the use to which I have put this help is, of course, entirely my own. I dedicate it to the people of St Matthew's Church, Brixton, in London, who have taught me a great deal about what it means to be part of the people of God in our day, so different from, and yet with such similarities to, the time of the Bible.

Introduction

"Of the making of many books there is no end" (Eccles.12:12). However true that may have been when those words were written, perhaps in the fourth or third century B.C., it is even more true in the twentieth century A.D. And it is astonishing how many of these books deal with one or other aspect of the Bible within whose pages Ecclesiastes is now to be found. (Surely to its author's wry amusement; for such a caustic critic of established religious belief to be part of the established canon is to see poacher turned game-keeper with a vengeance.) The first requirement of this introduction, therefore, is to justify yet another addition to the number of such books. This can best be done by explaining what it does and does not attempt to achieve.

As its title will already have revealed, its basic purpose is to give some indication of what may be known about the characters mentioned in the Bible. Not all of them, however: the majority of those referred to in its pages remain no more than names, concerning whom no other information is available to us, and such have not been included in an attempt to make a virtue out of completeness of coverage.

Secondly, this is not a re-telling of the scriptural account in different and almost certainly less vivid language. Rather, the concern is to assess what we may regard as reasonably probable in our knowledge of these characters. As a teacher of biblical studies, one is constantly asked: Is this a real-life figure? Are these stories simply pious imaginings? and so on. No generally agreed answer to questions of this kind is ever likely to be achieved, but an occasional progress report, on what scholars have been saying and how they are currently evaluating the evidence, may be useful. It is such a report that the present volume aims at presenting. The hope is that the reader will then turn, or return, to the biblical material, with a new kind of understanding open to him.

No apology is made, therefore, for the frequent note of question-ing and uncertainty which can be found in the pages that follow. If we are honest in our historical study of the Bible, we shall have to reckon with the fact that there are many areas where such doubt is the only appropriate response. Nor is it a matter for apology that the views here taken may be more sceptical than some scholars would feel to be necessary. (Certainly there is here no assumption made from the very outset that every word in the Bible is historically and geographically and scientifically reliable, so that the pages of the Bible come to be exempt from the normal use of our intellect.) Rather, the underlying assumption is that, if the Bible is a vehicle of faith, as for millions it is, it becomes the more essential to test, by every proper means available to us, the nature of the data it contains. It will be a matter for continuing dispute how far inaccuracies in matters of this kind reflect upon, or even undermine, belief in the inspiration of the Bible; what is certain is that questioning in these matters cannot be stilled.

One of the many difficulties experienced by those who come to the serious reading of the Bible for the first time arises from ignorance of the historical setting of the events described in the Bible. What follows, therefore, is a rapid sketch of the more important developments which relate to the biblical story; a diagrammatic outline will be found on p.14-18.

It is not possible to trace historical developments with dates accurate to within a decade, and cross-references to extra-biblical material, until the first millennium B.C., but the Old Testament enshrines many traditions which go back to a much earlier period. As presented in the books of Genesis, Exodus, Numbers, Joshua, and Judges, it appears as if they form one continuous story, but we need always to remember that this may be a misleading impression, owing more to the judgement of those who assembled the material in its final form than to accurately transmitted historical accounts. In particular, it is not clear whether the traditions relating to the 'patriarchs' (Abraham, Isaac and Jacob) originally concern the same group of people as those who took part in the exodus from Egypt.

With qualifications of this kind in mind, we may regard it as likely that the stories of the patriarchs originate from a period in the second millennium B.C., though no certain correlations with other known events from that period are possible. The stories of the patriarchs are not often referred to in the Old Testament outside the book of Genesis, but the deliverance from Egypt forms a constant theme in all parts of the Bible. The historicity of the departure of some of Israel's ancestors is not seriously in question; Moses is almost certainly to be linked with this event, which is commonly placed in the thirteenth century B.C.

There is as yet no agreement among scholars as to the circumstances of Israel's establishment in Canaan. Some are ready to accept as historical the picture given in the book of Joshua of a violent invasion; others think a more piecemeal process of absorption fits the archaeological evidence better; while others again think not so much of incursion from outside the land as of a kind of peasants' revolt of the lower classes against oppression. In any case the stories of Joshua and the judges, though they reflect this period when Israel was becoming a nation, have been stylised into regular foty-year periods, in the interests of a particular religious interpretation of Israel's past.

With the establishment of monarchy around 1000 B.C., we are on firmer historical ground. The books of Samuel are rich in material describing the exploits of particular individuals, and so many of the characters whose story is evaluated in this volume were active in the early monarchy, the time of Saul, David and Solomon. Saul's status and achievement are very ambiguous, but it is clear that David and Solomon ruled over a united monarchy which established the country as a state among states. The account given is still not history in the strict sense — both David and Solomon are credited with the conventional forty-year period of rule, like the judges; but much of the detail relating to their period of rule reflects a more down-to-earth assessment of events than the legendary or folkloristic stories dealing with earlier periods. The account of the intrigues relating to the succession to David (2 Sam.9-20; 1 Kings 1-2) is story-telling of a very high order.

After Solomon's death the kingdom was divided, never again to be reunited. The larger part retained the name 'Israel', but the story is told from a southern standpoint, and so it is the southern kingdom, Judah, and its capital, Jerusalem, which are the main focus of attention in the books of Kings and still more so in the later books of Chronicles, which deal with many of the same events from a slightly different theological standpoint. From the beginning of the ninth century reasonably precise dating of events becomes possible, and the year 853 B.C. provides the first relevant correlation from an extra-biblical source: the battle of Qarqar, fought in that year, is mentioned in Assyrian records, though ironically not in the Old Testament despite the participation of Ahab, king of Israel.

The eighth century saw the first in the series of great prophets whose oracles were collected, together with later additions and modifications, and formed into our 'books', and it was at that time that the greatest external threat to Israel developed with the rise of Assyrian power. (The development of prophetism and the external threat may have been related phenomena.) Israel's independent existence came to an end in 722 B.C., and Judah was reduced to vassal status. When the Assyrian Empire itself collapsed in the seventh century, there were hopes for a new period of independent Judahite power, but these were short-lived; the power gap was filled by Babylon under Nebuchadnezzar, who captured Jerusalem in 597 B.C. It has even proved possible to establish the precise date, 16 March. Continued disturbances in Judah led to a more drastic destruction of Jerusalem later in Nebuchadnezzar's reign; this time precision in dating is not possible, so that the fall of Jerusalem and the destruction of its temple may have taken place in 587 or 586 B.C.

These last years of the monarchy are fully documented, both within the Old Testament and by means of extra-biblical sources. For the following period, down to the second century B.C., our information is much more scanty. We know that some Judahites were exiled to Babylon and remained as a community there until the Babylonian Empire had in its turn given way to Persian rule. Under the Persians a measure of local autonomy was encouraged, and so the Jerusalem temple was rebuilt after encouragement from the prophets Haggai and Zechariah (c.520 B.C.). But after that the community in Jerusalem once again passes into obscurity, with occasional notices of their progress centring around religious and political leaders such as Ezra and Nehemiah. Even the most earth-shaking event of the period, the conquests of Alexander the Great (336-323 B.C.), which overthrew the Persian Empire, is passed over in silence by the Old Testament.

Our detailed knowledge begins again in the second century B.C. By that time the Jews formed a part of the Syrian Empire established by Alexander's successors with its capital at Antioch. The political and economic pressures experienced by that empire led to the attempt to bind it together more closely by a common religious policy. Such a move was unacceptable to some of the Jews, though others welcomed a closer degree of rapprochement with the surrounding Hellenistic world. But the literary evidence which has come down to us is sympathetic to those who resisted, notably the Hasmonaeans or Maccabees, who fought a war which lasted some twenty years beginning in 168 B.C., and were eventually able to claim independence. Unfortunately, the political manoeuvres involved in this struggle removed any claim on the part of the Hasmonaeans to be fighters for religious purity, and their later history is a sordid story of intrigues, both within the land and against the ever-increasing threat from Rome.

There is no biblical evidence bearing directly on the period between the late second century B.C. and the reign of Herod the Great (37-4 B.C.), but during that time Roman power in the area was established, with differing parts of the eastern Mediterranean being allowed differing measures of local autonomy. The traditions relating to Jesus' birth in Matthew and Luke date it before the death of Herod, which would mean that if they are reliable our conventional system of dating B.C./A.D. is erroneous; but it is impossible to work out the exact year of Jesus' birth. During his lifetime, however, the area of Judah was brought under direct Roman control and ruled by a series of prefects, of whom the most famous is Pontius Pilate. Further north, in Galilee, where Jesus exercised his ministry, another member of the Herod family was allowed a measure of independence. The Jews continued as resentful subjects of the Roman Empire until open rebellion broke out in A.D. 66. Jerusalem was captured and the temple destroyed in 70, and the final stages of the struggle were ended by 73.

The main geographical centre of the New Testament, however, has shifted from Palestine. Little is known of any Christian communities that may have existed there. Instead, the main witness of the New Testament writings is to the spread of Christianity among the other parts of the Mediterranean world. The preaching of the 'good news' or gospel was probably first undertaken among the many Jewish communities scattered through much of the eastern Roman Empire but, increasingly, Gentile sympathisers were accepted, and by the end of the first century A.D. Christian churches were established certainly as far west as Rome and probably even in Spain. The main agent in this remarkable development was Paul, but there is no doubt that the spread of the gospel owed much to many others whose names in most cases have not survived. This very fact means that the New Testament is much less involved than the Old in the political vicissitudes of the time, and we hear little or nothing in its pages of the great figures and events of the day.

*

This somewhat breathless introduction has been deliberately kept brief, both because many outline histories of Israel are available as well as full scholarly treatments, and also because it is hoped that entries in the main body of the book will for the most part be self-explanatory.

One concluding point must, however, be made. For a variety of reasons, scholarly study of the Bible during the last century has concentrated to an overwhelming extent on historical problems; and the result has been that, if the balance of probability has been against the historicity of a particular episode or individual character, either desperate attempts have been made to salvage some 'genuine' historical nucleus, or the conclusion has been reached that the Bible's authority and inspiration have in some way been damaged. To a considerable extent, the emphasis in this book is in line with this historical approach. But a welcome feature of more recent study has been the recognition of other proper types of approach. Stories in themselves may have much to teach us of different understandings of God and his dealings with man, regardless of the details of their historical accuracy; even genealogies could be used creatively as a kind of roll of honour, presenting the identity of the people of God in its extension through both time and space. History will undoubtedly continue to form an important part of biblical study; it must not be allowed to dominate all else. More specifically the negative historical judgements sometimes implied in the following pages should not be taken as having as their corollary the rejection of the value of the relevant biblical material.

The English translation used for this book is the Revised Standard Version. On occasions reference is made to the older King James or Authorised Version, or to other modern translations such as the New English Bible or the Good News Bible.

List of Abbreviations

The following abbreviations are used
for the books of the Bible

Genesis	Gen.
Exodus	Exod.
Leviticus	Lev.
Numbers	Num.
Deuteronomy	Deut.
Joshua	Josh.
Judges	Judg.
Ruth	Ruth
1 Samuel	1 Sam.
2 Samuel	2 Sam.
1 Kings	1 Kings
2 Kings	2 Kings
1 Chronicles	1 Chron.
2 Chronicles	2 Chron.
Ezra	Ezra
Nehemiah	Neh.
Esther	Esther
Job	Job
Psalms	Ps.
Proverbs	Prov.
Ecclesiastes	Eccles.
Song of Solomon	S. of Sol.
Isaiah	Isa.
Jeremiah	Jer.
Lamentations	Lam.
Ezekiel	Ezek.
Daniel	Dan.
Hosea	Hosea
Joel	Joel
Amos	Amos
Obadiah	Obad.
Jonah	Jonah
Micah	Micah
Nahum	Nahum
Habakkuk	Hab.
Zephaniah	Zeph.
Haggai	Hag.
Zechariah	Zech.
Malachi	Mal.

1 Esdras	1 Esd.
2 Esdras	2 Esd.
Tobit	Tob.
Judith	Judith
Wisdom	Wisd.
Ecclesiasticus	Ecclus.
Baruch	Bar.
The Song of Three Holy Children	Three Ch.
The History of Susanna	Sus.
Bel and the Dragon	Bel.
The Prayer of Manasses	Man.
1 Maccabees	1 Macc.
2 Maccabees	2 Macc.

*

Matthew	Matt.
Mark	Mark
Luke	Luke
John	John
Acts	Acts
Romans	Rom.
1 Corinthians	1 Cor.
2 Corinthians	2 Cor.
Galatians	Gal.
Ephesians	Eph.
Philippians	Phil.
Colossians	Col.
1 Thessalonians	1 Thess.
2 Thessalonians	2 Thess.
1 Timothy	1 Tim.
2 Timothy	2 Tim.
Titus	Titus
Philemon	Philemon
Hebrews	Heb.
James	James
1 Peter	1 Peter
2 Peter	2 Peter
1 John	1 John
2 John	2 John
3 John	3 John
Jude	Jude
Revelation	Rev.

CHRONOLOGICAL TABLE

DATE	ISRAEL	NEIGHBOURING POWERS	EGYPT
B.C.			
1800	The Patriarch		
1700	(Abraham, Isaac Jacob), sometime during the second millennium B.C.	Babylonian Power c. 1700 (Hammurabi)	
1600			
1500			
1400		Hittite Empire	
1300			XIXth Dynasty 1310-1200
1200	Exodus c. 1250, Moses Entry into Canaan c. 1200 Joshua		Rameses II 1290-1224
1100	Judges Period Saul, Samuel	Rise of Philistine Power	
1000	David Solomon		

DATE	JUDAH	ISRAEL	NEIGHBOURING POWERS		
			Egypt	*Assyria*	*Damascus*
	Rehoboam 922-915	Jeroboam I 922-901		Revival of Assyrian Power	
900	Abijam 915-913 Asa 913-873	Nadab 901-900 Baasha 900-877 Elah 877-876 Zimri 876	XXIInd Dynasty 935-725 Shishak 935-914		Ben-hadad I ?900-860

14

Jehoshaphat 873-849

Omri 876-869
Elijah
Ahab 869-850
Ahaziah 850-849
Joram 849-842
Jehu 842-815
Jehoahaz 815-901
Jehoash 801-786
Jeroboam II
786-746

Shalmaneser III
859-824

Ben-hadad II
?860-843

Hazael 843-796

800

Jehoram 849-842
Ahaziah 842
Athaliah 842-837 Elishah
Joash 837-800
Amaziah 800-783
Azariah (Uzziah)
783-742

Amos
Hosea

Zechariah 746-745
Shallum 745
Menahem 745-738
Pekahiah 738-737
Pekah 737-732

Tiglath-Pileser III
745-727

Rezin c. 740-732
Fall of Damascus 732

Ben-hadad III
?796-770

Jotham 742-735

Isaiah
(active
c. 742-
700)

Ahaz 735-715

Micah

Hoshea 732-724

Fall of Samria 721

Shalmaneser V
727-722
Sargon II 722-705
Sennacherib 705-681

Hezekiah 715-687
Invasion of Judah 701
Manasseh 687-642

Esar-haddon 681-669
Ashur-bani-pal 669-
633?

XXVIth Dynasty

700

Amon 642-640
Josiah 640-609

Zephaniah
Jeremiah (active
626-c. 580)

Babylon

Jehoahaz 609
Jehoiakem 609-
598

Nahum
Habakkuk

Fall of Nineveh 612

Necho II 609-593

Nebuchadnezzar
605-562

15

NEIGHBOURING POWERS

DATE	JUDAH	Egypt	Babylon	Persia
600	Jehoiachin 598-597 (deported)			
	Jerusalem captured 597; First Deportation			
	Zedekiah 597-587/6	Apries (Hophra) 588-569		
	Fall of Jerusalem 587/6. Temple Destroyed; Second Deportation			
	The Exile Ezekiel			
			'Evil-Merodach' 562-560	
	Governship of 'Deutero-Isaiah'		Fall of Babylon 539	Cyrus 550-530
	Zerubbabel 520			
	Temple rebuilt 520-515			
	Haggai			
	Zechariah			
	'Malachi'			
500				Darius I 522-486
				Xerxes 486-465
	Governorship of Nehemiah			Artaxerxes 465-424
	445-433			Darius II 423-414
	432-?			
	Sanballat I, Governor of Samaria			
400	Ezra's Mission 398 (or 458)			Artaxerxes II 404-358
				Darius III 336-330

	Greece
Greece	Alexander the Great (336-323)

DATE	JUDAH	Ptolemies	Seleucids
300	Ptolemies rule Palestine	*Ptolemies*	*Seleucids*
		Ptolemy II Philadelphus 285-246	Seleucus I 312-281
		Ptolemy III Euergetes 246-221	Antiochus II 261-247
		Ptolemy IV Philopator 221-203	Antiochus III 223-187
		Ptolemy V Epiphanes 203-181	

	Jewish / Palestine	Ptolemies	Seleucids
			Seleucus IV 187-175
			Antiochus IV Epiphanes 175-163
			Antiochus V Eupator 163-162
			Demetrius I Esoter 161-151
			Alexander Balas 152-145
			Demetrius II Nicator 146-139, 129-125
			Antiochus VI Epiphanes 145-142 (Trypho 142-138)
		Ptolemy VI Philometor 180-146	Antiochus VII Sidetes 139-128
200	Seleucids rule Palestine		
	Profanation of the Temple 167-(?168)		
	Maccabaean Revolt		
	Book of Daniel 167/4		
	Rededication of the Temple 164 (?165)		
	? Qumran Sect established		
	Hasmonaean Rulers		
	Judas Maccabaeus 166-160		
	Jonathan 160-142		
	Jewish Independence granted 142	Ptolemy VIII Euergetes 146-117	
	Simon 142-134		
100	Herod the Great 37-4 B.C.		

17

ROMAN EMPRERORS	THE ROMAN EMPIRE & DEPENDENCIES	JUDAH
Augustus 27 B.C. - A.D. 14	Aretas, Nabataean king (9 B.C. - A.D. 39)	Birth of Jesus ?c.5 B.C.
	Herod Antipas, tetrarch of Galilee (4 B.C.-39 A.D.)	Archelaus (4 B.C.–A.D.6)
	Philip, ruler of 'Ituraea & Trachonitis' (4 B.C. - A.D. 34)	*Roman Prefects*
Tiberius 14-37		Pontius Pilate 26-36
	Quirinius, legate of Syria (6)	Felix 52-60
Claudius 41-54	Herod Agrippa I, king (41-44)	Porcius Festus 60-62
	Herod Agrippa II (50-c. 100)	*High Priests*
Nero 54-68	Gallio, Proconsul of Achaia (51-52)	Annas 6-15
		Caiaphas ?18-36
Demitian 81-96		

THE CHRISTIAN CHURCH

Ministry and Death of Jesus ? c. 27-30
Conversion of Paul ? 33
Martyrdom of James son of Zebedee c. 43
Pauline Epistles c. 50-60
Martyrdom of James the brother of Jesus c. 62
?Martyrdom of Peter and Paul, Rome 64
Fall of Jerusalem 70
Composition of Gospels c. 70-90

The Old Testament

AARON is mentioned more than three hundred times in the Old Testament, and yet he remains a curiously shadowy figure. The great majority of references are simply to Aaron as the representative priestly figure, carrying out the Lord's requirements. When Israel was established in the land of Canaan, it became customary to trace back the pattern of her worship to the very beginning of her history, and this is done by the repeated implication that Aaron himself, the 'founder' of Israel's worship, had established the different ritual arrangements. This is very markedly the case in Leviticus and Numbers.

In two episodes Aaron seems to have a more distinctive role. In Exod. 4:14 he is called the 'Levite', and this seems in imply a particular function, rather than be a family or clan name. More specifically, in Exod.32 he plays a prominent and somewhat disreputable part in the story of the golden calf. This story is remarkably similar in many of its details to a quite separate incident — the setting up of the golden calves in the northern kingdom of Israel (1 Kings 12:28-32) — and it looks as if the tradition may have been handed down in circles which opposed Aaron's claim to be the only true priesthood.

This gives a clue to the special significance of many of the references to Aaron. At a later date, there were many disputes concerning true priesthood, and in the end it was those who could establish a genealogy going back to Aaron such as Ezra (Ezra 7:5) that came to be regarded as valid priests.

ABDON is described in Judg. 12:13-15 as one of the judges of Israel, but nothing is known of him save for this brief note. He and the other 'minor judges' appear to have been local leaders before Israel became a kingdom, perhaps in the eleventh century B.C.

ABEL, according to the story in Gen. 4, was Adam's second son. The account of his rivalry with Cain his brother symbolises the ancient rivalry between the nomad and the settler, the shepherd and the farmer. His death has also been seen in both Jewish and Christian tradition as symbolic of the innocent martyr (Matt. 23:35). His name means 'vanity', and this may be a deliberate reference to the transitory character of his, and perhaps of all, human existence.

21

ABIATHAR is frequently mentioned in 1 and 2 Samuel as one of the two leading priests in the royal service (1 Kings 4:4 is the last such reference). Whereas his colleague, Zadok, may not have been of Israelite origin, Abiathar was a descendant of Eli, the former priest of Shiloh, and accompanied David in his time as an outlaw before he became king. His particular concern was apparently with the ephod, here described as a cult-object used in divination (1 Sam. 23:6f.; 30:7). He remained loyal to David during Absalom's rebellion (2 Sam. 16-19), but eventually fell into disfavour, since he backed Adonijah instead of Solomon as successor to David, and was exiled. Others who had not supported Solomon were killed, but his early loyalty to David probably saved his life (1 Kings 2:26). He is mentioned once in the New Testament (Mark 2:26), but the reference is erroneous, because Abiathar was not the priest at the time of the incident referred to.

ABIGAIL is the heroine of the vivid tale in 1 Sam. 25, in which her beauty and her good sense each play a major role in saving her family from the revenge of David, pictured as a freebooter living on the fringe of society. Her wisdom is in contrast to the arrogance of her first husband Nabal (whose name means 'stupid'); she became one of David's wives, but her children were not involved in the later intrigues concerning the succession to the throne.

ABIHU (who is always mentioned in conjunction with his brother Nadab) was the second son of Aaron the brother of Moses, but no priestly line descended from Abihu or Nadab (Num. 3:4). Two traditions relate to the brothers: a favourable one which speaks of their being privileged to draw near to God with the other leaders of the people (Exod. 24), and an unfavourable one which describes their death for an unspecified ritual offence (Lev. 10:1-8).

ABIJAH There are nine different Old Testament characters called Abijah; since it meant 'The Lord is my father' it was understandably a popular name. Of these nine, some are known only from their occurrence in lists of names; one is also known as Abijam (q.v.). Of the rest, one is a son of the prophet Samuel, condemned for his wickedness (1 Sam. 8:2), another was a son of Jeroboam, the first king of the northern kingdom of Israel, who died without succeeding his father, in accordance with the prophetic word spoken by Ahijah (1 Kings 14:1-18).

ABIJAM, also called Abijah, was the second King of Judah after its division from Israel, probably late in the tenth century, when the two countries were engaged in border warfare to establish their respective positions (2 Kings 15:7). 2 Kings condemns his conduct; the account in 2 Chron. 13 takes a more favourable view, though the details of its historicity are suspect.

ABIMELECH is described in Gen. 20 and 26 as 'king of Gerar', in south-west Palestine. (The reference to the Philistines in 26:1 is anachronistic, for they only arrived in Palestine at a later date.) The two chapters are different versions of the same story; in each case Abimelech (of whom nothing else is known) is deceived into thinking that the patriarch's wife is his sister.

ABIMELECH Another Abimelech plays an important role in one of the earliest attempts to establish kingship among the Hebrews. (The name means 'My (divine) father is king'.) Judg. 9 describes his attempt to establish himself as ruler over what appears to have been a mixed Hebrew-Cananite group based on Shechem in central Palestine. The attempt was premature and ended in failure, and thus supports the view of the biblical editors that no kingship before that of David could be legitimate.

ABINADAB Several characters called Abinadab appear at the time of Saul and David, each of whom had a member of his family with this name (1 Sam. 31:2; 16:8; another Abinadab looked after the Ark on its return from the Philistines (1 Sam. 7:1).

ABIRAM: see *Dathan*.

ABISHAG was the beautiful girl from Shunem who twice played a significant role in the involved account of Solomon's succession to David (1 Kings 1-2). First, David's failure to have intercourse with her showed his loss of vitality and hence the need for a successor; secondly, Adonijah, Solomon's rival, sought her as his wife, and this was interpreted by Solomon as a bid for the throne.

ABISHAI the son of Zeruiah first appears as one of David's followers during his time of estrangement from Saul (1 Sam. 26:6-9), and the role in which he is presented in that incident, where he advocates killing Saul, typifies his behaviour. He kills Saul's general Abner (2 Sam. 3:30), and urges David to let him kill Shimi, another opponent (2 Sam. 16:9). His mother Zeruiah was probably David's sister, and Abishai seems to have formed part of a kind of family bodyguard, along with his brother Joab who shared his violent characteristics. Nothing is said of Abishai's ultimate fate.

23

ABNER was related to Saul, probably as first cousin (1 Sam. 14:50f.). Whilst Saul was alive he seems to have been the strong man behind the throne and after Saul was killed Abner attempted to maintain his dynasty as rulers over Israel. During Saul's lifetime the references to him are almost incidental: he explained to Saul the identity of David after the killing of Goliath (1 Sam. 17:55), and he acted as Saul's bodyguard on campaign (1 Sam. 26:5-15), but it is after Saul's death that Abner's role becomes important. 2 Sam. 2-3 are largely given over to his fate: how he established Saul's son Ishbosheth as king, killed Asahel the brother of Joab and Abishai and thereby involved himself in a family blood-feud, and was consequently killed when he tried to ally himself with David. In the context this is pictured as illustrating the divine support of David — all his potential enemies are removed without David himself being to blame. Indeed the story of Abner ends with a fragmentary lament over him attributed to David (2 Sam. 3:33f.).

ABRAHAM is the dominant figure in the stories of Gen. 11-25, and is dominant also in the later reflection of both Jews and Christians (and indeed Muslims) as being a founder-figure of their religion. His name is found in two forms: Abram and Abraham. The first means 'My father is exalted'; the exact meaning of the second is uncertain.

The extent to which the stories of Abraham have a basis in history is much disputed. Modern critical study of the historical background of Genesis has gone through three main phases. At first, scholars were inclined to dismiss the whole account of Abraham as unhistorical, perhaps enshrining the folk-memory of various later groups of people. Then extensive archaeological excavations at different Near-Eastern sites, such as Mari on the River Euphrates and Nuzi on the Tigris, led to the suggestion that the movements of Abraham described in Gen. 12-13 fit into what can be known of ethnic movements in the early second millennium B.C. It has also been claimed that the detailed arrangements for the succession to Abraham such as allowing a child born to a concubine to be the heir (Gen. 16:1-6) and the later revocation of such rights (Gen. 21:1-21) find a parallel in other texts from the second millennium texts and not in Israel's own later history.

The third phase of study is once again more cautious. Not all of the alleged parallels seem to be valid, and too often ancient texts have been combed to find some detail similar to a biblical incident without recognition of the larger context, which may give a very different picture. The wisest course, therefore, seems to be to recognise that the story of Abraham almost certainly includes ancient features, but to accept that it is not easy to decide which they are, or to map out a precise historical background against which they should be set. Some details, such as Abraham's great age, and the birth of his first-born son when he was nearly a hundred years old, clearly reflect later elaboration and cannot be taken as simple statements of fact.

The place of Abraham's origin is traditionally 'Ur of the Chaldees' (Gen. 11:31). The city of Ur, on the lower Euphrates, in modern Iraq, was an important city in the early second millennium B.C.; but to describe it as 'of the Chaldees' (i.e. Babylonians) is misleading, and there is no evidence to suppose that any ancestors of later Israel came from that area. By contrast, the links with Harran, much further north and a staging post in Abraham's migration (Gen. 12:5), are stronger and recur in the story of Jacob (Gen. 28:10).

A further difficulty arises from our uncertainty whether Abraham is to be understood as leading a semi-nomadic existence, wandering from place to place, or whether he should be associated with one or other of the various settlements mentioned in his story, such as Shechem (Gen. 12:6), or Beersheba (Gen. 22:19). The only chapter which appears as if might be helpful in supplying a historical context for Abraham is Gen. 14; unfortunately none of the figures there mentioned can be identified, and the usual modern opinion is that this is a late story with little independent historical value.

It seems, therefore, that the likelihood of establishing any reliable historical nucleus for Abraham is remote. We need not doubt that various of the traditions which have grown up around him are ancient, and that they originated some time in the second millennium B.C., but greater certainty is unattainable. The stories were handed down for perhaps a thousand years before being committed to writing, and were used as the vehicle of Israel's faith in God's promise to the fathers. As such they will have been elaborated by later understanding, and what they tell us of religious ideas may well be more important than the uncertainties of historical reconstruction.

References to Abraham in the remainder of the Old Testament are surprisingly few, though the Lord is often referred to as 'the God of Abraham'. But toward the end of the Old Testament period there is evidence of increasing interest in the great figures of the people's past, which is carried on in the Apocrypha and reaches a climax in the New Testament. Both for the fourth Gospel and for Paul, Abraham was clearly a figure of dominating importance, the one to whom God's promises had first been made. Paul is thus able to illustrate his great theme of faith by reference to Abraham, in

25

the epistle to the Romans, as does also James, with a somewhat different understanding of faith. Thus in both Jewish and Christian tradition Abraham is pre-eminently the example of faith, summed up supremely in the haunting and never fully explained story of the sacrifice of Isaac (Gen. 22).

ABSALOM, son of David, played an ill-fated part in the story of the succession to his father. It is a vivid picture of what would nowadays be called a 'love-hate' relationship. The story begins with Absalom killing his half-brother Amnon in revenge for his raping Absalom's sister (2 Sam. 13:20-34). He fled for fear of David's possible reaction, and even when summoned back to Jerusalem it was two years before a formal reconciliation took place (2 Sam. 14:28). Eventually Absalom rebelled and attempted to set himself up as king in David's place, and 2 Sam. 15-18 give a dramatic account of his rebellion and its consequences. It is clear that David's throne was in great danger, but his superior organisation prevailed, and Absalom was killed — against David's express orders (2 Sam. 18:9-15). The account ends with a broken-hearted David mourning the death of his rebellious son who had driven him away from Jerusalem and nearly cost him his throne (2 Sam. 18:33). For drama and psychological insight it is one of the most remarkable episodes in the Old Testament.

ACHAN is a figure of whom little is known historically: he is the central character in one story, which is told to illustrate a theological point. Josh. 7 tells how, after the capture of Jericho, Achan hid some of the spoil, and when his offence was discovered by casting lost, he and all his family were stoned to death, all being held corporately responsible. It has been suggested that Achan is not a historical character at all, but that the name is an explanation of a place-name of some geographical feature.

ACHISH was the ruler of Gath, one of the five chief Philistine cities, with whom David took refuge while a fugitive from Saul (1 Sam. 21-29). He himself wished to involve David in the fight against Saul, but the other Philistine leaders suspected David's loyalty and refused to accept his presence. David was thus spared a painful choice, and the incident was seen as another sign of the divine favour working on his behalf (1 Sam. 29:1-11).

ADAM is the Hebrew word for 'man' — man in general, as against a particular individual — and in the stories in Gen. 1-5 it is not always easy to tell when the word is being used to describe newly-created humankind, and when the reference is to the particular individual. Adam as an individual is the Hebrew equivalent to the mythical 'first man', stories about whom are found in many cultures.

After the Genesis accounts, most other biblical references to Adam occur in genealogies, but in the New Testament Paul in particular developed a theme, found also in Jewish writings of the period, of Adam as typifying man in his limitation, the means by which sin and wrong-doing entered into the world. Paul develops this idea by a comparison and contrast with the figure of Christ whom he regards as the last or new Adam (Rom. 5; 1 Cor. 15).

ADONI-BEZEK is described in Judg. 1 as a king of Jerusalem who was captured and mutilated by the invading Israelites. He is probably identical with Adoni-zedek, also a king of Jerusalem, mentioned in Josh. 10. The date is uncertain but may be around 1200 B.C.

ADONIJAH, a son of David, was one of those involved in the struggle to succeed his father as king. Adonijah attempted to secure his position by a *coup d'état* (1 Kings 1), but the supporters of his half-brother Solomon proved more adroit in gaining the support of the senile David. Adonijah attempted after David's death to be allowed to marry his father's former concubine Abishag, and this was regarded by Solomon as implying a plot which justified him in having Adonijah killed (1 Kings 2:13-25).

ADONIRAM, whose name is also found in the form Adoram, was in charge of forced labour from the time of David, through Solomon's reign and until the beginning of that of his successor Rehoboam. His position at a time of great building activity — for example Solomon's palace and temple — was an important one, but one which aroused great hostility and led to his being stoned to death (1 Kings 12:18).

ADONI-ZEDEK.
See *Adoni-bezek*.

ADORAM.
See *Adoniram*.

AGAG was a ruler of the Amalekites, a nomadic group traditionally hostile to Israel, at the time of Saul (c. eleventh century B.C.). The war against him was to be one of complete annihilation — what is sometimes called 'holy war', waged against a people utterly unacceptable to Israel's God — and his death is described in 1 Sam. 15:32f. in gruesome terms.

📖 **AHAB** is the earliest king of Israel to be mentioned in non-biblical sources apparently contemporary with the events described. He is referred to in Assyrian records as having made a substantial contribution to the anti-Assyrian coalition at the battle of Qarqar, in modern Syria, in 853 B.C. In the Old Testament he is best known as the opponent of the prophet Elijah (1 Kings 17-21). For the most part he is pictured as dominated by his Tyrian wife Jezebel, but both the Assyrian record and isolated notes in the Old Testament show that in fact he may have been a strong and effective king. He played a major part in establishing Samaria as the capital of the country. Even in religious matters it is by no means clear that his policy was so far from true Israelite worship as a cursory reading of the Elijah stories might suggest. Nevertheless, he came to be regarded later as the typical wicked king (2 Kings 21:3).

📖 **AHASUERUS**, the Persion king, is better known by the Greek form of his name, Xerxes (q.v.).

📖 **AHAZ** was king of Judah at the time when the Assyrian Empire was extending its power into Syria and Palestine (c. 730 B.C.). He is condemned in the Old Testament for his apostasy (2 Kings 16; Isa. 7), but modern readers might be inclined to feel that he had little freedom of choice in his policy; to accept Assyria's overlordship meant the acceptance also of Assyrian gods. The particular event associated with his reign was the attempt of his northern neighbours, Pekah of Israel and Rezin of Damascus, to form a coalition against the Assyrians; when Ahaz refused to join they threatened to overthrow him and establish their own puppet in Jerusalem (Isa. 7:1-9). Isaiah agreed that Ahaz was right in not joining the coalition, but he maintained that he should have turned to God for help instead of calling in the Assyrians, to whom he remained loyal for the remainder of his reign. These events took place c. 735-732 B.C., but the exact dates of his reign cannot be worked out, as it appears that there may have been some co-regencies — sons associated with their father's rule — at this period.

📖 **AHAZIAH** is the name of two kings almost contemporary with each other. One was the son of Ahab who reigned briefly in the northern kingdom of Israel about 850 B.C., and the other was a king of Judah who ruled a little later. Ahaziah of Israel is condemned by Elijah for relying on foreign gods, and his death follows (2 Kings 1); Ahaziah of Judah, who was a cousin of his namesake, paid a fatal visit to the northern kingdom and was killed in Jehu's *coup d'état* there (2 Kings 9).

AHIJAH the prophet from Shiloh is the most prominent of several Old Testament characters of that name. He played a significant part in the division of the kingdom after the death of Solomon. He is pictured as first encouraging and then condemning the first northern ruler, Jeroboam (1 Kings 11 and 14). The stories reflect the important role of prophets in establishing and over-throwing kings in Israel, and may also indicate a measure of hostility between the old sanctuary of Shiloh and the new southern capital of Jerusalem. Perhaps Jeroboam's failure to re-establish Shiloh accounted for Ahijah's change of attitude to him.

AHIKAR is found in the book of Tobit as a historical character, nephew of Tobit himself and a high official in the Assyrian Empire, but the name usually refers to a collection of wisdom sayings, possibly of Asssyrian origin and very widely disseminated in the ancient world and used as a source by the author of Tobit. There may have been an historical character of this name, but essentially he was regarded as a legendary figure of wisdom.

AHIMAAZ was the son of David's priest Zadok. He played a vital role on two occasions in helping to put down Absalom's rebellion, first as a spy in the enemy camp, then as the bearer of the news of victory (2 Sam. 17-18).

AHIMELECH was a priest at Nob (the location of which is unknown) during the reign of Saul. His friendly reception of David (1 Sam. 21) led to the slaughter of all the priests of Nob by the suspicious Saul. Only Ahimelech's son Abiathar escaped and survived to become one of David's priests.

AHITHOPHEL, the counsellor of David, appears to represent an early example of what we should regard as a leading civil servant. His shrewdness was proverbial, and his defection to David's enemies regarded as potentially disastrous. He carried his own principles to their logical conclusion; when his counsel was not accepted, he saw the hopelessness of the situation and committed suicide — an action which is recorded with no trace of moral censure (2 Sam. 15-17).

ALCIMUS played an important part in the second stage of the revolt of the Hasmonaean family against Syrian rule, as described in 1 Macc. 7-9. One of the claimants to the high-priestly office, he is regarded by the author of 1 Maccabees as a 'godless renegade', but other groups in Israel were more sympathetic to his

29

policy of co-operation with the authorities. 1 Maccabees regards the stroke which led to his death as a clear sign of divine displeasure (1 Macc. 9:55f.).

ALEXANDER the Great is on any showing one of the most remarkable leaders the world has ever known, and it is a continuing mystery why the Old Testament, some parts of which were written after his reign (336-323 B.C.), makes no mention of him. There is a veiled allusion to him in Dan. 11, which sets out the history of the time as if it were a prophecy of the future, and 1 Maccabees takes his reign as its starting-point (1:1). Elsewhere the lack of reference only serves to remind us that the Old Testament writers only mentioned foreign powers when their action was seen as indicative of God's dealings with his own people; as far as the Jews were concerned the transition from Persian rule to that of Alexander apparently passed relatively smoothly.

ALEXANDER BALAS, known also as Epiphanes, was one of the claimants to the Syrian throne in the troubled period 152-143 B.C., described in 1 Macc. 10-11. The divided nature of Syrian power played an important part in enabling the Jews to gain their independence.

AMASA played an important role in the intrigues against David described in 2 Sam. 17-20. He was the general of the rebels under Absalom, but despite this he was pardoned after his defeat and put in charge of David's own forces — a development which led to his death at the hands of the jealous Joab. 'Amasai' of 1 Chron. 12:18 is probably a variant form of the same name.

AMAZIAH was king of Judah in the early ninth century B.C., the exact dates not being recoverable (2 Kings 14). During his reign Judah seems to have been little more than a vassal of the more powerful northern kingdom of Israel.

AMNON, son of David, is known only for his rape of his half-sister Tamar (2 Sam. 13), which led to his own death at the hand of his brother Absalom, and is presented as a major cause of the bitter struggles within the royal family.

AMON ruled briefly over Judah (642-640 B.C.) at a time when the decline of Assyrian power was leading to renewed hope for the country's independence. His murder was probably due to differing views of the political situation thus caused (2 Kings 2:18-26).

AMOS was the first of the prophets whose words have been collected into a book of their own. He was the heir to a long tradition, including figures such as Samuel and Elijah, but never before had such a separate collection been made. Perhaps the fact that he prophesied doom on the whole nation of Israel at a time of prosperity helped his followers to realise the depth of his insight into God's actions.

We know nothing of Amos save for the evidence of the book, and the biographical information is included not for its own sake but as an illustration of his message. He was active around 750 B.C.; a southerner from Tekoa near Bethlehem but preaching in the northern kingdom; not a professional prophet by background but the recipient of a direct call from God to become a prophet (7:10-17). (It is not clear whether he had formerly been a simple shepherd or something more substantial — a sheep-breeder.)

His message is one of virtually unrelieved gloom. Israel had been more favoured by God than any other people, yet had utterly failed to realise the responsibility involved in this privilege (3:2). Social and religious corruption are vigorously denounced; injustice and fraud are rampant (2:6-8; 5:1-24). Amos's contemporary, Hosea, condemned the people for the worship of false gods; Amos himself is more concerned with the false worship of the true God (4:4-5). No prophet before had carried his attack to the logical conclusion, that the Lord would be prepared to reject his own people, since they had so utterly rejected him.

Amos does not mention Assyria (the reference in 3:9 of some modern translations is a conjectural emendation), but no doubt the Assyrian invasion thirty years later was seen as fulfilment of his warnings. The last few verses with their hopeful note (9:8-15) are usually regarded as a later addition, when it was realised that the doom had not after all been total extinction.

AMRAPHEL king of Shinar (Gen. 14) played a major part in a war in which Abraham was involved. 'Shinar' is elsewhere in the Old Testament used of Babylon, and so the attempt has often been made to identify this Amraphel and thereby date Abraham. But there is no known king of Babylon of such a name — Hammurabi has often been suggested, but the similarity is not a close one — and it is more likely that the story is a later one with little historical foundation. Certainly the other kings mentioned in Gen. 14 are entirely unknown.

ANTIOCHUS. After the death of Alexander the Great his empire was divided; Asia Minor, Syria and for a time Palestine were ruled by the Seleucid dynasty, no fewer than thirteen of whom took the name Antiochus. They are not mentioned by name in the Old Testament, though the veiled survey of history under the guise of prophecy in Dan. 11 is thought to refer to Antiochus II (vv.6f.), III (vv.10-19) and IV (vv.21-45). As the number of verses devoted to each shows, the purpose of the author of Daniel was to show the historical development to the time of Antiochus IV, that is, his own time of writing, and this is brought out more specifically in the books of Maccabees where there are explicit references to Antiochus III-VII.

ANTIOCHUS III, the Great (223-187 B.C.) raised the Syrian Empire to hits greatest power, but then suffered a crushing defeat from the Romans (1 Macc. 8:5-8) in the battle of Magnesia, in Asia Minor, in 190 B.C. He had to pay enormous tribute, and the financial difficulties of his successors stemmed in part from this.

ANTIOCHUS IV, called Epiphanes ('God Manifest') in his own official title, but Epimanes ('Madman') by his enemies, ruled at the time of crisis for the Jews (175-164 B.C.). Conscious of the divisions within his empire he attempted to unify it, and in particular to bring a greater measure of religious unity. Some Jews accepted and indeed welcomed this (1 Macc. 1:11-15) but there were others to whom this was apostasy, and they fought bitterly to preserve their distinctive status. A large part of 1 and 2 Maccabees is given over to description of Antiochus' action, on which the worst possible construction is always put. The opposition of the Jews was not his problem: he had wars on his eastern frontiers, the constant threat of the Romans, and family disputes at home to contend with, and it is likely that the Palestinian campaign occupied much less of his attention and resources than 1 Maccabees, in particular, implies. Eventually his death is described in considerable detail, in 1 Macc. 6:1-17 and 2 Macc. 9.

ANTIOCHUS V Eupator (264-161 B.C.) at first renewed the campaign against the Jews (1 Macc. 6: 18-54), but further internal disputes led first to his offering terms to the Jews and then to his being murdered by a rival claimant to the throne (1 Macc.6:55-7:4).

ANTIOCHUS VI was set upon the throne as nominal ruler when little more than five years old (1 Macc. 11:54f.), never being more than a puppet, and was murdered when he had served his turn (1 Macc. 13:31). His notional rule was from 145 to 142 B.C., and intrigues of the sort that surrounded him showed the depths to which the once impressive empire had descended.

ANTIOCHUS VII Sidetes is the last of the dynasty to be mentioned in the books of Maccabees. He ruled 138-129 B.C., and by this time he was reduced to bargaining with the Jewish leaders in the hope of gaining their support against other claimants to his own throne — a far cry from the days when the Jews had been regarded as a minor nuisance within a powerful empire. 1 Macc. 15:1-9 shows him currying favour with the Jewish leader Simon; later, after the events recorded in 1 Maccabees, he did in fact renew the attack upon Jerusalem, but the Syrians never controlled the area effectively again.

ARAUNAH (called Ornan in 1 Chron. 21) was the owner of the threshing-floor in Jerusalem which, according to the story in 2 Sam. 24, became the site of the future temple. The story has a number of curious features, and it has often been suggested that Araunah was a prominent figure in the religion of pre-Israelite Jerusalem and that his 'threshing-floor' was really an existing place of worship now taken over by Israel.

ARTAXERXES. There were three rulers of the Persian empire named Artaxerxes, during the fifth and fourth centuries B.C., a period when the Jews were under Persian rule. The books of Ezra and Nehemiah contain numerous references to Artaxerxes as emperor, and though the biblical editors almost certainly understood such references (as Ezra 7:7 and Neh. 2:1) as being to the same ruler, it has often been suggested that Nehemiah was active under Artaxerxes I about 445 B.C. and Ezra under Artaxerxes II about 398 B.C. This would help to explain certain pointers to the fact that Nehemiah's mission may have preceded that of Ezra. However that may be, Artaxerxes, like other Persian rulers, is described in very favourable terms as one who showed kindness to his Jewish subjects (e.g. Ezra 7:27). The Old Testament view of the Persian Empire is much more approving than that of the classical Greek writers who are our other main source of knowledge.

ASA was king of Judah for forty-one years in the late tenth and early ninth century B.C., and is one of the few kings to be praised by the biblical authors (1 Kings 15:9-24; 2 Chron. 14-16). The earlier account in Kings tells us little of the historical situation save for its description of the border-warfare which was endemic between Israel and Judah; the account in Chronicles is much fuller, but — though it no doubt enshrines some ancient traditions — is in part of a legendary character, best illustrated by the defeat of the Egyptian king Zerah (otherwise unknown), with an army of a million men, by means of prayer rather than any military prowess (2 Chron. 14:8-15).

ASAHEL. Of four Old Testament characters named Asahel the best known is the nephew of David and brother of Joab whose killing by Saul's general Abner (2 Sam. 2) brought about a blood-feud which long haunted David's entourage. Asahel was apparently renowned for his swiftness of foot, but little is otherwise said of him.

ASAPH. During the later Old Testament period the 'sons of Asaph' had an important role in the music of the Jerusalem temple; a number of Psalms (50, 73-83) is associated with them. The books of Chronicles ascribe all the arrangements for the temple to David, and they accordingly speak of an Asaph who was a contemporary of David (1 Chron. 6:31-48, especially v. 39). It must remain very doubtful whether Asaph was a historical figure.

ASHER was one of the tribes of Israel, occupying the coastal area in the north of Palestine. As with the other tribes, stories in Genesis attribute its beginning to an individual, Asher, one of the twelve sons of Jacob or Israel. Tradition holds Asher, along with Gad, to have been born to Jacob by his slave-wife Zilpah (Gen. 30: 12f.). But there are no traditions relating to Asher as an individual, and it is probable that the name should be confined to that of the tribe.

ASSUR-BANIPAL was the last great king of the Assyrian Empire, his approximate dates being 669-633 B.C. After his death the Assyrian Empire, which included Syria and Palestine, rapidly broke up. Among the most impressive of archaeological discoveries has been the excavation of his library, much of which is now in the British Museum, London. He is not referred to in Old Testament books dealing with the period of his rule, but it is likely that 'Osnappar' (or Asnapper) in Ezra 4:10 is a corrupt form of his name.

ATHALIAH was the daughter of Ahab and Jezebel, rulers of the northern kingdom of Israel, and her brief reign in the southern kingdom was the only interruption in an otherwise continuous line of descendants of David during more than four centuries. Having married king Jehoram of Judah, she seized power by a murderous *coup d'état* (2 Kings 11) after the death of her husband and her son; in due course she became the victim of an equally violent counter-revolution. Nothing is known of events during her reign; her religious apostasy earns her the condemnation of the editors of the books of Kings.

AZARIAH. More than twenty characters mentioned in the Old Testament bore this name, about only two of whom any detailed knowledge is preserved — the king known also as Uzziah (q.v.), and one of the three companions of Daniel who, in the popular story recounted in Dan. 3, were preserved from death in the 'burning fiery furnace'. This Azariah is probably better known by his Babylonian name of Abednego: see *Shadrach*.

BAASHA was the third king of the northern kingdom of Israel, whose reign occupied approximately the first quarter of the ninth century B.C. (1 Kings 15:33-16:7). His actions are condemned by the biblical writers and he appears to have fallen foul of the prophets of his own time, who took an active part in political matters, but there are also indications that he was a strong and successful king, dominant over the weaker southern kingdom (1 Kings 15:16ff.).

BACCHIDES was a Syrian general and governor of the Syrian province which included Palestine at the time of the rising led by Judas Maccabaeus. He achieved what previous attempts by the Syrian authorities had failed to bring about — the defeat and death of Judas, as well as a victory over Judas' brother and successor Jonathan. But the rebellion could not finally be put down and eventually Bacchides came to terms with Jonathan and withdrew from Palestine (1 Macc. 7-9).

BALAAM, a seer or diviner, plays the major role in the stories in Num. 22-24, but there are numerous later references to him which illustrate the distinctive way in which the traditions about him — already very complex in the book of Numbers — developed.

The outline of the story seems clear; Balaam was a famous diviner hired by Balak of Moab to curse Israel and so restrain their passage through his land. Balaam is represented as worshipping Yahweh, Israel's God, though he came from many hundreds of miles away, near the Euphrates. The present form of the story shows obvious inconsistencies — first God commands Balaam to go to Balak, but then he is angry with him for doing so. This is usually explained as the secondary joining together of distinct literary or other traditions. The talking ass incident shows the influence of folk-lore.

When Balaam reached Moab his oracles were consistently favourable to the Israelites, and such was the power attributed to his words that Balak took emergency measures to reverse or at least neutralise their effect. Despite this, the later tradition about Balaam was consistently hostile, both in the Old and the New Testaments. He is accused of excessive greed (2 Peter 2:15) and of leading Israel into pagan practice (Rev. 2:14) — neither accusation being supported by the stories about him that have survived.

BALAK was the king of Moab who hired Balaam (see above) in the attempt to thwart Israel. It is difficult to fit Balak into any known outline of Moabite history, and it was not Balak but Sihon and Og (qq.v.) who came to be regarded as the typical enemies of Israel on her journey through the wilderness.

BARAK is associated with Deborah in the great victory gained by an Israelite confederation over Sisera (Judg. 4-5). The exact relation between the two leaders is not clear, but Barak was in charge of the Israelite forces; the prose account in ch. 4 implies that victory owed much to his skill as a general, given suitable encouragement by Deborah; the poem in ch. 5 stresses to a much greater extent the direct action of God. The victory was clearly a major one, but it is not placed in any larger historical context and cannot be dated with confidence.

BARUCH is several times mentioned in the book of Jeremiah (especially chs. 32 and 36) as Jeremiah's faithful disciple and secretary. The story in ch. 36 in particular has led scholars to attempt to isolate those parts of the book of Jeremiah which might have formed part of his scroll, but such attempts are almost certainly fruitless. Nothing is known of his eventual fate, but his loyalty led to the development of later traditions about him, including a number of writings ascribed to him, one of which is to be found in the Apocrypha. It is a work of Jewish piety of a much later date and has no connection with the historical figure of Baruch.

BARZILLAI was a wealthy trans-Jordanian landowner who offered sustenance to David when the king was driven out of Jerusalem (2 Sam. 17). He later declined a permanent position at the royal court, in phrases which illustrate the difference between the new courtly style of life and the more traditional ways of the country (2 Sam. 19:31-39).

BATHSHEBA was the wife of Uriah the Hittite, one of David's bodyguard. Her beauty led David to desire her for his own harem, and when she was found to be pregnant, he arranged for the 'accidental' death of Uriah. The child she was bearing died, but she later became the mother of Solomon and an influential power behind the throne (2 Sam. 11-12; 1 Kings 1-2). In 1 Chron. 3:5 she is called 'Bathshua', which may be an error, but — since Bathshua was the name of the wife of David's ancestor, Judah — is more likely a deliberate means of showing how the power of Judah had passed to David.

BEELIADA, a son of David (1 Chron. 14:7) is notable, not because anything is known of him as an individual, but because his name, formed as it is from that of the great Canaanite god Baal, shows that even so devout a ruler as David was happy to give his son a name of this type.

BELSHAZZAR is described in the book of Daniel as if he were king of Babylon at the time of the Jewish exile about 540 B.C.; in fact he was the son of Nabonidus, the last king of Babylon and never succeeded to the throne, though he was crown prince and co-regent with his father. This is one of many historical inaccuracies in the book which, it is now generally agreed, was not finally compiled until the second century B.C. The story of 'Belshazzar's feast' (Dan. 5) has some parallels in the accounts of Babylon's fall given by Greek historians, though their accounts lack the dramatic climax of the writing on the wall.

BELTESHAZZAR was the Babylonian name given to Daniel (c.v.).

BENAIAH. Of numerous Old Testament characters called Benaiah, only one emerges as more than a name. This was the chief of David's personal bodyguard, a group whose loyalty was to the king in person, as against the old tribal militia. This was of crucial importance in the disputes concerning the succession to David (1 Kings 1), for whereas others supported Adonijah (another son of

David), Benaiah and his troops remained loyal to Solomon, and this in turn led to Benaiah being made the commander of Solomon's army.

BEN-HADAD was the name of three, or possibly only two, rulers of the Aramaean (Syrian) kingdom whose capital was at Damascus, and which during the ninth century B.C. was in continual rivalry with Israel. Hadad was the name of one of their chief gods, the equivalent of Baal, the storm god, and so the name Ben-hadad means 'son of Hadad', and may have been an official title rather than a personal name. The main Old Testament references are probably to Ben-hadad II, and describe his wars with Israel in 1 Kings 10 and his death in 2 Kings 8; the same king is probably referred to under the name Hadad-ezer in an Assyrian inscription describing the battle of Qarqar (853 B.C.), which provides our first certain dating reference in the Old Testament period.

BENJAMIN is described as the youngest son of Jacob and as such plays a vital role in the story of Joseph in Egypt (Gen. 42-45). Yet is is probable that the name originally referred to a tribal group; the word means 'southerner', and the link with Joseph expressed in terms of the two of them being the sons of Jacob's favourite wife Rachel may well originate from the fact that these two tribal groups together occupied the main central area of Palestine. Many of the stories of Israel's conquest of the land may have originated among the Benjaminites, and many traditions picture them as a warlike people.

Though these tribal traditions are the most ancient, it is also clear that Benjamin (unlike some of the other patriarchal figures) is described as a real individual in Genesis, but there is no agreement among scholars as to the date and origin of this tradition.

BEZALEL is singled out in Exod. 31:2, along with Oholiab, as a skilled craftsman involved in the preparation of the furnishings of the tabernacle. The wilderness-setting is a conventional one; it is likely that these were representative figures of guilds of craftsmen in Jerusalem.

BILDAD is one of the three 'comforters' who visited Job in his affliction (Job 2:11). His speeches throughout the book, like those of his two friends, represent the orthodox belief that sin and suffering are causally connected; it is doubtful whether any particular viewpoint is to be associated with Bildad over against that of his friends.

BILHAH, Rachel's maid, was given by her mistress to her husband Jacob, and she became the mother of Dan and Naphtali (Gen. 30:1-8). Whether any historical event underlies this story is not known, but one of the points of the story is to explain the later, slighting reference to these groups as 'handmaid tribes'.

BOAZ, the main male character in the book of Ruth, is attractively presented: a wealthy and kindly figure whose generosity rescues Ruth and her mother from their poverty. The genealogy which makes him the great-grandfather of David (Ruth 4:18-22) is almost certainly a later addition, but it may help to explain the preservation of this charming tale as holy scripture.

C

CAIN is, of course, best known as the murderer of his brother Abel, in a story which symbolises the perennial clash between the farmer and the shepherd (Gen. 4). But the Old Testament tradition is not wholly hostile: he is given divine protection (v. 15), and is regarded as the founder of the Kenites (vv. 17-24), a tribe with whom Israel was on friendly terms.

CALEB is one of those figures, of whom there are many in the earlier books of the Old Testament, who are presented sometimes as individuals, sometimes as representative of a larger group. He is pictured as an individual in the story of the spies reconnoitring the land of Canaan (Num. 13); but the capture of the city of Debir (Josh. 15) was probably accomplished by a whole tribe rather than an individual. In later times the Calebites were a group living in friendly relations with Judah, though never regarded as one of the 'tribes of Israel'.

CHEDORLAOMER is one of the kings mentioned in Gen. 14 as taking part in a major battle in Palestine. Despite many attempts, it has proved impossible to identify him and so provide a date and historical context for Abraham, who was also involved. See also *Amraphel*.

CUSHAN-RISHATHAIM is the name given to an oppressor of Israel during the time of the Judges (Judg. 3:8-10). Further identification is impossible, for his name (which means 'doubly-wicked Cushan') is in its Old Testament form almost certainly a parody of his real name, and no known king in Mesopotamia is connected with any tradition of oppression reaching to Palestine in the time of the Judges.

CUSHI, presented in some Bible translations as a proper name (e.g. at 2 Sam. 18:21ff.), is really the generic name given in Hebrew to dark-skinned Africans.

CYRUS, the founder of the Persian Empire and one of the greatest conquerors of the ancient world, became king in about 558 B.C., overthrew the Babylonian Empire in 539 and by the time of his death in 530 had extended his rule almost to Egypt. His policy of attempting to gain the loyalty of subject peoples by allowing them to practise their own religion led to the Old Testament writers taking a favourable view of him. The unknown author of Isaiah 40-55 envisages him in the service of Israel's god (Isa. 44:28-45:1), and Ezra 1 and 6 spell out, in somewhat different terms, the decree he issued allowing Jews to return from Babylon to Palestine and to rebuild the Jerusalem temple.

DAN is presented, like the other 'sons of Jacob', both as an individual and as a tribe. As an individual he has no distinctive role, being listed simply as born to Jacob by Rachel's handmaid Bilhah (Gen. 30:6). This 'hand-maid' status is reflected in the history of the tribe, which found it extremely difficult to gain a foothold in Canaan (Judg. 1:34f; 18) and the tribe was held in so little regard that the latest list of the tribes of Israel (Rev. 7:4-8) omits it entirely.

DANIEL illustrates perhaps better than any other individual the difference between traditional and historico-critical approaches to the Old Testament. Traditionally Daniel has been regarded as one of those exiled from Judah to Babylon by Nebuchadrezzar, one who proved a skilled interpreter of dreams and portents, and survived until the coming of the Persian Empire some sixty years later (including a miraculous demonstration of the power of his God when he was thrown to the lions). He had visionary powers, and his book has been regarded from New Testament times onwards (Matt. 24:15) as the work of a prophet.

The critical study of the Bible during the last century has thrown all of these matters into question. Apart from a general scepticism about the miraculous elements in the book, many historical details have been shown to be inaccurate — for example, the reference to 'Darius the Mede' (q.v.) — and the book is not now regarded as part of the prophets. The Jews have always classed the book among the miscellaneous 'Writings' rather than with the Prophets, and it is now usually considered that it reached its final form about 165 B.C.; that it was written to provide the loyal Jews with an example and encouragement when they were being persecuted by Antiochus Epiphanes (q.v.); and that the literary genre of the book is apocalyptic rather than prophetic.

Whether there was an historical individual called Daniel cannot be decided with certainty. There is a tradition of a folk hero, renowned for his righteousness (Ezek. 14:14) which may have given rise to the stories in our present book; but it is also possible that there was an actual Daniel among the exiles about whom stories came to be told. From the second century B.C. on, the book of Daniel became very popular; additional stories about its hero came to be told (two of them, 'Susanna' and 'Bel and the Dragon' are included in the Apocrypha); and it had important influence on the New Testament — for example, in the book of Revelation, and in the title 'son of man', found in Dan. 7:13 and widely used of Jesus in the Gospels.

DARIUS There were three Persian Emperors named Darius. Darius I (522-486 B.C.) was ruler at the time of Haggai and Zechariah, and in each case their prophecies are dated by reference to the years of his reign. It was only after a struggle against rival claimants that he established himself on the throne, and it is sometimes held that these prophecies are a direct reflection of this period of unrest. More important for the Jewish community, however, was the generally benevolent attitude of Darius towards them, which allowed the Jerusalem temple to be rebuilt in 516/5 (Ezra 5-6). Darius II (423-404 B.C.) was much involved in the struggle with the Greek city-states; there is no certain Old Testament reference to him, but a possible one in Neh. 12:22, where no date is

given. Alternatively this might refer to Darius III, the last Persian ruler (336-330 B.C.) who was defeated by Alexander the Great — an event which forms the starting-point for 1 Maccabees (1:1-8) and is also referred to cryptically in the veiled 'prophecy' of Daniel (the 'fourth king' of Dan. 11:2).

DARIUS THE MEDE is known only from the book of Daniel (5:31; 6), and is almost certainly a fictitious character. The author of Daniel, writing some centuries after the event, received only confused traditions about the order of the Persian rulers, and also supposed there to have been a Median Empire interposed between the Babylonian and Persian. Despite many attempts, it has not proved possible to identify this Darius with any known historical character. (See also *Daniel,* for the historicity of the events recorded in that book; *Cyrus,* for the actual conqueror of Babylon.)

DATHAN and his brother Abiram feature in an exemplary story in Num. 16 designed to show the importance of obedience to the properly designated authority. Their stubbornness leads to their being swallowed alive in the ground. The story was used later to illustrate the absoluteness of God's power and the constant sinfulness of the people (Deut. 11:6; Ps. 106: 17), and has also been important in modern source-critical study, since Num. 16 in its present form illustrates the interweaving of two originally separate stories, one dealing with Dathan and Abiram, the other with Korah.

DAVID is one of the great heroic figures of Israel, and like his many counterparts in the history of other nations, fact and legend have become intermingled in the stories about him. Even so, there is a substantial body of tradition concerning him which can be regarded as well established. Here the attempt will be made, first to set out an outline of what we may know historically with fair confidence; then some indication will be given of the ways in which traditions about David developed in later centuries.

David was the son of Jesse, from Bethlehem, in the land of Judah. No dates can be established, but some time around 1000 B.C. is probable. Israel was scarcely established as a nation, but its first experiments with monarchy were beginning under Saul. David's relations with Saul were ambivalent. Sometimes he appeared as a loyal vassal and supporter; at other times he acted as an independent local chieftain on the southern borders of the country (1 Sam. 16-31). After Saul's death, not all would accept his son as king; others advanced the claims of David, who was established as a successful fighter and one who commanded the loyalty of his followers.

David thus became king over the southern area, at Hebron; divisions within the house of Saul eventually led to the rest of the country also turning to David in the search for a successful king (2 Sam.1-5).

David thus became king of a joint monarchy of Israel and Judah. At about this time he captured Jerusalem, a city which had not previously been controlled by Israel, and made it into a distinctively royal city and the capital of his kingdom which he then proceeded to organise with a centralised administration, perhaps based on Egyptian models. Jerusalem also became the religious centre of the kingdom; some elements from the existing, non-Israelite tradition were probably incorporated, but the city was now 'taken over' by Israel's God, Yahweh. In many respects David became a typical oriental monarch: waging successful war, building up a corps of mercenaries responsible to himself (as against the older tribal militia), and with a sizeable harem. This last led to intense and bitter intrigues as the sons of his different wives attempted to establish themselves as his designated successor (2 Sam. 6-20). In his last years he is pictured as a pathetic figure: sexually impotent and unable to curb the divisions within his own household, who were nevertheless dependent upon his decision as to the succession (1 Kings 1).

This basic picture has been elaborated in three main ways, two of which are very closely related. The first concerns David's exploits as a hero. The characteristic example here is the familiar story of Goliath, whose defeat is elsewhere attributed to Elhanan (2 Sam. 21:19). It seems as if the story in 1 Sam. 17 originally concerned an anonymous Philistine. This enhancement of David's prowess may well have been linked with a concern to legitimise his power, since it appears to be set as a deliberate contrast to the withdrawal of power (and therefore divine favour) from Saul.

The second development has its most characteristic expression in the attribution of a great number of Psalms to David. His skill as musician and poet are attested in what may well be early stories, and psalms as a literary genre may have been particularly characteristic of the worship of the royal court. While it is therefore unlikely that he himself was the composer of any of the Psalms that have survived (some would see a possible exception in the psalm-like lament over Saul and Jonathan: 2 Sam. 1:19-27) it is characteristic of the Psalms that they were composed under royal patronage and are especially linked with the worship of Jerusalem.

The third and associated development concerns the religious achievement of David in more general terms. In the account of David in 1 Chron. 1-29 he is credited with all the arrangements for the worship of the Jerusalem temple, only the actual building being left to his son Solomon. Again this is an idealisation, reflecting the concerns

43

of the Chronicler's own time (about 350 B.C.); Israel then was primarily a religious community, and so David's secular exploits were put in a context which emphasised their religious motivation.

One last development may be noted, even though it is not directly concerned with the historical figure of David. In the later Old Testament period, and in the time of Jesus, there is evidence of a belief in a 'new David', a 'messiah' (i.e. anointed one) who would be raised by God to deliver Israel from her oppressions. There is some evidence of this in the Old Testament (e.g. Micah 5:2; Isa. 11:1); the New Testament begins with the statement of Jesus' descent through the Davidic line (Matt. 1:1); and many other New Testament passages exhibit the same concern for a right understanding of the role of Jesus as 'son of David' (e.g. Rom. 1:3).

DEBORAH is described as both a prophet and a judge (Judg. 4:4), and she appears to have played a major role in encouraging Barak and the Israelite tribal levies to resist the military threat posed by the Canaanite general Sisera. She is most likely to have been a charismatic figure associated with the one particular occasion rather than a member of any recognisable succession. The vigorous and graphic poem describing the defeat and death of Sisera (Judg. 1:5), though ascribed to both Deborah and Barak, is always known as the 'Song of Deborah', and is usually held to be an almost contemporary account of the event. Unfortunately it is not possible to correlate the event with anything known from other historical sources and the uncertainty of the biblical chronology at this period makes dating impossible.

DELILAH is known only as the betrayer of the gullible Samson into Philistine control (Judg. 16). It is not stated whether she herself was a Philistine, and the folk-tale elements in the story make any historical judgements suspect.

DEMETRIUS I became king of Syria in 161 B.C. (1 Macc. 7) and was able to achieve what his predecessor had failed to accomplish — the defeat and death of Judas Maccabaeus, the leader of the Jewish uprising. Subsequently the threat of rival claimants to his throne led him to take a more conciliatory attitude to the Jews, but he was eventually killed by supporters of his enemy after his horse had been bogged down in a swamp (151 B.C.), a detail not mentioned in the account of his death at 1 Macc. 9:50.

DEMETRIUS II, son of the above, was also king of Syria in times of great disturbance (146-149 B.C.; 1 Macc. 11-14). By this time Syria had given up all effective control over the Jews, though the correspondence preserved in 1 Maccabees suggests that Demetrius maintained the fiction of suzerainty.

DINAH was the daughter of Jacob and Leah. Her birth is described without any of the elaborate word-play used in explaining the names of her brothers (Gen. 30:21), and, unlike theirs, her name was not associated with that of one of the tribes of Israel. The most famous episode relating to her is her rape by the men of Shechem (Gen. 34); this and the subsequent episodes involving Simeon and Levi appear to be a way of describing the relations between early Israel and the Canaanite inhabitants of Shechem.

DOEG was an Edomite, a servant of Saul whose exact position is not clear (the traditional 'chief of Saul's herdsmen' seems scarcely apt for the role he played). He is credited with the slaughter of eighty-five religious officials at the sanctuary of Nob, on Saul's orders, after he discovered that they had assisted his rival David (1 Sam. 21-22). The presence of an Edomite in Saul's entourage is noteworthy — his kingdom was not, as is sometimes asserted, a purely local tribal office.

EBER appears in Genesis as simply a name in an extended list (Gen. 10:21-25). The point of interest is that he is regarded by the Old Testament as having given his name to those subsequently called 'Hebrews', and is linked with Shem, the purported ancestor of all Semites, in the genealogy. These are not scientific etymologies, but popular fancies based on like-sounding names; Hebrews appear to have been a stratum of society widely attested in the ancient Near East under forms such as 'Habiru' and unconnected with any individual named Eber.

EHUD is known only for the gruesome story of his deliverance of the people from Moabite oppression by his murder of the fat Moabite ruler Eglon, who was tricked by Ehud's left-handedness. He is not specifically called a judge in this story (Judg. 3:15-30), but it appears as if the editors of the book of Judges have used this local folk tale as part of their framework of a series of 'deliverer' judges.

ELDAD and Medad were two Israelite elders who displayed the gift of prophecy according to the story in Num. 11:26f. If the tradition underlying this is ancient, it would point to the existence of prophets in Israel before the settlement of Canaan, but the names are of a Canaanite type, and it is widely maintained that the story comes from a later period in Israel's history.

ELEAZAR. Of seven Old Testament figures named Eleazar, the most significant is the son of Aaron through whom in later days the priestly line was reckoned. There are no stories in which he plays a distinctively individual role, but in the last centuries B.C. it was regarded as essential to the exercise of true priesthood that a descent from Eleazar (preferably) or his brother Ithamar should be established (1 Chron. 24).

ELI was the priest of Shiloh at the time of the birth of Samuel, when Israel was just becoming established as a nation, and he and his family played an important role as custodians of the Ark which symbolised the divine presence (1 Sam. 1-4). According to one tradition he was judge over Israel (1 Sam. 4:18), but for the most part he is pictured as playing an entirely religious role, and the stories about him are told in such a way as to emphasise that his family was ill-fated: his sons are condemned for their greed, Samuel (rather than anyone from his own family) is presented as his successor and eventually he dies because of the shock caused by the loss of the Ark to the Philistines. Late traditions claimed that he was descended from Aaron, and it is possible that David's priest Abiathar was a descendant, but in effect nothing is known of his family apart from the stories in 1 Samuel.

ELIAKIM was the name of the son of king Josiah chosen to succeed his father by the Pharaoh Necho of Egypt, who claimed overlordship of Palestine. He showed this by having the king's name changed to Jehoiakim (q.v.). Two other characters of the same name are referred to in the Old Testament and two in the New Testament.

ELIASHIB. Of six Old Testament characters of this name the most significant is the high-priest who is referred to in Nehemiah (3:1; 12:10; 13:4). It is not clear that all these references are to the same person, but if they are he will have been high priest and therefore a person of great significance in the Jerusalem community in the mid-fifth century B.C.

ELIEZER was the servant of Abraham referred to in Gen. 15: 2, a verse whose exact translation is uncertain, but which appears to imply that Eliezer had been adopted as heir to the childless Abraham. Attempts have been made to associate this with what is known of adoption customs in the ancient Near East. It is possible, though not stated, that Eliezer was the servant involved in the beautiful story of the finding of a wife for Isaac (Gen. 24).

ELIHU is the name of four historical characters in the Old Testament, but better known than any of them is the young man suddenly introduced into the story of Job (Job 32-37), who attempts to persuade Job that his sufferings must be due to the sins he had committed. It is generally held that his speeches represent an addition to the original dialogue of which the main part of the book consists, and it is unlikely that there is any historicity in the character as portrayed.

ELIJAH is regarded by the New Testament as *the* typical Old Testament prophet, pointing forward to Jesus. One tradition regards John the Baptist as a new incarnation of Elijah (Matt. 11:13); Elijah's presence with Jesus on the mount of Transfiguration (Mark 9:4) symbolises the prophetic role of pointing forward to Jesus. This expectation that Elijah would return is already found in the Old Testament (Mal. 4:5).

The original traditions concerning Elijah are found in 1 Kings 17 to 2 Kings 2. This cycle, and the closely related Elisha stories, are more full of miraculous elements than any other part of the Old Testament, and this, coupled with signs of later editing, makes it difficult to be confident about the historical role of Elijah. There seems no reason to doubt, however, that he was active in the mid-ninth century B.C., as part of that succession of prophets in the northern kingdom of Israel who were consistently hostile to the kings, particularly when the latter attempted to set up a dynastic succession or became involved in the religious practices of surrounding countries. Much of his activity is also associated with what appears to have been a particularly severe drought, interpreted as a sign of God's displeasure with his people.

Around this nucleus have been woven a number of miraculous stories — the meal and oil which never diminished, the raising of the widow's son, instantaneous translation from place to place, the calling of fire from heaven, the crossing of the Jordan dry-shod, and the final assumption into heaven — the historical value of which will be very differently assessed in accordance with one's presuppositions about the miraculous. Despite these uncertainties, it is still clear that the Elijah stories — particularly that of Naboth's vineyard (1 Kings 21) — enshrine the determination of the old order in Israel, loyal to its God and the traditions that it had received, not to give way to the pretensions of an absolutist ruler. Here, above all, the Elijah tradition is in full harmony with that of the later prophets of Israel.

ELIPHAZ is the oldest of the three friends of Job who come to offer him their sympathy in his distress, but whose comfort soon turns to condemnation of the supposed wrongs that Job had committed. It is doubtful whether Eliphax is to be understood as having a different point of view from that of his friends, Bildad and Zophar; probably the variations are due simply to dramatic effect. Eliphaz is said to have come from Teman, in Edom (Job 2:11) but the point of view he expresses is typically Israelite.

ELISHA was the successor of Elijah, two accounts (1 Kings 19; 2 Kings 2) being given of his call to that role. Whereas Elijah is usually presented as a solitary figure, Elisha has a band of followers (2 Kings 4:38-42), and appears to have been in closer and more positive relations with the king than Elijah had been (2 Kings 3; 13:14-21).

To an even greater extent than with Elijah the traditions concerning Elisha have a miraculous, and at times even magical, element. Some of the stories appear to be variants of those told about Elijah (the healing of the widow's son; the miraculous jar of oil); others (the curse which brings death to the children mocking his baldness, 2 Kings 2:23-25) are little more than popular tales of a crude wonder-worker. Despite this, and his sometimes bloody role in the political intrigues of the day (2 Kings 9), there are elements in the Elisha cycle which show that he, like his master, stood for the maintenance of the traditional worship of Israel's God against any dilution with foreign cults; this emerges especially in the story of the cure of Naaman (2 Kings 5).

ENOCH is mentioned in the list of patriarchs said to have lived between the time of Adam and the great flood (Gen. 5:17-24). He is differentiated from the others in that list by the fact that his life-span, though remarkable (365 years) was much less than that of the other figures on the list, and by the description of his end: 'he was not, for God took him'. This cryptic statement gave rise to a great variety of legends about him in the last pre-Christian centuries, with one such allusion in the New Testament (Jude 14), as well as his inclusion among the heroes of faith in Heb. 11:5. As for the list, comparable lists of figures from remote antiquity living to a great age were widespread in the ancient world.

EPHRAIM was the dominant group in the northern kingdom of Israel during the period of the divided monarchy, so that frequently in the eighth-century prophets Ephraim is used as a way of referring to the whole kingdom (e.g. Hosea 4:17; Isa. 7:2). Originally the name seems to have referred to a district of central Palestine, but as with the other tribal names, Ephraim came to be regarded as a personal name. Ephraim and his brother Manasseh were said to have been born to Joseph in Egypt (Gen. 41:50-52), so that in the lists of the twelve tribes, Joseph is sometimes found as a single tribe whereas on other occasions Manasseh and Ephraim are listed separately. The description of their birth in Egypt has led to it being widely held that at least these groups were involved in the Exodus. There are many indications in the Old Testament of tension amounting to hostility between Ephraim and other groups (cf. e.g. Judg. 12:1-6; Ps. 78), but we do not know the history of this or the other tribes in detail before they were joined in the monarchy.

EPHRON the Hittite is referred to in Gen. 23 as the owner of the piece of land which Abraham bought for a burial-place, thereby giving himself rights of possession in Palestine. Nothing else is known of Ephron and the description of him as a 'Hittite' is very curious — there was a Hittite empire in Asia Minor in the middle of the second millennium B.C., but it is difficult to connect this in any way with the Abraham story or other Old Testament references to Hittites.

ESARHADDON was king of Assyria 681-669 B.C., a period during which the former northern kingdom of Israel had been absorbed into the Assyrian Empire and Judah was forced to remain a loyal vassal. Old Testament references to him are only incidental: one mentions his accession following the murder of his father (2 Kings 19:37, repeated in Isa. 37:38), the other alludes to a campaign in Palestine which involved the settling of inhabitants of other parts of his empire in Palestine (Ezra 4:2).

ESAU, the older son of Isaac (Gen. 25:21-26) is seen by Paul (Rom. 9:13) and the writer of Hebrews (Heb. 12:16) as the typical figure of divine rejection because of ingratitude. Many

49

moderns have regarded him as the simple dupe, easily outwitted by his subtle brother Jacob. The Old Testament accounts of his loss of his birthright (Gen. 25:27-34) and of his father's blessing (Gen. 27) are not only stories about individuals but also explain the relation between Israel and the neighbouring people of Edom, whom Israel both despised and feared. Esau is thus described both as an individual and as the ancestor of a people, a combination which helps to explain some otherwise curious features of the stories (e.g. Gen. 25:30, with its play on the word *edom* meaning 'red' but also the name of the people).

 **ESDRAS.**
See *Ezra*.

ESTHER is the heroine of the book named after her. The story tells how the beautiful Jewish orphan Esther was chosen as his queen by the Persian king Ahasuerus (Xerxes) when she won a beauty competition. Hearing of a plot against her people instigated by the wicked grand vizier Haman, she risked the king's displeasure by requesting an audience instead of awaiting the king's summons. Haman's plot was revealed, he himself was accused of trying to seduce Esther and was hanged on the gallows he had prepared for his enemies, and the Jews were spared. Such an outline shows the fairy-tale elements that are present in the story, and it is most unlikely that there is any historical basis for the account, none of whose significant details are supported by external evidence. It is better to take the book as a story told to illustrate God's care for his people, protecting them against all attacks; and in particular to explain the origin of the popular Jewish feast of Purim, said to be the commemoration of the escape from the massacre intended by Haman. The lack of obvious religious reference in the book led to early additions being made in the form of prayers, and these additions are found in the Apocrypha.

EVE. The woman created by God to be a partner for Adam (Gen. 2:22) is at first unnamed, but after the story of the temptation by the snake she is given the name Eve (Gen. 3:20). Her name is there said to be linked with the Hebrew word for 'life', but there is also an ancient tradition linking it with a similar word which means 'snake'. Apart from her failure to resist the snake's suggestions — a point twice picked up in the New Testament (2 Cor. 11:3; 1 Tim. 2:13) — she is mentioned only as the mother of Cain and Abel, and later of Seth and other unnamed children.

EVIL-MERODACH is the Hebrew version of 'Amel-Marduk', who ruled the Babylonian Empire in succession to his father Nebuchadrezzar, 562-560 B.C., but our knowledge of him is virtually confined to the note in 2 Kings 25:27, which interprets his favourable treatment of the exiled Jehoiachin king of Judah as a sign that the disaster of exile was still not without hope for the Jews.

EZEKIEL is one of the most mysterious of Old Testament figures whose personality and psychology have attracted attention far beyond the range of professional biblical scholarship. He is known only from the book named after him, which presents him as both priest and prophet, exercising his ministry in Babylonia, where he had been exiled, presumably with those involved in the first deportation of 597 B.C. Many of his prophecies are dated, and they cover the period 593-571 B.C.

No part of the Old Testament has occasioned more diverse scholarly views than Ezekiel. The dates, now generally taken as genuine, were once widely questioned, and debate still rages about the place of his ministry — for much of his preaching seems to be addressed directly to those still in Jerusalem (cf. especially chs. 8-11). Perhaps 'the Spirit . . . brought me in visions of God to Jerusalem' (8:3) should be taken as a literal journey; more probably it expresses the close link between those exiled to Babylon and those still in Jerusalem. Psychological speculation about Ezekiel has been widespread — his dumbness (3:26), his lying motionless for more than a year (4:4-8), and many other strange manifestations of his personality have made this inevitable. But it is a fruitless exercise, not only because of the distance in time that separates us from him, but also because we only know of Ezekiel through the book which was gathered together over an extended period by those who saw the hand of God at work in this strange figure.

Until the final fall of Jerusalem in 587 B.C., Ezekiel's message was one of uncompromising doom, a summons to the community to accept responsibility for what had come about. After the city had fallen, when all his fellows were despairing of the future, Ezekiel looked forward to a restoration, symbolised in the vision of the dry bones (37:1-14). And overarching the whole of his prophecy is the conviction of the supremacy and absolute sovereignty of Israel's God, even in a foreign land. From the mysterious vision in ch. 1 to the closing words 'the Lord is there' (48:35) the glory of God dominates the words of Ezekiel.

EZRA is one of those Old Testament figures whose achievement has been so much elaborated by later legend that it is

51

extremely difficult to identify the original historical nucleus of the tradition. Some, indeed, have denied his very existence; but it seems probable that he was a member of the Persian imperial service, sent to Jerusalem to ensure the stability and loyalty of the empire's vulnerable south-western frontier. This took place under the Persian ruler Artaxerxes (Ezra 7:7), but it remains a matter for debate whether this was Artaxerxes I (465-424 B.C.) or — as many modern scholars have held — Artaxerxes II (404-358 B.C.). His mission would thus be dated around either 458 or 397 B.C.

If his mission was originally in part at least political, it is described in Ezra 7-10 and Neh. 8 in strongly religious terms. Two key issues are involved: the ending of intermarriage by Jewish men with foreign women (Ezra 9-10), and the proclamation of the law to the people (Neh. 8). Both have at their heart a concern to spell out in detail the implications of being a religious community, set apart from all outsiders for the service of God. In more modern terms we might speak of helping the community to resolve a crisis of identity.

It is impossible to be certain what constituted the law which Ezra proclaimed but from an early date it came to be held that it was the Pentateuch, the first five and the most sacred books of the Hebrew Bible. From this fact there developed elaborate traditions about the role of Ezra in establishing Judaism as the religion of a book, and he has sometimes been given the description 'father of Judaism' on this account, implying that he set down in their final form the ancient traditions of his people. This veneration led to later writings being associated with him, and two such books have come to be included in the Apocrypha — 1 and 2 Esdras, the Greek form of the name Ezra.

GAD was one of the twelve tribes, and the tradition in Genesis describes this group as having originated from one of the sons of Jacob: like Asher, Gad's mother was the hand-maid Zilpah, a reference that probably indicated the inferior status of the tribe at some point in its history (Gen. 30:11). (The name means 'good fortune' and is also found as the name of a heathen god in Isa. 65:11.) The later history of the Gadites is better known than that of some other tribes, for they inhabited the area east of the Jordan known as Gilead — the names Gad and Gilead are sometimes confused — and they therefore stood somewhat apart from the main body of Israel west of the Jordan, as is shown in the stories in Num. 32 and Josh. 22. The tribe was distinctive also in being one of the very few to which an extra-biblical reference has been found. The ninth-century B.C. 'Mesha stele', from the neighbouring kingdom of Moab, refers to the 'men of Gad' having occupied part of the land which king Mesha claimed as his own.

GAD was also the name of one of David's court officials; the name may imply an origin in the tribe of Gad. He is described as both prophet and seer (2 Sam. 24:11), and it may be that the two roles are virtually identical. He was already David's adviser before he became king (1 Sam. 22:5), and brought God's word to David in the census episode, with its strange twist which led to the purchase of what would later become the site of the Jerusalem temple (2 Sam. 24).

GEDALIAH Of several Old Testament characters called Gedaliah the most important is the member of a leading Jerusalemite family during the last days of the monarchy. Both his grandfather Shaphan and his father Ahikam had played a prominent part in affairs of state in the late seventh and early sixth centuries B.C., and when Nebuchadrezzar finally captured and destroyed Jerusalem in 587 B.C., Gedaliah was made governor with his headquarters at Mizpah, just north of the ruined city of Jerusalem. We are not told the exact length of his governorship, which is referred to briefly in 2 Kings (25:22-25) and more fully in Jeremiah (40:5 — 41:18) but we know that he met a violent death at the hands of a gang led by Ishmael, a member of the royal family who no doubt saw Gedaliah as both a usurper of a position which should have been his and a traitorous collaborator with the Babylonians.

GEHAZI, the servant of Elisha, is usually described in unflattering terms; he rudely attempts to keep the Shunammite woman grieved by the death of her son from asking Elisha's help (2 Kings 4:27), and when his greed impels him to ask a gift from the Aramaean general Naaman who Elisha had cured of his skin disease he is afflicted with the same disease (2 Kings 5:20-27). (The disease was almost certainly not leprosy, as in older translations.)

GERSHOM/GERSHON. The relation between different people with these names appears already to have caused some difficulty even before the Old Testament reached its final form. Gershom

53

the son of Moses (Exod. 2:22) is also mentioned in Judg. 18:30 as the ancestor of the first priest of the sanctuary of Dan. Otherwise his name is found only in lists of the descendants of Moses (e.g. 1 Chron. 23:15f.).

Another member of the tribe of Levi is sometimes called Gershom (e.g. 1 Chron. 6:16) and sometimes Gershon (e.g. 1 Chron. 6:1). Nothing is known of him as an individual, but as descendants of Levi (Gen. 46:11) his family were reckoned among those responsible for the service of the Jerusalem temple, and as such play an important part in the early chapters of Numbers and in 1 Chronicles, both books being much concerned with the setting-out of proper ritual arrangements.

GESHEM was one of the opponents of Nehemiah's work in rebuilding Jerusalem in the time of Persian rule, probably c.445 B.C. He is called 'the Arab' (Neh. 2:19; 6:1) which may imply that he was the official in charge of some kind of Arab confederacy within the Persian empire. An alternative form of his name, Gashmu, is found in Neh. 6:6.

GIDEON's exploits as a judge of Israel are described in Judg. 6-8. He is remembered as a skilled guerilla fighter, who brought about the defeat of the Midianites, invaders from the desert fringes who were attempting to press into more fertile territory. (These are the 'troops of Midian' of the hymn 'Christian, dost thou see them?') It seems probable that two distinct accounts of the same, or related incidents, have been preserved: one in Judg. 7:1-8:3, the other in 8:4-21. As the tradition now stands, Gideon is presented as a loyal follower of Yahweh, but it is noteworthy that he has an alternative name Jerubbaal, which may suggest that he was a worshipper of Baal. The date and precise historical circumstances of his career are unknown; the final editors of the book of Judges have incorporated as many ancient traditions as possible to illustrate the theme that 'the spirit of the Lord took possession of Gideon' (Judg. 6:34), and at a later time 'the day of Midian' (Isa. 9:4) was symbolic of the defeat of Israel's enemies.

GILEAD is not a proper name, but a geographical area, the fertile lands east of the river Jordan. However, in a way that has happened with a number of such names in the Old Testament it has come to be applied first to the inhabitants of the area, and then those inhabitants are regarded as the descendants of an individual whose name they came to bear. So in the tribal lists, which were mostly composed much later, Gilead is regarded as an individual (e.g. Num. 26:29f; Josh. 17:1).

GOG of Magog is the enemy whose overthrow is described in highly symbolic language in Ezek. 38-39. Attempts have been made to identify him with a sixth century B.C. king of Lydia called Gyges, but it is most unlikely that any historical figure underlies the description. The oppression of Babylon may once have been in the prophet's mind, but the picture has been universalised in visionary ways to stand for the overthrow of all human wickedness.

GOLIATH. There will be few readers who do not know the story of Goliath, the Philistine giant, but the problems associated with the familiar tale in 1 Sam. 17 are greater than at first sight appear. Basically the giant in that story is anonymous, being referred to simply as 'the Philistine' except for the identifying notes in vv. 4 and 23. Furthermore, 2 Sam. 21:19 states that Goliath was killed by an otherwise unknown hero called Elhanan. Some have suggested that this was another name for David; more probably David's victim was once unnamed, and later tradition has given him the name Goliath. The story has much of the romantic character of 'Jack the giant killer' stories; there is no evidence to suggest that the Philistines as a whole were of unusual stature.

GOMER was the wife of the prophet Hosea (Hosea 1:3). She is described as a prostitute, and it appears that two of the children she bore were not Hosea's. The story is told primarily as symbolising Israel's unfaithfulness in her 'marriage' with her god Yahweh. It is likely that the story in ch. 3 describes the same events in a different form, but some have maintained that the (unnamed) woman there was someone different.

GORGIAS was one of the generals sent by the Seleucid kings to attempt to quell the guerilla uprising led by Judas Maccabaeus c. 165 B.C. Though he met with some success (1 Macc. 5:59-61), he was unable to counter Judas' surprise tactics (1 Macc. 4:1-25).

H

HABAKKUK is unknown save for the book named after him. Though brief, it poses some of the most difficult problems for the interpreter of the Old Testament, since it differs in many respects from the other prophetic books. One suggestion is that Habakkuk may have been a 'cultic prophet', that is, a member of the staff of the temple, who uttered divine oracles either of his own initiative or in response to requests from worshippers. There is no certainty about his date, but the reference to the Chaldeans (i.e. Babylonians) (1:6) has usually been taken to imply the seventh or sixth centuries B.C. The name Habakkuk is not a usual Hebrew one. There is some evidence of a later interest in Habakkuk; he is mentioned in a curious episode of the apocryphal book Bel and the Dragon (vv. 33-30), where he is carried in the air by an angel to take food to Daniel in the lion's den: a version of Hab. 1-2 was one of the first of the Dead Sea Scrolls to be discovered: and Paul made use of Hab. 2:4, 'the righteous shall live by his faith' when setting out his theme of justification by faith (Rom. 1:17).

HADADEZER was king of Zobah, an Aramaean kingdom north of Israel, at the time of David (tenth century B.C.). It would seem that both David and Hadadezer were attempting to gain control of the area of Syria and Palestine at a time when the great powers were quiescent. 2 Sam. 8 and 10 describe David's success in wars between the two states. Hadad was a divine name, another form of the storm-god better known from the Old Testament as Baal.

HAGAR, the maid of Abraham's wife Sarah, was the mother of his first-born child Ishmael. The Old Testament contains two accounts of her expulsion when Sarah herself bore a son (Gen. 16; 21:8-21), which are probably variants of the same story. The stories reflect both the kinship which the Israelites acknowledged with the nomadic Ishmaelites and the mutual hostility between the two groups. It has sometimes been alleged that the custom of giving a slave-girl to the head of the family that he might have children by her if his wife was barren reflects established custom in the mid-second millennium B.C., but the evidence for this practice is very ambiguous.

HAGGAI was a prophet active in Jerusalem around 520 B.C., whose words have come down to us in the short book named after him and who is also referred to in Ezra 5:1 and 6:14, dealing with the same period. This was the time when Persian rule was being established in Palestine, and new opportunities were offered to the Jews, no longer as a nation-state, but as a religious group devoted to the worship of their God. This is the background of Haggai's concern for the purity of the people (2:10-14) and especially for the rebuilding of the Jerusalem temple (ch. 1). At this period many Jews had returned from exile in Babylon, but there is no certainty that Haggai was one of them — his message seems to have been intended to stir the people of Jerusalem from their lethargy.

HAM is described as the second son of Noah (Gen. 5:32), who was saved with the rest of his family from the flood. After the flood a cryptic story in Gen. 9:20-27 condemns Ham when he 'saw the nakedness of his father and told his two brothers outside'. Despite many speculations it is not clear what the original point of the story was, or even whether Ham was always an integral part of it, since Noah's curses are directed against Canaan. In Gen. 10 the table of the nations apportions the world newly populated after the flood to the three sons of Noah; the Hamites are described in vv. 6-20, and include many peoples whom the Israelites hated or feared because of their remoteness; there is no scientific basis for the division, and certainly no biblical support for the idea sometimes still found that the 'children of Ham' include allegedly inferior races.

HAMAN is the villain of the piece in the book of Esther. His plotting against the Jews provides the occasion for Esther's heroism; his own fate is sealed when his desperate pleas for mercy are interpreted as sexual advances (Esther 7:8), and he is thereupon hanged upon the gallows he had prepared for his own enemies. Melodramatic touches of this kind make it clear that the story has been told so as to give it the maximum effect, and it is doubtful whether any actual historical figure underlies the representation of Haman, or of any of the other characters in the story.

HAMMURABI, king of Babylon probably in the eighteenth century B.C., is not mentioned in the Old Testament, though in the past attempts have been made to identify him with the Amraphel of Gen. 14:1. Little is known of the detailed history of his life and times, but it seems clear that he ruled at a time of great power for Babylon. The 'Code of Hammurabi', a series of laws first discovered in 1902, shows interesting parallels with Old Testament law-codes in the book of Exodus.

HANANIAH was a common Old Testament name. At least twelve different persons were so called, but the only one of whom we have any significant further knowledge is the prophet who opposed Jeremiah (Jer. 28). To all outward appearance each had a similar claim to be delivering a genuine divine message — Hananiah a word of hope, Jeremiah a warning of disaster — thereby vividly illustrating the problem of false prophecy. Jeremiah was vindicated in the most dramatic way; Hananiah died as he had foretold (Jer. 28:16f.).

HANNAH the mother of the prophet Samuel is an example of a characteristic biblical motif — the barren woman who subsequently bore a son who played a major part in his people's fortunes. As a thank-offering for the birth the child was dedicated to God's service (1 San. 1), and there follows a psalm (1 Sam. 2:1-10), on which the 'Magnificat', the song of the Virgin Mary in Luke 1, is based.

HANUN, king of the Ammonites at the time of David (tenth century B.C.) is known only because of the humiliating treatment he inflicted upon David's envoys (2 Sam. 10:1-5). According to the account in 2 Samuel, it was this episode which led to the war against the Ammonites which was so fraught with consequences for the royal succession in Judah (2 Sam. 11-12), and which led to a humiliating defeat for the Ammonites.

HASMONAEANS. This was the name of the family which ruled Judah from the time of the rising against the Seleucid rulers of Antioch in the 160s B.C. until Pompey's capture of Jerusalem in 63 B.C. Their ascent to power is described in 1 Maccabees. There was speculation in ancient times about an individual 'Hasmon' who would have been the founder of the family, but nothing is known about such a figure, and the family name is more likely to have been derived from a place name. (See also *Mattathias; Judas Maccabaeus; Simon; John Hyrcanus.*)

HAZAEL ruled the Aramaean kingdom of Damascus for some forty years during the last part of the ninth century B.C., and is pictured by the Old Testament as having reduced Israel almost to vassal status (2 Kings 13:1-7). But the Old Testament historian also saw this as a state of affairs brought about by Israel's god as a way of punishing his own people's wickedness and set in motion by a prophet from Israel, either Elijah or Elisha (1 Kings 19:15-17; 2 Kings 8:7-15). It appears that Hazael was a usurper, whose vigorous policy brought considerable success to his kingdom before it was overrun by Assyria at the beginning of the eighth century, and there are several extra-biblical texts which show that he was recognised as a powerful and effective ruler.

HEMAN is mentioned as a legendary figure of wisdom in 1 Kings 4:31, for the purpose of showing that the wisdom of Solomon outdid that of all others. In 1 Chron. 2:6 he has come to be treated as an Israelite, and in 1 Chron. 6:33 the tradition has developed still further to make him one of the leaders of the temple singing. To our eyes such a development is unhistorical and therefore unacceptable, but it is characteristic of some parts of the Old Testament to use this method of showing all revered figures of the past as being guided by the God of Israel.

HEZEKIAH was king of Judah at one of the most crucial periods of the nation's history. The rising threat of Assyria overran the northern kingdom of Israel and incorporated its territory into the imperial provincial system, but Judah was allowed a measure of independence, perhaps because of its greater remoteness, perhaps because its rulers had been willing to pay tribute. For much of his reign Hezekiah was also a vassal of Assyria, but he is remembered chiefly for his attempt at rebellion.

This rebellion came when Sennacherib (705-681 B.C.) was still establishing himself on the Assyrian throne, and reached its climax in 701 B.C. Sennacherib's own annals, and a brief account in 2 Kings 18:13-16, imply that a considerable humiliation was inflicted upon Hezekiah, who lost much of his territory and had to pay a heavy tribute. But Jerusalem itself, though besieged, was not captured, and it is this aspect of the revolt which the other biblical accounts have seized upon (2 Kings 18:17-19:37; Isa. 36-37). In this version (or versions: there are probably two parallel stories) Sennacherib's attack on Jerusalem ends with a crushing defeat inflicted by 'the angel of the Lord' and his ignominious retreat and subsequent murder. The exact nature of this event is still a matter of discussion and speculation.

Hezekiah is also remembered for a religious reform (2 Kings 18:1-8) and it is inherently likely that such measures would accompany a declaration of political independence. It is, however, unlikely to have taken the extensive form described in 2 Chron. 29-31, where it is probable that a measure of idealisation has taken place. It is striking that, by contrast with many kings of Judah, Hezekiah

59

is nowhere the subject of condemnation.

In view of the wealth of material, it is surprising that Hezekiah's dates remain uncertain. One tradition (2 Kings 18:1f.) begins his reign before the fall of the northern kingdom to the Assyrian threat, that is, in about 727 B.C. But this would have made Hezekiah only eleven years younger than his father Ahaz (2 Kings 16:2), and so it is widely held that a later date should be adopted for Hezekiah's reign — c.715-686 B.C. (cf. 2 Kings 18:13) — but certainty is impossible.

HILKIAH was the priest of the Jerusalem temple in about 622 B.C. under king Josiah. His discovery of the book of the law (perhaps Deuteronomy, as a whole or in part) led to the religious reform being carried out which forms the climax of the account of Judah in 1-2 Kings. The Hilkiah from whom Ezra claims descent (Ezra 7:1) is probably the same, but the father of Jeremiah the prophet (Jer. 1:1) is almost certainly a different, though approximately contemporary, individual.

HIRAM, king of Tyre at the time of David and Solomon (tenth century B.C.), is notable as the first neighbouring ruler with whom Israel, now a state among states, established friendly relations. The Tyrian craftsmen played an important part in supplying material and expertise in the building of Solomon's temple (1 Kings 5:1-12), and also supported various commercial developments undertaken by Solomon (1 Kings 9-10). Possibly Solomon's ambitions outran his ability to pay, for he had to cede territory to Hiram to pay his debts (1 Kings 9:11-14).

HOBAB is one name given to Moses' father-in-law, who is also called Jethro (q.v.).

HOLOFERNES may be described as the villain of the piece in the apocryphal book Judith. He is the commander of the Assyrian army sent to subjugate Judah and all other lands, but his strength is no match for the shrewdly pious Judith, who gets him drunk at a feast. The result is that, instead of Judith becoming Holofernes' victim, she cuts off his head, places it in her food-bag, and by showing it to the beleaguered Jews restores their courage and enables them to rout the Assyrians.

This entertaining story is a folk-legend, not to be taken seriously as history. If there was a real enemy general called Holofernes he must have been Persian rather than Assyrian, but we have no knowledge of any actual events which might have provided the nucleus of our story.

HOPHNI and Phinehas, the two sons of Eli, were priests at Shiloh, where the ark of God was kept before the establishment of the monarchy and the setting-up of Jerusalem as the central sanctuary. They are condemned for their greed in a curious story which throws light on the worship practice of early Israel (1 Sam. 2:12-17) and they were both killed by the Philistines when they accompanied the ark into battle (1 Sam. 4:11). A pathetic touch is added in the account of Phinehas' widow, who was pregnant, giving premature birth to a child named Ichabod ('The glory has departed') and then herself dying.

HOPHRA, pharaoh of Egypt 588-569 B.C., plays a part in Old Testament history during the last years of Judah's independent existence. He encouraged the small states of Palestine to rebel against their Babylonian overlords, promising them help in the rebellion. But his aid was quite ineffectual, and Jeremiah condemns both Hophra himself (44:30) and those Judaeans who trusted in him (37:5-10, where he is referred to simply as 'Pharaoh').

HOSEA was one of the remarkable group of prophets in the eighth century B.C. whose words have come to be regarded as epitomising the kind of demands which God makes of his people. We have no knowledge of him other than the book named after him, which is the first of the twelve 'minor prophets'. It is placed first either because it is the longest, or because Hosea was thought — probably wrongly — to have been the earliest of these figures. In fact, it is likely that Amos pre-dated him by a few years, and that Hosea was active in the period c.745-720 B.C. His book gives no precise dates, but is generally held to reflect the troubled conditions of the northern kingdom of Israel in the last years before it was conquered by the Assyrians, Samaria, the capital, being taken in 722. The Hebrew text of parts of the book is extremely difficult, and it has been suggested that this might be due to dialect differences: Hosea was a northern prophet, the only one whose words have been put in a book, though we have stories of many earlier northern prophets, such as Elijah and Elisha.

Much recent discussion of Hosea has centred around two questions. The first concerns how much we can know of the prophet as an individual. Chapters 1-3 are concerned with his personal relations with one or two women, a third-person account describing his marriage with Gomer in ch. 1, a first-person account of his dealings with an unnamed woman in ch. 3. Most probably these are different accounts of the same set of events. The patience with which Hosea

61

bears his wife's infidelity and his constant attempts to win back her love are symbolic of the love which the Lord bore for his people, and, as such, the message is more important than the personality of the prophet. In fact we know very little about his personal life. Whether he had been trained as a prophet, whether he was a city or country dweller — these are quite unknown to us.

The other disputed issue is whether Hosea's main emphasis should be regarded as significantly different from that of Amos. It is clear enough that Amos' word was one of doom, and there is much in Hosea that is equally full of foreboding. But there is also a strand which seems to imply that the doom will not be unmitigated disaster, that God's love for his people is such that he cannot simply destroy them (11:1-9). The Hebrew word which describes this attitude, *hesed*, is difficult to translate, but it implies a love which is both an obligation brought about by the terms of the covenant and also a free choice. In perhaps the most famous verse in the book (6:6) it is contrasted with cultic worship — 'I desire steadfast love, and not sacrifice, the knowledge of God rather than burnt offerings' — in terms which imply, not that worship as such is wrong, but that it is useless without the prior involvement implied in steadfast love (*hesed*) and knowledge of God. Twice quoted by Jesus in St Matthew's Gospel, (9:13; 12:7), it remains a basic test of any religious profession.

One other aspect of Hosea's message is of special significance. A long-standing problem for the people of the Old Testament was the nature of the difference between their God and those of the earlier inhabitants of Canaan, the baals. Hosea sets out a remarkable solution to this problem. Instead of stressing the difference between Yahweh and the baals, he emphasises the fact that Yahweh is the true giver of what the people vainly sought from the baals (ch. 2). Thus the images of marriage and fertility, which might have been thought totally abhorrent to the religion of Yahweh, were brought into it and have continued to have an important function in the Judaeo-Christian tradition ever since.

HOSHEA was the last king of the northern kingdom of Israel. (The name in Hebrew is the same as that of the prophet, and is also found in Num. 13:8 as a different form of the name of Joshua, q.v.) Hoshea was established on the throne in Samaria as a vassal of Assyria, but in a bid for independence he was involved in a rebellion (2 Kings 17:3). It was a hopeless cause, and the Assyrians besieged and captured Samaria and incorporated it into their empire (722 or 721 B.C.). Nothing is known of Hoshea's own fate.

HULDAH is the subject of only one incidental reference in the Old Testament, (2 Kings 22:14), but it is of interest in that it shows that women might not only be prophetesses — a fact illustrated much earlier by Deborah (q.v.) — but also that they might be in an official position and consulted on matters of great moment. Her prophecy in the following verses was fulfilled, as regards both the state as a whole and the king; but this may be due to the work of the final editors, who would have set down the prophecy in terms of the subsequent events.

HURAM/HURAM-ABI is said in both 1 Kings and 2 Chronicles to have played an important part in supervising the construction of Solomon's temple. It seems that the Israelites lacked building skills, and so this Tyrian expert was enrolled, though it is noted, as a sop to national pride, that he had an Israelite mother (1 Kings 7:14). The confusion of names may be due to the fact that 'abi', which in Hebrew means 'my father' is really a title. So the New English Bible at 2 Chron. 2:13 has 'master Huram'.

HUSHAI, a counsellor of David, played a vital role in helping David overthrow the rebellion of his son Absalom. When many of David's friends were deserting him, Hushai pretended that he also had switched his allegiance (2 Sam. 15:32-37; 16:15-19) and then gave misleading advice which prevented Absalom from following up his initial success (2 Sam. 17:5-16). The subsequent career of many of the actors in this drama is described later, but no further word is heard of Hushai.

I

IMMANUEL, is the name given by Isaiah (7:14) to the child whose birth would be a sign to the king of God's intervention in the historical crisis of the time. It is disputed whether the child should be identified with anyone known by some other name from the Old Testament (e.g. was he the son of Isaiah himself or of the king?), and whether the prophecy was originally one of hope or of threat. Christian interpretation, from St. Matthew's Gospel onwards, has applied the prophecy to Jesus (see the New Testament section).

ISAAC, the son of Abraham, is a shadowy figure by comparison with his father and with his own younger son Jacob. Indeed, there are no stories in Genesis which can truly be said to have Isaac as their central character; he appears either as the intended victim of Abraham's sacrifice, or as the old man tricked into giving his blessing to his younger son. Even in the apparent exception — the story of Isaac's dealings with Abimelech in Gen. 26 — it is noteworthy that the same story, of a beautiful wife being passed off as a sister, has already been told twice of Abraham in chs. 12 and 20, and the Isaac version can hardly be true as it stands, since the Philistines (v. 1) did not settle in the land until long after any possible date for Isaac. It may well be, therefore, that Isaac is really a link figure whose role is to join two originally separate sagas, those which told of Abraham and of Jacob. This is not to make a judgement concerning his historicity, which raises the same problems as those relating to Abraham and Jacob, but simply to note that he has not become, like them, a figure which has stirred the creative enthusiasm of later generations.

ISAIAH has been, on any showing, one of the most creative figures in the whole Judaeo-Christian tradition, and a good deal of information is available to us about his life, as well as the remarkable witness provided by the great prophetic book named after him. Here, we will deal first with what is known of his life, and then give an outline of the relation of the book to the prophet.

The earliest recorded experience is found in ch. 6, the vision of the Lord which took place 'in the year that king Uzziah died'. The chronology at this period is uncertain, but the approximate period is 740 B.C. This vision is not specifically described as the beginning of his ministry, but a clear account is given of his call to be a prophet with a warning of the doom-laden consequences of his message (6: 9-13). It appears that this took place in the Jerusalem temple, and throughout his life Isaiah was closely associated with Jerusalem. It is noteworthy that his message, like that of the other great prophets of the eighth century B.C. (Amos, Hosea, Micah) was essentially one of doom and judgement (6:9f.). Many of the oracles in chs. 1-12 and 28-32, which are those which most certainly go back to Isaiah himself, are of this nature.

In around 735 B.C. the various small states of Syria and Palestine joined together to resist the threat from the Assyrian Empire. King Ahaz of Judah thought this a hopeless venture and preferred to become an Assyrian vassal. Isa. 7 shows that the prophet shared Ahaz' view of the possiblity of the alliance being effective, but maintained that instead of turning to Assyria he should have put his trust in God. These are the background circumstances of the famous 'Immanuel' prophecy in 7:14, where the original reference was possibly to the child soon to be borne by the king's wife. What may have originally been a threat came to be understood as a promise, and to it were added in 9:2-7 and 11:1-9 other oracles looking forward to a time of prosperity under an ideal king. Whether these passages come from Isaiah himself or from a later stage in the development of the book is much disputed.

The other great historical crisis with which Isaiah is associated came a generation later, when Sennacherib of Assyria threatened Jerusalem. On this occasion Isaiah was confident that the threat would be repelled and counselled resistance. The historical details are unclear, but it is certain that Sennacherib failed to capture Jerusalem, though there is no external confirmation of the alleged mass slaughter of the Assyrian army (37:36). We know nothing more of Isaiah himself; there is a late but historically worthless tradition that he was martyred during the reign of Manasseh, early in the seventh century.

It has long been recognised by Old Testament scholars that a large part of the book of Isaiah appears to come from quite a different historical background from that outlined above. In particular chs. 40-66 seem to presuppose a setting in the Babylonian exile, in the sixth century, at a time when Cyrus king of Persia (550-530 B.C.) was already active (44:28-45:1). Detailed study of other parts of the book has led to the conclusion that our present book of Isaiah forms a kind of library inspired by Isaiah himself and handed down and added to by his followers and disciples. The words of Isaiah himself are found for the most part in chs. 1-12, 28-32, and in some of the oracles directed against foreign nations in 13-23. Chapters 24-27 seem to be a later addition, displaying the bizarre imagery and vivid symbolism of later apocalyptic writings; 40-55, often called 'Deutero-Isaiah', are a great proclamation of salvation from the time of exile; 56-66 probably come from a date a little later in the sixth century, after some of the exiles had returned to Palestine. This grouping of material under the name of 'Isaiah' should not in any way be thought of as fraudulent; it is rather a kind of family tradition, applying the message of Isaiah to new and changing circumstances. In particular the remarkable oracles of 'Deutero-Isaiah' lose nothing of their authority or inspiration simply because they come from a date different from that which was formerly believed.

ISHBOSHETH, son of Saul, succeeded his father as king of Israel (2 Sam. 2:8-10). He appears to have been little more than a figurehead for the general Abner, who was the strong man behind the throne, and when Abner deserted to join David,

Ishbosheth's reign came to an ignominious end (2 Sam. 4:1-12). The name Ish-bosheth means 'man of shame' and it is probable that his actual name was Ish-baal, 'man of Baal' (Eshbaal in 1 Chron. 8:33). The change was made because the editors of 2 Samuel found proper names compounded with that of the Canaanite god Baal unacceptable, and also to indicate that the divine favour was no longer with the line of Saul.

ISHMAEL is a name found several times in the Old Testament, but the only individual of whom any detailed information is added is the son of Abraham, born to him by the concubine Hagar (Gen. 16:15) and driven away after the birth of Isaac to Abraham's wife Sarah. The Genesis stories give us no real individual picture of Ishmael; most of what is told of him really refers to the semi-nomadic groups of Ishmaelites, of whom he is regarded as the eponymous ancestor. This explains both the references to Ishmael as a great nation and an expert bowman (Gen. 21:18-20) and the lists of Ishmaelite chiefs named as his sons in Gen. 25:12-16.

ISRAEL is an alternative name for Jacob (q.v.), given to him after the story of his wrestling with the angel in Gen. 32:23. In the Old Testament it is never a name for a geographical area; it either denotes a nation (the northern kingdom as against the southern kingdom of Judah) or a religious community (the people who were devotees of the god Yahweh). There is dispute as to whether there was already a recognisable entity known as Israel which sojourned in Egypt and was delivered at the Red Sea, or whether Israel only came into existence on Palestinian soil. In any case it seems that the naming of Jacob as 'Israel' is a later reflection about the people's origin, analogous to the claim that the tribes of Israel were named after the twelve sons of Jacob.

ISSACHAR was primarily the name of a tribal group who occupied a northern area and whose most spectacular role in history occurred at the time of the great battle against Sisera described in Judg. 4-5. It is possible that Deborah, who seems to have inspired the people on that occasion, was from Issachar (Judg. 5:15). As with the other tribes, the ancestry of Issachar is traced back to an individual, a son of Jacob (Gen. 30:18). As a northern group, Issachar played only a minor role in the later Old Testament story, which was edited from a southern viewpoint.

ITHAMAR was the fourth of the sons of Aaron according to Exod. 6:23, but his importance for later Judaism lies not in any personal details of his life, of which nothing is known, but in the fact that he and his brother Eleazar were regarded as those through whom the Aaronic priestly succession was handed down. The line through Ithamar was regarded as valid but less honourable than that through Eleazar, and so most of the priestly families claimed to be descended from Eleazar (1 Chron. 24:1-4).

ITTAI was one of the leaders of David's forces who remained loyal to him during the revolt of his son Absalom (2 Sam. 15: 19-22). This is remarkable in that Ittai was an alien who remained loyal to a king whose own son was fighting against him, and also because he was a Philistine, a representative of Israel's former enemies, and probably therefore a mercenary soldier in David's service.

JABIN, king of the Canaanite city of Hazor, was one of the local rulers overcome by Israel during the course of her establishment in Canaan. Josh. 11:1-13 provides an account of his defeat and death at the hands of Joshua; Judg. 4:2, 24 describes the defeat of his army by forces inspired by Deborah. It is not likely that there were two separate kings called Jabin, but more probable that these are two accounts of the defeat of the same ruler, and it is noteworthy that in Judg. 4 the real enemy is not Jabin but Sisera. Some modern archaeologists have suggested that the excavations of Hazor, showing extensive devastation in the thirteenth century B.C., provide an illustration of the defeat of Jabin and the Israelite occupation of the area.

JACOB, the third of the patriarchs whose story is told in Genesis, is also called Israel, and is therefore regarded as the founder of the people, a point which is emphasised by the fact that the 'founding fathers' of the twelve tribes are regarded as sons of Jacob. Yet compared with the idealisation that has taken place in regard to other possible 'founders' of the nation, Abraham and Moses, the portrait of Jacob is a very ambiguous one. He obtains the birthright and the blessing by deceit, taking full advantage of his brother's folly and his father's blindness (Gen. 25:29-34; 27: 1-40), and outwits his crafty father-in-law Laban as he amasses

67

greater wealth (Gen. 31:25-43). Indeed he is not above doing a deal with God which he regards as likely to be advantageous to both of them (Gen. 28:18-22). These stories reflect something of the delight commonly found in folk-tales when the cunning hero triumphs over a stronger but less skilful rival. But they also reflect a belief in divine justice: Jacob is long an exile from his own land, and his story ends with his anxiety over the fate of his sons, and even when reunited with his family it is no longer in the promised land of Palestine.

Two other major elements in the Jacob stories are important. The first is the role he is given in the foundation of what were later to be important holy places, notably Bethel (Gen. 28:11-22). It was important for a sanctuary to be able to claim that it originated with one of Israel's great figures. The same motif can be found in the association of Christian churches with particular saints.

The second important theme is that of Jacob as founding father. This is exemplified in his alternative name, Israel; the description of the birth and naming of his twelve sons is given in detail (Gen. 29:31-32:24; 35:16-21); and the last part of the Jacob story is largely given over to the exploits of the twelve brothers, their father now being regarded as a feeble old man. Sometime the brothers are pictured as individuals (e.g. in the selling of Joseph into Egypt, Gen. 37), sometimes they appear to personify tribes (e.g. in the assault of Shechem, Gen. 34).

Ancient traditions undoubtedly underlie these stories, but they are not history in the sense in which that term would nowadays be understood. Dates ranging from the eighteenth to the fourteenth century B.C. have been proposed for these events; it is argued whether the descent into Egypt should in some way be associated with the Semitic rulers of Egypt known as the Hyksos (seventeenth century), or with the troubled conditions revealed by the archaeological finds known as the Amarna letters (fourteenth century). In other words, closer investigation shows that is is not possible to trace a succession from Abraham through Jacob and Joseph to Moses. This material should be understood as story, incorporating much ancient material, rather than more narrowly as history.

JADDUA was said by the Jewish historian Josephus to be the Jewish high priest at the time of Alexander the Great (c. 330 B.C.). It is likely that this is the same as the priest mentioned in Neh. 12:11, 22, and, if so, he would be the latest person mentioned in the Old Testament save for the 'prophetic' references to later figures in Daniel. Unfortunately, Josephus' dating is not always reliable, so this point cannot be certainly established.

JAEL, the wife of Heber the Kenite, is praised in Judg. 4 and 5 for what might appear to be a remarkably unscrupulous act. Having granted hospitality to the beaten general Sisera, she then killed him, either as he drank the milk she offered him (5:25-27) or while he slept (4:17-22). Whatever the detail, the sense of exultation of the Israelite poet at the removal of a dreaded emeny led him to gloss over the circumstances of the deed and to proclaim Jael as 'blest above all women'.

JAIR is both a personal and a district name in the Old Testament, and the relation between the two is not always clear. One person named Jair is described in Num. 32:41 and elsewhere as one of the heroes of Israel's settlement in Canaan, after whom the area of Havvoth-Jair was named. But in Judg. 10:3-5 this district is said to have been named after a different Jair, who was a judge of Israel, one of the 'minor judges', so called because of the paucity of our information about them. Probably these are variants of the same trans-Jordanian tradition.

JAPHETH, the second son of Noah, is regarded by the table of nations in Gen. 10 as one of the three from whom all the nations of the world are descended. Not all the descendants of Japheth in vv. 2-5 can be identified, but they appear to be those peoples of whom Israel was aware who lived to the north of Palestine. There is no scientific basis for the table of nations.

JASON is one Greek form of the Hebrew name Joshua, for which a more familiar Greek form is Jesus. Two very different characters of this name are referred to in 2 Maccabees. First, the whole book is described as an abridgement of a more substantial history written by Jason of Cyrene (2 Macc. 2:19-24), of whom nothing else is known. He was presumably a Jew who originated from Cyrene in modern Libya. Secondly, one of the principal characters of the book — and, to the author, one of the villains of the piece — was the high priest Jason, who obtained the office by bribery in 174 B.C. (2 Macc. 4:7-10), and in return introduced hellenistic practices which were anathema to the strict Jews of Jerusalem. Outbidden by a rival claimant to the high priesthood, he tried to regain it by force, but was beaten off and died an exile in Sparta, in Greece (2 Macc. 5:10). Like others involved in the great struggles of this period, it may well be that he has suffered from having only a hostile view presented of his activity.

JEDUTHUN is the name given at 1 Chron. 25:1 to the founder of one of the three musical groups; elsewhere the equivalent name is Ethan. As usual in the Chronicler's accounts of the worship

69

of the temple, it is probable that he was describing what would have been familiar to his contemporaries, so we cannot be certain whether there was an actual individual named Jeduthun at the time of David.

JEHOAHAZ. Three kings of Israel or Judah bore the name Jehoahaz. The name is a variant of 'Ahaziah' (with the divine element as a prefix instead of as a suffix) and the first one, who ruled over Judah in the 840s B.C., is more usually known as Ahaziah (q.v.). Some thirty years later another Jehoahaz ruled Israel (2 Kings 13:1-9), at a time when the country was little more than a vassal of her northern neighbour, the Aramaean kingdom of Damascus. Finally, in the last years of the southern kingdom, Judah, an attempt to establish another Jehoahaz as king after the death of his father Josiah was thwarted by the Egyptians who were trying to establish control over Palestine at that time (609-8 B.C.) (2 Kings 23:30-33). This Jehoahaz is also known as Shallum (1 Chron. 3:25; Jer. 22:11); it is likely that the latter was his personal name, Jehoahaz being his official name given when he became king. It is likely that he was the 'young lion' referred to in Ezekiel's lament over Judah's kings (Ezek. 19:3).

JEHOIACHIN was the last king to rule a free and independent Judah — for just three months! (2 Kings 24:8). It appears that the Babylonian siege was already far advanced when he became king, and the city was captured in March 597 B.C. Because he surrendered, his life was spared, though he and his entourage were deported to Babylon. It is clear that some of the people continued to regard him as the legitimate king: the dates in Ezekiel are based on the years of his reign (1:1 and elsewhere) and jar-handles mentioning his name have been found which imply the same thing. More remarkably a set of tablets excavated in Babylon proved to give details of the rations to be allocated to 'Yaukin king of Judah' and his family. We last hear of him in the epilogue to 2 Kings (25: 27-30), where the author provides a kind of hopeful coda to the book, by describing Jehoiachin's restoration to favour at the Babylonian court.

JEHOIADA. Of several Old Testament figures with this name, the most significant is the priest whose actions played a major role in maintaining the purity of religion and the Davidic succession in the ninth century B.C. (2 Kings 11). He organised the coup which led to the overthrow of the usurping queen Athaliah and the stamping-out of the false worship she had introduced. 2 Chronicles supplies the further details that he was the son-in-law of the former king of Judah, and that his Davidic protege Joash neglected his good advice after Jehoiada's death and fell away.

JEHOIAKIM, king of Judah 609-598 B.C. is condemned by all the biblical sources which refer to him. He lived at a difficult time, when Egypt and Babylon were each trying to establish control over Palestine after the collapse of Assyrian power, and some of the condemnations may appear too severe because of the external difficulties, but it still seems probable that he was a harsh and unscrupulous ruler. Put on the throne by the Pharaoh of Egypt (2 Kings 23:34), he later transferred his allegiance to the Babylonians after they defeated the Egyptians at Carchemish (605), and then rebelled against his new masters in about 601, after they had been unsuccessful in a further battle with Egypt. But Nebuchadnezzar and the Babylonians were still much too strong for Judah, and Jerusalem was besieged and fell in 597. Jehoiakim had died shortly before the city fell: peacefully according to 2 Kings 24:6, but Jer. 22:18 implies an ignominious death. That verse comes in a passage sharply condemning the king, and Jer. 36 also illustrates his contempt for God's word spoken through his prophets, in the vivid story of the king attempting to thwart the prophecy by cutting the scroll in pieces (Jer. 36:21-32).

JEHOSHAPHAT was king of Judah in the mid-ninth century B.C., but the accounts in Kings and Chronicles pose acute historical problems. 1 Kings 22:41-50 gives a brief summary account of his reign, which implies that he apparently prospered save for the ship-wreck described in v. 48. But the earlier part of the same chapter describes a joint expedition by Jehoshaphat and Ahab, the king of Israel, against Ramoth-Gilead, which ended in disaster. There the impression is given that Jehoshaphat was little more than a vassal of the much more powerful northern king. Many modern scholars, however, feel that both the kings in this story were originally anonymous, and the adding of the names of Ahab and Jehoshaphat was a later detail to give greater vividness to the story.

Even more disputed is the lengthy account praising Jehoshaphat in 2 Chron. 17-20. These chapters describe a kind of teaching mission to expound the law of the Lord (17:7-9); a great legal reform (19) and a victory over an enemy army which is achieved by prayer rather than by force of arms (20). Since none of these events is mentioned in sources earlier than the Chronicler (fourth century B.C.), and since they accord so well with his theological ideas, we should be cautious about their historicity. They seem rather to be stories told to illustrate the meaning of the name Jehoshaphat — 'the Lord judges'.

71

JEHOVAH is the name given in some English translations for the God of Israel (Exod. 3:15 and elsewhere) and is an artificial name devised by translators. The actual name of Israel's God was most probably *Yahweh*, but for reverential reasons this was never pronounced, the form *Adonay*, meaning 'lord' or 'master' being used instead. In writing, the consonants of the divine name YHWH were supplied with vowels to form YaHoWaH — from which the form Jehovah was derived. In this book, and in most modern translations of the Bible, the generalised form 'Lord' is used instead.

JEHU, king of Israel in the second half of the ninth century B.C. has given his name to the English language as a description of one who 'drives furiously' (2 Kings 9:20). The reference occurs in the middle of the account of the coup d'etat by which Jehu seized the throne from Joram, the last king of the dynasty of Omri (q.v.). It seems to have been felt in prophetic circles that that dynasty had compromised itself by its attachment to foreign religious practices and must therefore be removed. Hence Jehu's rising is instigated by the prophet Elisha (2 Kings 9:1-13) and supported by the religious leader Jonadab the son of Rechab (2 Kings 10:15-23). It is questionable whether much was gained, for the revolt was accomplished by bloody massacre, not only of the surviving members of the royal family (2 Kings 9:30-10:14) but also of all those involved in idolatrous worship (2 Kings 10-15-27), and a century later the prophet Hosea still had a vivid idea of the damage done by the slaughter (Hosea 1:4).

Jehu has the unique distinction of being the only Israelite king of whom we have a pictorial representation. In about 841 B.C. he was forced to pay tribute to the Assyrian king, Shalmaneser III — an incident not mentioned in the Old Testament — and an Assyrian obelisk depicting Jehu and other subject kings grovelling before Shalmaneser was discovered in 1846 and is now in the British Museum, London.

JEHU is also the name of a prophet mentioned, both in 1 Kings 16, as warning of the destruction which would befall the dynasty of Baasha, king of Israel, and in 2 Chron. 20:34, where he is said to have been the author of a 'history' of which nothing is known; it may simply be a reference to the part played by him in the books of Kings.

JEPHTHAH was one of the judges whose exploits are described in the book of Judges. Like the others he is pictured as if he ruled all Israel (Judg. 12:7), but his sphere of activity seems to have been limited to trans-Jordan. All the other major judges are credited with having ruled Israel for a round number of years, in each case a multiple of twenty, but Jephthah's 'six years' link him with the minor judges of Judg. 10 and 12, while his exploits against the raiding Ammonites are more akin to the stories of the major judges.

There are other features of the account of Jephthah which make it distinctive among the judge stories. He is first rejected because of his mother's status (Judg. 11:1f.), and this suggests some form of hereditary succession, even in days before there was a king of Israel. The end of his story shows that there were divisions within Israel as well as enemies external to her, and different parts of the country varied in their dialects. The word *shibboleth* (originally an ear of corn) has come into English with the sense of 'stumbling-block' (Judg. 12:6). Finally, Jephthah is also remembered for the story of the tragic fate of his daughter, sacrificed to God in accordance with the vow he had made (Judg. 11:30-40). The story should probably be understood as an explanation of a ceremonial believed once to have been practised in Israel.

JEREMIAH is one of the great religious figures of history, who has been ill-served by the association with the word 'jeremiad' meaning a 'doleful complaint'. There is much in the book that is of this nature, but a great deal more beside. As is usually the case with Old Testament prophets, our only knowledge comes from the book named after him; he is mentioned in later Old Testament writings (Chronicles, Ezra and Daniel) as well as the Apocrypha (the pseudonymous Letter of Jeremiah), but these allusions are based on the tradition now enshrined in the book, and convey no reliable separate information. The book of Lamentations, with which he has traditionally been associated, may be contemporary with him, but there is no reason for supposing it to be by him.

The period of Jeremiah's ministry was one of dramatic and disastrous changes in the life of his people. His call came in about 626 B.C. (Jer. 1:2), at a time when Judah's future seemed bright. The Assyrian Empire, which had dominated Palestine for over a century, was in a state of collapse, and Judah seemed likely to gain real independence under Josiah. Political independence often entailed religious independence, and there was a revival of the pure worship of Israel's own God with the destruction of foreign forms of worship.

Within a few years all this had changed; Josiah met an ignominious death at the hands of the Egyptians (2 Kings 23:29f.), and instead of gaining independence, Judah found herself forced to serve first Egypt and then the new power of Babylon. Attempts at rebellion proved futile, and led first to the capture of Jerusalem and the reduction of Judah to vassalage in 597 B.C., and then — after another rebellion — to the destruction of Jerusalem and its main buildings, including the temple, in 587/6 B.C. The leading citizens were exiled, and the state of Judah as a distinct entity came to an end.

Jeremiah was active throughout these events, and his message was a grim one. Earlier prophets had warned of the Lord's anger against his people if they failed to mend their ways; Jeremiah saw those warnings coming into effect and refused to modify them. Any who prophesied a happy ending to the crisis were false prophets (Jer. 28), and only by surrender to the king of Babylon could the Lord be served (Jer. 27). It is no wonder that at a time of intense patriotism such words were regarded as treason, and Jeremiah was nearly a victim of lynch-law (Jer. 37 and 38 — these may be two different accounts of the same events). The worship of the people had previously been intimately connected with the land itself, but Jeremiah was convinced that the only hope for the future lay with those exiled away from the land, in Babylon, and in a letter he urged them to settle in Babylon, to pray for its rulers, and to set aside hopes of a speedy return (Jer. 29). He himself was taken against his will to another Jewish community in Egypt (Jer. 43-44), and it is probable that he died there.

Jeremiah had incurred the wrath of kings, priests, prophets and many other of his fellow-countrymen, yet is is clear that there were others who realised the truth of his words. The scribe Baruch is mentioned several times as one such (e.g. ch. 36), and it is probable that the stories about Jeremiah which make up much of chs. 26-45 of his book were brought together by a group whom we call 'Deuteronomists', because their style and theological interests are akin to the book of Deuteronomy.

But Jeremiah's own words, found mainly in chs. 1-25 of his book, bring out another aspect of his ministry. In a series of psalm-like laments addressed to God, he bemoans his lot, and, in astonishingly direct language, blames God for getting him into his predicament (e.g. Jer. 20:7). It is much disputed whether these 'confessions', as they are often called, give us an insight into the mind of the man himself, or whether they should be regarded as liturgical pieces. What also emerges from these earlier chapters of the book is the extent to which he set himself against all the established religion of the day: he preaches against the temple (ch. 7), he condemns his fellow prophets (23:9-32), he attacks the king himself (ch. 22).

Despite all this, when things were at their darkest, he was able to discern hope for the future. This is symbolised in the care with which he arranged for the transfer of a piece of family property (32:6-15), and in particular by the vision of a new covenant, after the breakdown of the old one. The words of Jer. 31:31-34 may be those of the Deuteronomists, but the basic theme is likely to go back to the prophet himself — a conviction that God's grace toward his people would outlast all their failings. It is not surprising that these words were taken up in the New Testament (Heb. 8:8-12) or that some of his contemporaries saw Jesus as a newly arisen Jeremiah (Matt. 16:14).

JEROBOAM I was the first ruler of the northern kingdom after the death of Solomon and the division of his empire (late tenth century B.C.). The immediate impression given by the Old Testament account (1 Kings 11-12) may be misleading, since it pictures the secession as if it were a small group of disaffected rebels; in fact the greater part of the kingdom followed Jeroboam, leaving Solomon's son Rehoboam with the capital, Jerusalem, and a small surrounding area. It is appropriate that the name Israel should be given to Jeroboam's kingdom, as much the more powerful and politically significant. The main problem was the lack of a suitable capital, and this was not finally overcome until Samaria was built half a century later. Jeroboam first established himself at Shechem, an ancient site, then at Penuel in trans-Jordan (1 Kings 12:25), and finally at Tirzah, near Shechem but more easily defensible (1 Kings 14:17). It may be that these moves were connected in some way with the raids on Palestine carried out by the Egyptian Pharaoh Shishak (1 Kings 14:25 refers only to Judah, but Shishak's own records make it clear that his attack was more far-reaching).

The biblical attitude to Jeroboam is ambivalent. At first he is treated sympathetically (1 Kings 11:26-40), and the rebels' cause in ch. 12 seems to be a just one. Yet when the kingdom is established under Jeroboam it is consistently denigrated; only in Jerusalem and by the properly appointed cultic staff could the Lord be worshipped, and so Jeroboam's religious measures gave particular offence (1 Kings 12:26-33). After him, virtually every king of the northern kingdom is characterised as following 'all the ways of Jeroboam the son of Nebat, which he made Israel to sin' (e.g. 2 Kings 13:2). It is clear that this is a judgement from a particular, Deuteronomic, religious standpoint, rather than an attempt at historical impartiality of the kind we might attempt nowadays.

JEROBOAM II was the last king of the northern kingdom, Israel, before the period of chaos which marked its last years. His reign is briefly described in 2 Kings 14:23-29, and appears to have been a time of prosperity. Assyria was unable to mount a threat and Jeroboam extended his frontiers to an extent unknown since the days of Solomon. The prophets Amos and Hosea were active at this time, warning that the prosperity would be short-lived, but it is impossible to tell whether the social injustice which they condemn so vigorously (e.g. Amos 2:6-8; Hosea 4:1-3) was something particularly characteristic of this period, or whether the prophets focused attention upon a weakness that was endemic in Israel's society. Jeroboam's long reign ended in about 746 B.C., just before the accession of the first great conquering Assyrian king, Tiglath-Pileser III.

JERUBBAAL is the name given to the judge Gideon after his destruction of the Baal altar (Judg. 6:32). Subsequently it is specified that he was the father of Abimelech (9:1). It is possible that this was an alternative name of Gideon, but more probably two separate heroes have been confused in folk memory, partly because each of them was associated with an alter story, and so they have become assimilated. The name Jerubbaal suggests that he was in fact a Baal-worshipper, and it is noteworthy that in 2 Sam. 11:21 he is called Jerubbesheth, with the word 'shame' (*bosheth*) being substituted for the detested name Baal.

JESHUA is a variant of the more familiar name Joshua, but for convenience we may use this form for the high priest of the sixth century B.C., leaving the more usual name for the hero of Israel's settlement in Palestine. For the high priest the form Jeshua is used in Ezra and Nehemiah, and Joshua in Haggai and Zechariah.

He may well be the first figure to whom the title of high priest can appropriately be given, and from his time on, with no king, the Jerusalem community turned increasingly to the high priest as its leader in all aspects of its life. He was exhorted by Haggai to lead the people in the rebuilding of the temple (Hag. 1), and the visions in Zechariah foreshadow something of the exalted role the high priest was to play (Zech. 3:1-5). In the earlier oracles he is mentioned along with Zerubbabel, who was a member of the royal family, but later Zerubbabel disappears from the scene and Jeshua is left alone as the recipient of the divine promises (e.g. Zech. 6: 9-14, where the mention of 'two crowns' makes it likely that once Zerubbabel was mentioned alongside Jeshua).

JESSE, the father of David, is mentioned in the Bible only in stories whose real subject is David. All we really know of him is that he lived in Bethlehem, though the impression given (e.g. by

1 Sam. 16:1-13) is that he was a man of some substance. The tradition in 1 Sam. 17:13, 28 seems to imply that he had four sons, whereas 1 Sam. 16:10f. implies eight and 1Chron. 2:15 seven; exactness in details of this kind is often lacking in Old Testament traditions. The term 'son of Jesse', at first used slightingly of David (1 Sam. 20:27) came eventually to be a title of honour for the expected messianic ruler (Acts 13:22), and the expression 'stump' or 'root' of Jesse was used similarly (Isa. 11:1, 10), giving rise ultimately to the 'Jesse-windows' found in some of our great cathedrals, portraying the descent of Jesus from Jesse.

JESUS
See *Sira*.

JETHRO, the father-in-law of Moses, has occupied the attention of biblical scholars for two main reasons. First, his name presents a problem. Jethro is the name given in Exod. 3:1; 4:18; 18:1-12, whereas in Exod. 2:18 and Num. 10:29 he is called Reuel, and in Judg. 4:11 his name is Hobab, who in Num. 10:29 is the son of Reuel. Some scholars have felt that it is inevitable that complex traditions should arise around great figures like Moses, and that it is impossible to reconcile them. If reconciliation is possible, it may be along the lines that Reuel is a clan or family name, and that Hobab was Moses' brother-in-law rather than his father-in-law.

A more important point is the suggestion that Moses received the knowledge of Yahweh, who came to be the God of Israel, from his father-in-law, and that Yahweh had originally been the god of the Kenite clan. This argument is supported by reference to Exod. 18:10-12, where Jethro takes the initiative in offering sacrifices to Yahweh (English versions: the Lord), and it is speculated that Moses first learnt of Yahweh during his sojourn with Jethro. Support for this idea is found in the fact that the Kenites — to whom Jethro belonged according to one tradition — are always sympathetically described in the Old Testament. But the theory, though ingenious, has too many gaps to be more than a theory. What is established is the kinship between earliest Israel and other semi-nomadic groups inhabiting the desert fringes.

JEZEBEL, the Tyrian-born wife of Ahab king of Israel, is, to a far greater extent than her husband, the villain of the Elijah stories. It is her prophets whom Elijah confronts on Mount Carmel (1 Kings 18:19); it is she who vows to be revenged on Elijah (1 Kings 19:2); it is she who engineers the death of Naboth when he thwarts the royal will (1 Kings 21:5-16). Behind the dramatic confrontation of the story-teller we may discern two different conceptions of royal power. For Jezebel, the king was the earthly embodiment of the divine will, and laws were made — and could if necessary be un-made — by him. This view seems sometimes to have been espoused by members of the Davidic line in Jerusalem, but was always opposed in the northern kingdom by the prophets like Elijah, who regarded the whole people as being in covenant with God, so that the king could not impose his wishes on them. The prophetic view was exclusive in another sense — that only the Lord could be worshipped in Israel. The conflict on Mount Carmel was designed to show that Baal had no power, and therefore no right, in Israel.

Jezebel's death came about in the bloody purge initiated by Jehu (q.v.). Her final act of defiance and her gruesome fate are vividly described in 2 Kings 9:30-37. Her influence continued after her death, in that her daughter Athaliah was able to seize power in Judah, and in another sense has continued much longer: already in the New Testament the name is used to typify false religious pretensions (Rev. 2:20) and it has come into the English language as a more general term of abuse against women whose behaviour is disapproved of; curiously the name Isabel, which appears to have the same derivation, has remained entirely acceptable.

JEZREEL was the name given by the prophet Hosea to one of his children (Hosea 1:4f.). As is often the case in the Old Testament (particularly in connection with prophets) the name had a symbolic significance. Jezreel was the place of the massacre by which the ruling dynasty had come to power (2 Kings 9:30-37), but the new line of kings had proved no better than its predecessors, and would itself be destroyed. We are not told how the symbolism in the child's name was to be recognised by the rulers; the fact is simply recorded in the book of Hosea.

JOAB was David's leading general, and his fortunes are interlocked with those of his master throughout David's reign. He appears to have been the king's nephew, since he is always called 'son of Zeruiah', and she was apparently David's sister (1 Chron. 2:16). (The cautious 'apparently' is necessary, because it is only in 1 Chronicles, written much later, that this relationship is stated, and that may itself be an attempt to explain the unusual prominence given to a woman; we never hear of the identity of her husband.)

Joab's career shows that at that time (tenth century B.C.) only a very thin veneer of civilisation covered the endemic warfare and intrigue in which government was involved. He first appears in an account of single combat which turned into a mass slaughter (2 Sam.

2:12-17); he was involved in a blood-feud against Saul's general Abner (2 Sam. 2:18-32) whom he eventually murdered in cold blood (2 Sam. 3:26-30); he connived at the murder of Uriah so that David might have his wife Bathsheba (2 Sam. 11:14-21), and when David's son Absalom rebelled against his father, Joab killed him in express defiance of the king's commands (2 Sam. 18:5-15). He lost his position as commander of David's forces and once again took a treacherous revenge on Amasa, who had replaced him (2 Sam. 20:4-10).

It is also clear that Joab had his redeeming qualities. He was brave, playing a major part in the capture of the apparently impregnable stronghold of Jerusalem (1 Chron. 11:4-8), and utterly loyal to what he considered to be David's best interests, even if this involved disobeying his commands. But he lived at a time when something more than heroism was needed; the old society was giving way to a more sophisticated structure in which subtlety as well as violent deeds of valour was required. Inevitably his end was violent; in the intrigues concerning David's successor, he supported Adonijah rather than Solomon, (1 Kings 1:7) and when Solomon had gained power he lost no time in having Joab eliminated, even though he had claimed sanctuary at God's alter (1 Kings 2:28-35). The manner of his death matched much of his life.

JOASH is a shorter form of the name Jehoash. In the Hebrew Bible both forms are used without discrimination; English versions have varied customs, some following the Hebrew, others giving a uniform rendering in either the short or the long form. Here Joash will be used throughout. It is probable that eight different men of this name are found in the Old Testament, of whom four may be noted here.

JOASH the father of Gideon was a member of the clan of Abiezer (Judg. 6:11-32). The site of his home, Ophrah, has not been identified. Judg. 6:26 might suggest that he was a Baal-worshipper, but it is likely that the two names apparently given to his son (Gideon and Jerubbaal) really enshrine traditions about two different people; if so the tradition of the Baal altar would involve Jerubbaal and his (unnamed) father, and not relate to Joash or Gideon. Since the name Joash means 'yahweh has given', a Baal connection seems unlikely.

JOASH the son of the king of Israel is mentioned in 1 Kings 22:26 as being given responsibility for the recalcitrant prophet Micaiah. If the king of that story is really Ahab (v. 20) nothing else is known of this Joash, but it may well be that the kings in this story were originally anonymous, in which case this Joash might be identical with the last one mentioned below.

JOASH king of Judah in the last third of the ninth century was the child who escaped the slaughter of the royal family by Athaliah (2 Kings 11:1f.) and was subsequently brought to the throne by a counter-coup (2 Kings 11:4-12); the account of his accession is of special interest as being the only one in the Old Testament providing any detail of the ceremonies. It is indicative of the particular concerns of the editors of the book of Kings that the main incident recounted of his long reign is his repair of the temple, presumably because of its desecration under Athaliah (2 Kings 12:4-16); there is also a brief note of a humiliating defeat at the hands of the Aramaeans and of a revolt against him which led to his death (2 Kings 12:15-21). In Kings these are simply recounted as separate incidents, but the Chronicler characteristically explains these setbacks as being caused by Joash's own fall from grace which culminated in his having the priest-prophet Zechariah stoned to death. Joash's misfortunes are then seen as divine punishment (2 Chron. 24:17-27), but this should probably be regarded as sermon-illustration rather than accurate history.

JOASH king of Israel came to the throne just before the death of his namesake in Judah (2 Kings 13:10). His reign appears to have been successful, at least in the military sense, for he won victories over the Aramaeans (2 Kings 13:24f.). In this he may have been helped by Assyrian pressure on other fronts, as is now described in Assyrian records, one of which mentions his name in a list of subject kings. He reduced Judah to virtual vassalage (2 Kings 14:8-14, a passage which contains a rare Old Testament example of a short fable). Though the editors of 2 Kings condemn Joash for religious malpractice (13:2), it seems that his reign was in fact the beginning of one of her times of greatest prosperity, which reached its climax under his son Jeroboam II.

JOB is the central character in the book of that name. He is also referred to in Ezek. 14:14, 20, which may imply that he was regarded as a traditional righteous figure from remote antiquity, but we have no means of assessing the historicity of such a figure, or of suggesting a likely date. Older speculations that Job should be identified with the Edomite Jobab (Gen. 36:33) have now been abandoned. The prose prologue and epilogue of the book of Job are a folk-tale, which again offers no clues as to historical setting, and the poetry transcends details of this kind. (An ancient Near-Eastern text has sometimes been called 'the Babylonian Job', but this title comes from the similarity of theme, not from the presence in it of a figure named Job.)

The importance of Job lies, therefore, in the message of the book and not in any historical gleanings. The book has exercised unending fascination for artists of all kinds; here it is possible only to say that Job's suffering appears to draw out the theme of the transitoriness of man in his standing before God, a status which gives rise to problems which offer no easy solutions.

JOCHEBED was the mother of Moses (Exod. 6:20). Nothing is known of the details of her life, and the main interest has centred around her name. The 'Jo-' prefix is probably a short form of the divine name Yahweh, and this cuts across the view that Yahweh (the Lord) first revealed himself to Moses; probably his worship was already practised among some of Moses' ancestors.

JOEL is a common Old Testament name, borne by at least twelve different characters. Apart from the elder son of Samuel (1 Sam. 8:2), who is regarded as unworthy of following his father, all are simply recorded in lists without personal details, except for the prophet Joel after whom a book is named.

The prophet is called 'son of Pethuel' (1:1), but nothing is known of him as an individual. Even the date and place of his activity are obscure; the placing of the book second among the twelve minor prophets may have been influenced by the belief that he lived before the exile, perhaps in the eighth century B.C., but most modern writers take him to be a post-exilic figure, from perhaps the fifth century. Again, though there are no clear indications of place, it is likely that he was a member of the Jerusalem community, possibly involved with the second temple.

The imagery of the book uses the disasters of drought (1:8-12) and a plague of locusts (1:5-7) as symbolising the imminent day of the Lord (1:15). But beyond the immediate disaster lies hope for the future, if the people will repent, and take the appropriate ritual actions. There are elements here reminiscent of the visionary language of the apocalyptic writings, and many have seen both the theme of disaster leading to triumph and the vivid symbolism of the book as indicating a transition from the classical prophets of an earlier age to the apocalyptists of the last centuries B.C.

JOHANAN, the Hebrew form from which our name John derives, is a very common Old Testament name; fifteen characters bear either this name or the variant form Jehohanan. Of these only two fall to be treated here because of individual details recorded about them.

81

JOHANAN son of Kareah is mentioned only by name in 2 Kings 25:23, but plays a prominent part in Jer. 40-43. He was a military leader who, after the destruction of Jerusalem, gave his support to Gedaliah, whom the Babylonians had appointed governor, and warned him in vain of a plot to assassinate him (Jer. 40:13 – 41:3). He was the leader of those who restored some sort of order thereafter, but was unable to capture the murderers who had compounded their wickedness by killing a group of innocent pilgrims. Johanan felt that it was unlikely that the Babylonians would accept that he was entirely innocent, and decided to flee to Egypt, away from Babylonian reach. This was despite the advice of Jeremiah, whom Johanan and his followers took, protesting, with them.

JOHANAN was the high priest at Jerusalem in the year 410 B.C. This is attested by one of a series of papyri found at Elephantine in Egypt early this century. It is probable that he is also referred to in the books of Ezra and Nehemiah. In Ezra 10:6 Ezra went to the room of 'Johanan son of Eliashib', and in Neh. 12:22f. there is a reference to Johanan son of Eliashib in a context which makes it clear that both of them were high priests, though it remains uncertain whether Johanan was Eliashib's son or grandson. (The New English Bible translates 'grandson' throughout.) There has been much discussion of the date of Ezra, and if it can be established that the biblical references and the Elephantine papyri are speaking of the same individual, there would be a strong case for saying that Ezra came in 398 B.C., under the Persian king Artaxerxes II, and not sixty years earlier under Artaxerxes I, as has commonly been supposed.

JOHN is used in English Bibles as a translation of the Greek form of the Hebrew name Johanan (see previous entry), and so its use in the Old Testament is confined to the Apocrypha. There are four Johns in the book of Maccabees. For one of these, John Hyrcanus, see the next entry; of the others, the only one worthy of further note is the son of Mattathias, the oldest of five brothers (1 Macc. 2:2). But though he was the oldest, he played no significant role in the uprising, and we learn only of his being kidnapped and killed in a skirmish in Transjordan (1 Macc. 9:35-38).

JOHN HYRCANUS, the son of Simon, is the last person to be mentioned in 1 Macc. and therefore the lastest character to be mentioned in the Old Testament and Apocrypha. His father, the last of the Maccabee brothers, was treacherously killed along with the rest of his family (1 Macc. 16:14-17), but John managed to escape and was able to establish himself as king, in practice if not by name. His rule lasted from 134 to 104 B.C., and saw the end of any effective attempt by the Syrians to exercise control over Palestine. But the details of his period of rule are known only from extra-biblical sources; 1 Macc. 16:23-24 simply give a summary statement of his success.

JONADAB is the name of two very different Old Testament characters. The first, a nephew of David, is mentioned several times in 2 Sam. 13. In particular it is his plan that enables the love-lorn Amnon to rape his half-sister Tamar, and thereby bring about further bitterness within David's already divided family. It is note-worthy that his plan is described as 'wise' (2 Sam. 13:3; 'crafty' in some English versions is interpretive), an illustration of the point that wisdom implied know-how rather than any specifically moral judgements.

The other Jonadab lived more than a century later and was the leader of the Rechabites, an intensely conservative group who kept aloof from all association with things regarded as Canaanite — the produce of the vine, agriculture, even city-life itself (Jer. 35:6-10). (At the time of Nebuchadrezzar's siege of Jerusalem the Rechabites had to abandon their refusal to inhabit cities, but they are never-theless praised by Jeremiah in 35:18f.) Jonadab himself played a part in the violent reaction against Canaanite forms of religion associated with Jehu in the 840s (2 Kings 10:15-24). It appears that he was prepared to condone what proved to be a bloody massacre in the interests of the anti-Canaanite ideals he had espoused.

JONAH is the subject of two very different sets of traditions, one of which appears to be solidly founded in history, the other being a popular folk-tale used to draw out religious lessons.

The historical Jonah was apparently active during the eighth century B.C., and, unlike most of the prophets whose oracles have come down to us, he prophesied that Israel would be successful in its dealings with other nations. The prosperous reign of Jeroboam II was taken as fulfilling this word (2 Kings 14:25). All that can be said of this Jonah was that he came from northern Israel, and may have been active in the time of Jeroboam, or earlier, if his words had been handed down in some form of prophetic guild.

Since we know so little of the historical Jonah, there is no means of telling why he should have been chosen as the central figure — we can hardly say 'hero' — of the book named after him. It differs from all the other prophetic books in being a story told about the prophet rather than a setting-down of his oracles. Though the story is allegedly set in Assyrian times, since Jonah is commanded to go to preach in Nineveh, the Assyrian capital (Jonah 1:2), the legendary details about Nineveh in chs. 3 and 4 suggest that the story comes from a much later date. The most familiar episode in the book, Jonah's being swallowed by a sea-monster, is a typical folklore motif, and fits in well with the general popular piety of the whole story. Despite its wonder-working and magical elements, however, the book has an important message: God is in control even of those elements that might seem most alien from him — the heathen empire, the storm at sea, the monster — and it is demanded of Israel that she should welcome a turning to God even from those traditionally regarded as his enemies.

JONATHAN is a very common Old Testament name (probably seventeen different individuals, including those in the Apocrypha). Saul's son is the best known, but several others receive more than a passing mention. Those of whom some details are known are listed here in approximate chronological order.

JONATHAN the grandson of Moses is mentioned in Judg. 18:30, at the end of a long story in chs. 17 and 18 about the establishment of a sanctuary for the tribe of Dan. The priestly figure mentioned has previously been anonymous, but at the end of the story is revealed as being Moses' grandson. At a later date, it was felt inappropriate that Moses' grandson should have been mixed up with a sanctuary which fell into disrepute, and so the name Moses was changed into Manasseh, the 'n' being inserted in an unusual position, 'Ma^{n}asseh', and this accounts for the Authorised Version translation.

JONATHAN the son of Saul is described in 1 Samuel more sympathetically than any other member of his family, toward whom the compiler is generally hostile. This may be because of his evident bravery, which led to the defeat of the Philistines in 1 Sam. 13-14 or because of his great friendship with David, which has become legendary, and led to his helping David to escape from the jealous rage of Saul (1 Sam. 19-20). It is noteworthy that, whereas for much modern society affection between two people of the same sex often brings either indignant charges, or an equally indignant defence, of homosexuality, the biblical account is quite un-selfconscious. The most moving illustration of this is found in the lament uttered by David over Saul and Jonathan, following their death in battle:

I am distressed for you, my brother Jonathan,/very pleasant have you been to me;/your love to me was wonderful,/passing the love of women (2 Sam. 1:26).

It is futile to speculate what would have happened had Jonathan lived, when he and David might have become rivals for the kingdom; his only surviving son, Meribbaal, or Mephibosheth, was never an effective contender for the kingdom because of his physical weakness.

JONATHAN the son of Ahimaaz plays a significant role in two stories, in each case as a bearer of vital news at a time of rebellion. When Absalom rebelled against his father David, Jonathan was employed together with Ahimaaz as a courier to bring news of what Absalom intended; and despite one narrow escape, they were able to keep David informed of his son's plots (2 Sam. 15:35f.; 17:15-20). In the second episode Jonathan found himself on the losing side — he brought the news to the conspirator Adonijah of David's decision that Solomon should be his successor, and Adonijah's cause was consequently doomed (1 Kings 1:41-46).

JONATHAN son of Mattathias was one of the five brothers who are often collectively called the Maccabees, from the name of Judas Maccabaeus, the best known of them. Jonathan was the youngest of the brothers, but on the death of Judas in 160 B.C. he was chosen to carry on the struggle against Syrian rule (1 Macc. 9-12). But by this time the character of the struggle had changed very significantly; now the Jews were no longer a small guerrilla band waging war against a much superior army; divisions within the Syrian Empire meant that skilled diplomacy was as important as military ingenuity, and much of Jonathan's period of supremacy witnessed intrigues whereby he attempted to play off one faction among the Syrians against another. To a large extent he was successful, at least materially; but in the end he over-reached himself and was killed by treachery (143 B.C.). It can also be argued that his intriguing reduced those who struggled for independence to the same level as those against whom their struggle was directed, though 1 Maccabees always paints a favourable picture of all the brothers.

In one other case it is virtually certain, and in another highly probable that 'Jonathan' has been written in error for 'Johanan'. The first is 'Jonathan son of Kareah' (Jer. 40:8), altered to 'Johanan' in most modern translations; the second is the name in the list of high priests at Neh. 12:11, where it is usually held that the same individual is referred to as the 'Johanan' of v. 22. See under *Johanan* for both these figures.

JORAM is a shortened form of the name Jehoram and both the original Hebrew and modern translations have varied greatly in their use of the two forms. Confusion is liable to be increased by the fact that the two important figures with this name were virtual contemporaries, each a king, one in Israel, the other in Judah. It is possible that there was already some confusion in the mind of the editor of the books of Kings, but the main data can probably be established.

JORAM of Israel was the last king of the family of Omri to reign in the land. The tradition in 2 Kings 3:1 makes him contemporary with Jehoshaphat, with whom he waged war against Moab. But the chronological difficulties of the period were considerable, and it is impossible to fit in the twelve years with which he is credited in 2 Kings 3:1 with what is known from Assyrian records, which mention his father Ahab as king in 853 B.C. and his successor Jehu in 841. Jehu succeeded him as a consequence of a violent rebellion led by a group of army officers (2 Kings 9), in which Joram met a violent death (vv. 24-26).

JORAM of Judah was an almost exact contemporary of Joram of Israel, though according to 2 Kings 2:17 he became king before his namesake of Israel (contrast 2 Kings 3:1 and 8:16); since Athaliah, daughter of Ahab, was Joram of Judah's wife, the two men were probably brothers-in-law. The account of his reign in 2 Kings 8 is brief and uninformative; there is greater elaboration in 2 Chron. 21, where a most unfavourable judgement is passed, including details of a massacre committed by Joram within his own family. But, as with many stories peculiar to the Chronicler, there must be some doubt about the historicity of this episode.

JOSEPH is a common name in both Old and New Testaments, but only the patriarch whose adventures are described in Gen. 37-50 is more than a name to us. For the leading New Testament characters called Joseph, see the New Testament section.

The outline of Joseph's story is a familiar one. The child of his father's old age, his dreams of greatness evoke the jealousy of his brothers, who see him into Egypt and pretend to their father Jacob that they have found his coat (the 'coat of many colours' of the Authorised Version; the exact detail of the finery is still disputed). After various further mishaps he eventually rises to a position in Egypt second only to the Pharaoh himself, and finds himself confronted by his brothers when they come to buy corn to relieve their starvation. After he is satisfied that they have repented of their former treachery he reveals himself, Jacob and the brothers come to settle with him in 'the land of Goshen' and all ends happily. The two sons of Joseph, Ephraim and Manasseh, gave their names to two of the leading tribes of Israel, and in the reckoning of the twelve tribes these are normally included rather than Joseph himself.

There is no agreement among scholars as to the historicity of this story. There were periods when groups of Semites rose to considerable power in Egypt, including even one dynasty of Pharaohs, and it is possible that the story of Joseph should be associated with such a group; the difficulty would be that the periods of their influence were for the most part early in the second millennium B.C., and Joseph seems to be placed at a later period. For this reason, and because of the presence of various folk-tale elements in the story, some scholars are inclined to reject the whole as historically worthless. What does seem likely is that the way that the tale is told is intended to emphasise Joseph's *wisdom*. The wise man, in the sense of the shrewd man of affairs, able to see the correct solution to all problems, expert in the interpretation of dreams, and relying on his *savoir-faire* even when things seemed to be going wrong, was a type highly esteemed in Egypt and in some quarters in Israel, and the particular characteristation of the Joseph story brings out these points very vividly. One might almost be reading a story based on the maxims found in the book of Proverbs.

JOSHUA is the central figure of the account of Israel's settlement in Palestine. The book of Joshua is so called, not because he was its author, but because he is the central character. The book presents a most vivid account of Israel's dramatic and totally successful invasion of Palestine under Joshua's leadership. After the crossing of the river Jordan, the key city of Jericho is captured; then Ai, after an initial setback. After that decisive raids first in the south and then in the north of the country pave the way for the division of the land among the tribes under Joshua's direction, so that in the death-bed scenes of the last two chapters of the book, Joshua can regard his work as essentially completed and can bring it to a climax by binding the people on oath to remain loyal to their God.

In this achievement, Joshua is presented as having carried out the tasks for which he had been prepared during the lifetime of his great predecessor Moses; he is introduced in Exod. 33:11 as Moses' assistant, though he has already been referred to without detailed explanation in Exod. 17 and in the episode at Mount Sinai (Exod. 24 and 32). In the story of the spies sent to reconnoitre the land (Num. 13-14) he is one of the two who gives an encouraging report of the people's prospects. (In this story, at 13:8, he is given the alternative name Hoshea, a form found also in Deut. 32:44, but this appears to be no more than editorial variation.)

The most widely divergent opinions have been expressed by

scholars concerning the original role of Joshua. Some have been prepared to accept the biblical account as substantially historical, but there are formidable difficulties. The account of a rapid and successful conquest given in the book of Joshua seems to be sharply at variance with the account in Judg. 1 of a much more long and drawn-out piecemeal process of infiltration. Archaeological excavation has confirmed that there was widespread devastation in Canaan in the thirteenth century B.C. (the most likely date for Joshua), but has found little positive evidence to associate this with Israelite incursions, and at the sites most closely linked with Joshua — Jericho and Ai — there are no traces that the sites were occupied at this period. Literary examination of some of the stories in the book has shown that their primary purpose was aetiological, that is to say, they served as explanation of remarkable geographical features or local customs, and their historicity has therefore been suspected on these grounds. For all these reasons, many would take the view that Joshua was a local hero of the tribe of Ephraim, whose exploits came in the course of time to be magnified so that he was regarded as a judge over all Israel, and as previously having been directly connected with Moses. If this is so, perhaps we should suppose that the personality cult is not a peculiarly modern phenomenon.

JOSIAH, king of Judah from 640 to 609 B.C., was for the editors of the books of Kings the ideal ruler: 'he did what was right in the eyes of the Lord, and walked in all the way of David his father, and he did not turn aside to the right hand or to the left' (2 Kings 22:2). Modern estimates have not always been so enthusiastic.

The basic political background to Josiah's reign was the collapse of the Assyrian Empire, which had dominated the whole of the ancient Near East for more than a century. Though precise details are not known, it would seem that as the Assyrians became ineffective, Josiah attempted to fill the vacuum they left, and to build an empire comparable to that of his ancestor David. To this end he attempted to gain control of the territory of the former northern kingdom of Israel, and archaeological evidence has provided some confirmation of this aspect of his policy. The religious reform described in detail in 2 Kings 22-23 is also related to this: to declare political independence implied also a declaration of religious independence, and religious reform was thus a political act, an assertion of the power of the national god against that of the gods of the former overlords. This appears to be the essential basis of his actions, though the account that has been handed down has been elaborated by the editors of 2 Kings. They were of the group associated with the book of Deuteronomy, and they picture the reform in terms of the faithful carrying out of the requirements of the book of Deuteronomy. But this has always posed a problem, since there are few indications elsewhere in the Old Testament of a thorough-going reform, and it is likely that the reform was as much political as religious.

Josiah met his death in 609 at the hands of the Egyptian Pharaoh Necho, and it seems to have been a clear example of his attempting something beyond his strength, for he appears to have tried to prevent Necho marching through Palestine to the relief of the Assyrians, whose empire had by that time virtually collapsed. The details of his death are differently recorded in 2 Chron. 35:20-27 from the brief account in 2 Kings 23:29f., but the substance is similar. There are few references to him in other parts of the Bible, but the allusion in Jer. 22:15f., which speaks of his judging 'the cause of the poor and needy' suggests that his personal reputation lasted despite the collapse of his political ambitions.

JOTHAM the son of Jerubbaal (Judg. 9:5) is known for the fable associated with him in his condemnation of the attempt to set up a royal dynasty in Shechem (Judg. 9:7-20). After his veiled attack on his half-brother Abimelech he fled for his life (v. 21), and nothing is known of his subsequent fate. The fable itself is used in its present context as a condemnation of those who supported Abimelech's claim to kingship, and perhaps, by implication, of kingship itself; but it may well have existed in its own right simply as a folk-tale.

JOTHAM king of Judah ruled at an important historical period, when the growing power of Assyria posed a threat to Israel and Judah; but unlike other kings of the time, he remains a shadowy figure. The account in 2 Kings 15 mentions a reign of sixteen years, but this is taken to include the unspecified length of a time during which he acted as regent on behalf of his incapacitated father (v. 5). (The note in v. 30 referring to a twenty-year reign is almost certainly an error.) The total period will have been approximately 750-735 B.C., since he apparently died before the threat to Judah posed by the kings of Israel and Damascus in about 734. A somewhat more elaborate account is provided by 2 Chron. 27, but is is doubtful whether this preserves additional historical material.

JUBAL is mentioned in Gen. 4:21 as the progenitor of all musicians. The note can scarcely be historical, but it is another example of what is known as an aetiological legend; here it acts as a story giving the origin of a widespread custom or practice.

JUDAH

JUDAH is a name which has had a complicated history of development, and it is not surprising that confusion has often been the result. Originally, it was probably the name of a district in southern Palestine, near Jerusalem. The name was then given to the people who inhabited the area, and then, as with other groups which comprised the totality of Israel, it was given to an eponymous ancestor, that is, an individual from whom it was believed that the name of the area and its inhabitants had originated. Such stories were developed for all the supposed tribal founders, who were presented as twelve brothers, the sons of Israel. The account of Judah, with a popular etymology linking his name with the theme of praise, is found in Gen. 29:35. The clearest illustration that the stories of the patriarchs are in certain cases really concerned with whole groups of people is found in Gen. 38, where the development of the tribe is implied; and the references to Judah as the kindly disposed brother in the Joseph story (e.g. Gen. 37:26; 43:8f.) may also indicate the prominence of the tribe of Judah. Similarly the blessing of Jacob (Gen. 49:8-12) is concerned with the fortunes of the tribe.

Throughout the period of the monarchy Judah was the name given to the southern kingdom, with its capital in Jerusalem and its ruler a member of the family of David, a Judahite. There are many indications that, even when the kingdom was united, Judah stood somewhat apart from the rest of Israel (e.g. 2 Sam. 19:8-15, 40-43), so that it is likely that the dual monarchy of David and Solomon was an aberrant development rather than the normal state of affairs which the editors of the books of Kings took it to be. The Greek form of Judah is *Judea,* from which comes the word Judaism; while from the Hebrew word meaning an inhabitant of Judah, *Jehudi,* the word Jew is derived.

JUDAS MACCABAEUS, the hero of the Jewish campaigns against Syrian rule in the 160s B.C. is known to us primarily from the stories in 1 Macc. 2-9. In that book, Judas is the great hero, a freedom fighter giving his all to deliver his people from oppression. There are some indications that not every group of Jews regarded the Maccabaean revolt with such enthusiasm as did the author of 1 Maccabees.

Judas was the third son of the priest Mattathias, whose refusal to compromise his religious belief when required to sacrifice on a pagan altar led to the outbreak of the rising, probably in 167 B.C. (1 Macc. 2:23-28). After the death of his father Judas became the leader — no reason is given why the third son should have been the successor — and his subsequent actions are described in terms reminiscent of those applied to the heroes of ancient Israel. By 164 B.C. the campaign had been sufficiently successful for Jerusalem to be reoccupied by the patriotic forces and the temple cleansed and re-dedicated (1 Macc. 4:36-61), an event which was afterwards commemorated by the Feast of Hanukkah or Dedication (John 10:22). Judas continued the struggle, causing increasingly important Syrian forces to be involved in the war, until eventually he was defeated and killed at Elasa in 160 B.C. (1 Macc. 9:1-22).

The eulogy of Judas in 1 Maccabees continues until his death, which is described in terms deliberately reminiscent of David's lament over Saul and Jonathan; but other sources give a more reserved judgement. The book of Daniel describes the Maccabees as 'a little help' (Dan. 11:34), and for the more strictly religious groups it is clear that there were doubts about the aggressive policy pursued by Judas and his immediate followers. The purification of the temple might have served their purpose; further war in itself involved contamination with the very evils which the struggle was aimed at. Despite these doubts the successful struggle waged by Judas exercised a powerful fascination on Jews in the next two centuries, when some groups thought that a similar fight for freedom might be waged against the Romans, and on some movements within Judaism ever since.

JUDITH is the heroine of the story told in the book named after her which now forms part of the Apocrypha, though she plays a part only in the second part of the book (chs. 8-16). A pious and wealthy widow, she was one of the citizens of Bethulia when the city was besieged by Nebuchadnezzar's general Holofernes. The leaders of the city were ready to surrender, but she scorned such craven behaviour, and persuaded the citizens that her plan could save the city. She visited Holofernes, who was captivated by her beauty and held a feast in her honour; but he became so drunk that Judith was able to cut off his head, which she then brought back to the city in the bag in which she had carried her own specially prepared food. The coup brought new heart to the Jews and demoralised the besiegers, who were put to flight. Judith had delivered not only her own city, but the whole country.

This lively story is not historical. Nebuchadnezzar (the king of Babylon) is presented as king of Assyria; no actual city Bethulia is known; and many other details are legendary. Whether a historical nucleus can be detected is uncertain. But the story is basically a romance, setting forth the heroism of Judith (the name is simply 'Jewess') as an example encouraging the people to remain loyal to their faith at a time of oppression, perhaps in the first century B.C.

K

KETURAH, the second wife of Abraham, is mentioned in Gen. 25:1 without any personal details. The tradition describing her marriage to Abraham and the subsequent birth of six sons (Gen. 25:2-5) stands somewhat at odds with the main theme of the Abraham stories in Genesis, which is concerned with the birth to Abraham and Sarah of a son, Isaac, in his parents' extreme old age. It is at least unexpected that Abraham should have remarried and had several further children.

KISH, the father of Saul (1 Sam. 9:1) is mentioned only in the stories dealing with his son. The family lived at Gibeah and belonged to the tribe of Benjamin. Saul's assertion that his family was very insignificant is clearly intended as a polite disclaimer rather than a literal statement, and is in any case contradicted by the extensive family tree provided in 1 Chron. 8:33-40. (The Kish of 1 Chron. 8:30 is probably a different individual.)

KOHATH is named in various genealogical lists (e.g. Gen. 46:11) as a son of Levi. No traditions relating to him as an individual have been handed down, but his family came to be regarded later as especially important, since from it descended Moses and Aaron, and thus all the priestly groups. As with other biblical genealogies it is doubtful to what extent such details are based on factual memory and to what extent they are later idealisation.

KOHELETH.
See *Qoheleth*.

KORAH A good deal of confusion surrounds the various figures in the Old Testament who bore this name. Unrelated to the others are the Edomite chiefs listed in Gen. 36:5, 16. The difficulty arises from attempts to identify or distinguish between the heads of various priestly families of this name. In Num. 16 a story is told of Korah, the head of a priestly family, who claims for his family privileges reserved for Moses and Aaron (Num. 16:3). As a result of this presumption, God sent fire to kill the offenders (v. 35). This story is intertwined with what appears to be an entirely separate one, of the revolt led by Dathan and Abiram, which had no direct connection with religious matters. Another Korah is found in 1 Chron. 6:22, 37, in the priestly lists; and there is also mention of 'Korahites' in 1 Chron. 9:19, where they are doorkeepers, and in the titles of certain Psalms (Pss. 42-49; 84f.; 87f.). Most probably, all these references come from a late stage in the editing of the Old Testament, and reflect disputes concerning the precedence of different priestly families, so that Num. 16 would represent an anti-Korahite tradition propagated by other priestly groups. (The Korah mentioned in 1 Chron. 2:43 appears to be a place-name, though its whereabouts is unknown.)

LABAN plays a prominent but somewhat ambiguous role in the stories about Jacob in Genesis. He is described as an Aramaean (Gen. 25:20), whose exact dwelling-place is unknown, but was near Haran in northern Mesopotamia, which was Abraham's place of origin in one tradition (Gen. 12:4; 27:43). His sister Rebekah married Isaac, and his daughters Leah and Rachel both married Jacob and became mothers of the ancestors of Israel, those after whom the tribes were named.

In some of the stories Laban is presented in a favourable light. He is hospitable to Abraham's steward (Gen. 24:29-33), and he made a covenant with Jacob (Gen. 31:43-55). But elsewhere he is shown as motivated by self-interest. This is true already in the story in Gen. 24, where his hospitality is due in part at least to the hope of a rich reward, but it is much more marked in his dealings with Jacob. Gen. 29-31 tells how he first tricked Jacob by giving him his older daughter Leah rather than the beautiful Rachel as wife; then the deceit in the matter of wages; and finally his anger at Rachel's theft of the household gods (the Hebrew word *teraphim* is given this meaning, almost certainly correctly, by the Revised Standard Version at Gen. 31:34). There is much humour in the stories, which are told partly at least with a view to demonstrating how hopeless it is to attempt to get the better of Jacob, himself a master of deception. The stories may also reflect relations between different semi-nomadic groups which were akin to one another but not always on friendly terms.

LAHMI, mentioned in 1 Chron. 20:5 as brother of the giant Goliath, is almost certainly a fictitious character. The killing of Goliath is attributed in the books of Samuel not only to David but also to Elhanan. The Chronicler, writing much later, solved the problem by making Elhanan's victim 'Lahmi', which is really part of the place-name Bethlehem, and calling him Goliath's brother.

LAMECH is represented in Genesis as being either the sixth (Gen. 4:17f.) or the eighth (Gen. 5) in line of descent from Adam. The two accounts differ also in making his descent through Cain and Seth respectively, and in some of the names of the intervening figures. When these figures and their vast ages were taken as literal history, these differences posed acute problems; they are now seen as illustrative of the varied traditions underlying the ancient records of Genesis. Lamech is singled out for more detailed consideration than the other antediluvian figures. His two wives Adah and Zillah bear children from whom originate various basic human customs: tent-dwelling, musical ability, and the forging of tools (Gen. 4:19-22). These stories, again examples of aetiologies, explaining a characteristic feature of human behaviour, are prominent in the early part of Genesis. With Lamech is associated also the human trait of seeking vengeance (Gen. 4:23f.), in a poetic fragment which is alluded to by Jesus in his requirement of forgiveness on the part of those who would follow him (Matt. 18:22).

LEAH, the elder daughter of Laban (Gen. 29:16f.), became Jacob's wife through trickery; Jacob had courted her beautiful younger sister Rachel, but on the wedding night Leah was substituted for her (vv. 22-27). Leah bore six sons to Jacob (Gen. 29:31-35; 30:14-20), as well as a daughter, Dinah (30:21). These sons bear names which are also those of tribes of Israel, and it is much disputed whether the tribes were named after individuals, or, as seems more probable, the stories of individuals depend on established tribal names. In that case the six 'sons of Leah' may have represented a tribal grouping earlier than that of the whole of Israel.

LEMUEL, king of Massa is mentioned in Prov. 31:1 as the author of the following sayings, which, uniquely, are ascribed to his mother's teaching. But it is doubtful whether Lemuel is properly understood as a proper name, and the word *massa*, unknown as a place-name, elsewhere means an oracle. The exact significance of the phrase may already have been lost when the book of Proverbs was finally edited.

LEVI, the third son of Jacob by his wife Leah (Gen. 29:34) is singled out among the patriarchs for his cruel and violent behaviour, so that the 'blessing' of the dying Jacob upon his sons is in the case of Levi and Simeon turned into a curse (Gen. 49:5-7). The occasion for this condemnation was the manner in which the two brothers are said to have treacherously killed the inhabitants of Shechem and seized their possessions as spoil after the rape of their sister Dinah (Gen. 34:25-31).

This action, like others ascribed to individual patriarchs, was almost certainly a tribal memory, reflecting the unsettled conditions when Israel was establishing itself in Canaan. At a later date the tribe of Levi became the priestly tribe, with certain of its members set apart for full priestly office, while others 'the Levites' performed more menial ecclesiastical duties. It is by no means clear whether there is a relation between the secular group described in Gen. 34 and the priestly caste; some scholars have felt that the coincidence of names was such that there must have been a development from one to the other; but it may be more likely that the name Levi/Levite denotes a function, and that no connection between the two groups existed — a view supported by references to members of other tribes as Levites (Judg. 17:13).

LOT, the nephew of Abraham, plays a somewhat ambiguous role in the stories in Gen. 11-19. On the one hand he shared with Abraham the venture which brought them from their homeland to the promised land of Canaan, and Lot and his family were singled out from all the other inhabitants of Sodom to be spared when the city was destroyed. When God's messengers came to announce Sodom's fate, he was the only one to offer hospitality (Gen. 19:1-9). But the story is also told in such a way as to contrast Lot's character with that of Abraham; in Gen. 13 he chooses the more superficially attractive and fertile land to dwell in, but the real promised land is the bare upland where Abraham settles. In ch. 14 he and his dependents have to be rescued by Abraham after their capture by the marauding kings; and in ch. 19 this ambiguity reached its height. Though he does offer hospitality to the visitors, he shows no compunction in offering his daughters to his depraved fellow-citizens for their sexual pleasure (v.8). He and his family escaped from Sodom and were allowed to flee to a nearby city named Zoar. Probably one of the many saline pillars in the region was thought to resemble a human figure, and so there emerged the story of Lot's wife who looked back, and became a pillar of salt (v. 26) — a story used by Jesus to show the need for urgent decision (Luke 17:32). Finally Lot is the victim of an insulting story aimec against Israel's neighbours and inveterate enemies, the Moabites and Ammonites. Lot became drunk and while he was in this state his daughters had intercourse with him and their children were the ancestors of Moab and Ammon. The crude humour of this tale suggests that Lot was not wholly revered by later tradition.

LYSIAS was one of the Syrian generals who had the task of putting down the rebellion led by Judas Maccabaeus from 168 B.C. onwards. 1 Macc. 3:31-38 describe how Lysias was left by king Antiochus Epiphanes as viceroy of Syria and Palestine. At first he sent subordinates to quell the insurgents; later he attempted to do so himself (1 Macc. 4:28-35; 6:28-63), but in the end was forced by changing political circumstances to abandon the war, which enabled Judas and his followers to re-establish the worship of the Jerusalem temple. Subsequently Lysias was heavily involved in the struggles between rival claimants for the Syrian throne, and it was in this situation that he was killed by a rival in about 162 B.C.

MAACAH is a name found in the Old Testament of both men and women. Almost all the people so named are mentioned only in lists, the exception being the queen-mother referred to in 1 Kings 15 and 2 Chron. 11-15. She was remembered as the daughter or grand-daughter of David's son Absalom, though another tradition asserts that he died childless (2 Sam. 18:18). The queen-mother played a much more important role than the king's wife in the ancient world, and Maacah's devotion to heathen practice represented a danger to true religion (1 Kings 15:13). She is said to have been the mother of two succeeding kings, Abijam and Asa (1 Kings 15:2, 9). Both statements cannot be true, since Asa was Abijam's son; it is possible that Maacah was Abijam's mother, but continued to exercise the queen-mother's role during Asa's reign.

MACCABAEUS was the surname, or perhaps nickname, of Judas, son of Mattathias, who led the rebellion against Syrian power in the years after 168 B.C. The name came to be applied to his brothers who succeeded him, and eventually to the whole family; hence the 'Books of Maccabees', which deal with other subjects as well, though 1 Maccabees in particular is an apologia for Judas and his brothers. See under *Judas*.

MACHIR is described in Gen. 50:23; Josh. 17:1 as the eldest son of Manasseh, and further details are supplied in the genealogical lists in 1 Chron. 2:21-23; 7:14-28. But references in ancient sources to Machir are to a clan (Judg. 5:14), and it is probable that historically Machir was a clan which later became absorbed within the larger unit of Manasseh, and only later reflection presented this relationship in individual terms.

MACHIR, clearly the name of an individual, is mentioned in 2 Sam. 9:4f.; 17:27, in the story of the rebellion against David. He is shown as giving hospitality first to Mephibosheth (Meribbaal), the crippled grandson of King Saul, and then as dealing generously with David in his time of flight. Though nothing else is known, these isolated references shown him to have been a man of some substance.

MAHER-SHALAL-HASH-BAZ was the son of the prophet Isaiah (Isa. 8:1, 3). Nothing is known of him save the name, which was given because of its symbolic meaning, 'Spoil speeds, prey hastes' (the two halves of the name being synonymous), to give vivid point to the prophet's conviction that Damascus and Samaria, then threatening Jerusalem, would be destroyed by the greater power of the Assyrians. Isa. 8:18 refers to Isaiah himself and his children (and, presumably, their names) being 'signs and portents' (see also *Shear-Jashub*).

MALACHI is the last book of the Old Testament in the usual order found in English Bibles, though not in the Hebrew, where it concludes the second, or prophetic, section of the threefold canon. Whatever order is used, it is not likely that it is the last in date. Though clear indications are lacking, a date in the fifth century B.C. has been the most widely supported.

The word Malachi means 'my messenger'. Though this is treated as a proper name at 1:1, it is more likely that the book is anonymous, the name Malachi originating from the reference to 'my messenger' in 3:1. As in other post-exilic prophetic collections, this book shows great concern for the Jerusalem temple and the proper worship of God, and there is a hostile attitude to other neighbouring peoples, especially Edom. Over against this rather negative attitude must be borne in mind the universalistic vision of the worship of God in 1:11. The book concludes (4:5f.) with the divine promise that Elijah would be sent back to earth before a final day of judgement, a prophetic vision whose consequences have been important for both Jews and Christians. In strict Jewish circles the custom of leaving a vacant place for Elijah at the Passover celebration is still observed, while early Christian writers interpreted the ministry of John the Baptist as that of a new Elijah preparing the way for Jesus (Matt. 11:14).

MANASSEH is described in Old Testament tradition both as a son of Joseph and as the name of one of the tribes of Israel. As with other tribal groups, the older view, implicitly supported by the biblical text itself, is that the tribe consisted of the descendants of the founding father; but the usual modern view is that the tribe already existed as an entity before the stories of the ancestors were elaborated. Manasseh and Ephraim differ from the other tribes in that they were the 'sons', not of Jacob but of Joseph, and the tribal lists differ in that sometimes Joseph is found in them (e.g. Gen. 49:2-27), whereas other lists include both Ephraim and Manasseh but omit one of the others (e.g. Num. 1). These two tribes became the most important in the central territory of Israel, but Ephraim's increasing precedence over Manasseh is reflected in the incident in Gen. 48:8-22 which describes how Jacob deliberately blesses Ephraim over his older brother Manasseh.

Later accounts of the tribe of Manasseh often refer to it in two distinct sections, one on each side of the Jordan (e.g. Josh. 17: 1.6). The Transjordanian area may once have been associated with Machir, described as a separate group in some parts of the Old Testament (e.g. Judg. 5:14), and integrated within Manasseh by being called his first-born (Gen. 50:23; Josh. 17:1).

MANASSEH, king of Judah, enjoyed the longest reign of any king in the Old Testament — fifty-five years (2 Kings 21:1). The probable dates are 696-642 B.C., though the first part of his reign may have been as co-regent with his father. He appears to have been a loyal vassal of Assyria, whose control of Palestine was complete throughout the period, and this implied that he had to accept the religious practices of the Assyrians. For all of this he is bitterly condemned by the author of 2 Kings, who regards him as the worst of all Judah's rulers, upon whom was to be laid the blame for the final destruction of the kingdom fifty years later (2 Kings 21:10-13).

The account in 2 Chronicles, written much later, differs sharply in describing Manasseh's repentance from his evil (2 Chron. 33:12f.).

The general view is that this tradition is not likely to be historical, but has been influenced by the Chronicler's distaste for all-or-nothing judgements, and by the length of his reign as an apparent mark of divine favour. The tradition of Manasseh's prayer of repentance gave rise to various later writings including the Apocryphal Book called the Prayer of Manasseh. Manasseh — whose name has sometimes been taken to imply northern links, with the tribe of the same name — is also mentioned in Assyrian records, as a vassal who remained loyal when others were rebelling.

MANOAH, the father of Samson, is mentioned only in Judg. 13 (apart from an allusion to his burial-place at Judg. 16:31), in the story relating the circumstances of the conception of his son. In fact, though only Manoah is named, it is his wife who is the central figure in the story. She was barren, and so we have a favourite motif, of the birth of a hero-child to the formerly childless woman. It was to her that the divine visitation came (vv. 3-5, 9); she was the one whose abstinence from particular forms of food and drink prefigured Samson's own vow (v. 14). She reassured her husband when he was afraid that the sight of God must lead to their death (vv. 22f.). Manoah's own role is little more than that of an intermediary between the divine messenger and his wife.

MATTATHIAS is the earliest member known to us of the family of the Hasmonaeans, or Maccabees, who played a decisive role in the struggle for deliverance from Syrian oppression, in the years following Antiochus Epiphanes' attempt to impose religious unity on his empire, c. 168 B.C. Mattathias himself was a priest and a member of one of the 'courses' into which the Jerusalem priesthood was divided; he would only be required to officiate at rare intervals, however, and so his family home was at Modein, nearly twenty miles from Jerusalem (1 Macc. 2:1). His refusal to engage in pagan sacrifice, and his slaughter of a fellow-countryman whom he regarded as a traitor for doing so, precipitated the rebellion (1 Macc. 2:15-28). Mattathias was involved in the important decision to fight even on the Sabbath if they should be attacked on that day (vv. 29-41), and already during his lifetime guerilla activity was making the way of those who accepted the imperial command a risky one (vv. 42-28). Finally, after a death-bed blessing reminiscent of Israel's heroes from the past, Mattathias died and bequeathed the task of leading the struggle to his sons (vv. 49-70). Though 1 Maccabees is to a large extent an apologia on behalf of the Maccabee family, there is no ground for questioning the importance of the principle for which Mattathias stood, or for the courage with which he carried it out.

MEDAD.
See *Eldad*.

MELCHIZEDEK is described in Gen. 14:18-20 as 'king of Salem' and 'priest of God Most High'. This mysterious figure is introduced without further explanation into the story of Abram (later Abraham) and the coalition of kings in Gen. 14, a chapter which stands quite apart from the main body of stories relating to Abraham. Some scholars have maintained that this chapter contains very ancient historical notes, by which Abraham might be placed in his original historical context, but the more general view is that the story is a later construction, and that any ancient fragments that it may contain have lost their original context.

We cannot, therefore, be certain about Melchizedek's historical context, but it is likely that his kingdom of 'Salem' was Jerusalem, and that the 'God Most High' whom he served was the Canaanite god El-Elyon (cf. the footnote in the New English Bible), a god whose worship was later absorbed into that of Israel's own god. Ps. 110:4, the other Old Testament reference to Melchizedek, may reflect this process, where the king in Jerusalem is associated with the priestly order of Melchizedek.

Later Jewish and Christian speculation about this enigmatic figure was wide-ranging and often fanciful. In the New Testament the author of the Epistle to the Hebrews used his priesthood as an appropriate analogy for his understanding of Jesus (see the New Testament section), and many later Christian writers saw in Melchizedek's offering a foreshadowing of the Christian.offering of the Eucharist.

MENAHEM was king of the northern kingdom of Israel at a time when it was torn by internal dissension and gravely threatened by the growing power of Assyria. 2 Kings 15:14-22 illustrates both these points. Menahem seized power from Shallum, another contender for the throne, and his atrocity described in v. 16 was probably directed against supporters of his rival. Verses 19f. make clear that Menahem's independence was severely limited. He had to pay tribute to the king of Assyria, 'Pul' (better known as Tiglath-Pileser), in order to maintain his throne. The recovery of Assyrian royal annals provides independent evidence of this, for Menahem is listed among the kings who paid tribute to Tiglath-Pileser in the period 743-739 B.C. Despite all these crises the note recording Menahem's death (v. 22) suggests that he died peacefully, unlike all the other kings in the last years of Israel.

MENELAUS is the Greek form of the Hebrew name Menahem. The fact is relevant to our appreciation of the only biblical character with this name — the high priest who is condemned bitterly in 2 Macc. 4:23-5:23. An important element in this condemnation was Menelaus' willingness to espouse Greek customs, and thereby (as it appeared to the author of 2 Maccabees) betray his own native traditions. According to 2 Maccabees, Menelaus obtained the high-priesthood, for which he was not qualified by birth, by bribery in about 171 B.C. The subsequent account accuses him of every form of evil, not only betraying his own people but also attempting to be disloyal to his new masters. How far these condemnations are justified we have no means of establishing. He is not mentioned again until the account of his death in about 163, when 2 Macc. 13:1-8 describes how he was killed by asphyxiation, being thrown into a tower of ashes.

MEPHIBOSHETH, the son of David's friend Jonathan, is also known as Meribbaal (1 Chron. 8:34). The latter form is no doubt closer to the original, and means 'May Baal contend' (on behalf of the one who bears his name). But to the editors of 2 Samuel this compounding of a name with the (to them) alien god Baal was abhorrent, and so they substituted a form including the word *bosheth*, meaning 'shame' (See *Ishbosheth* for another example of a similar change.)

The unhappy life of Mephibosheth is presented in 2 Samuel in such a way as to justify this negative verdict. His father and his grandfather Saul were both killed when he was still a child, and he himself was a cripple (2 Sam. 4:4). Though he found favour with David (2 Sam. 9), he was then betrayed by his own servant Ziba (2 Sam. 16:1-4) and ended by losing half his possessions (2 Sam. 19:24-30). Thus the editor makes it clear that there is no possibility of the throne returning to the family of Saul.

MEPHIBOSHETH who is listed in 2 Sam. 21:8 as having been killed with David's connivance is a distinct figure, presumably the uncle of the Mephibosheth described above.

MERAB the daughter of Saul was at first promised to David as wife in return for his valiant deeds on behalf of her father (1 Sam. 18:17-19), but in the event she was given to another, Adriel. But one purpose of the editors of the books of Samuel is to show that Saul can never get the better of David, and the family of Merab ends by being given up to their enemies and put to death in gruesome circumstances (2 Sam. 21:1-14).

MERIBBAAL.
See *Mephibosheth.*

MERODACH-BALADAN is only referred to briefly in the Old Testament, but is known as an important figure from other ancient Near Eastern texts. There is a brief note in 2 Kings 20:1, which refers to Merodach-baladan sending gifts to Hezekiah, apparently as a friendly gesture, 'for he heard that he had been sick'. (Isa. 39:1 provides a virtually identical version of the episode.) Wider knowledge of the history of the eighth century B.C. shows that Merodach-baladan was a rebel against Assyria, which claimed to rule over the whole of Mesopotamia, and his message to Hezekiah was aimed at enlisting his support in the rebellion. Various of Assyria's enemies contrived to maintain Merodach-baladan's rebellion with intermittent success for nearly thirty years, c. 721-692 B.C., and more than once the Assyrian rulers had to come to terms with him, though no lasting peace was reached. (The Hebrew of 2 Kings 20:12, by a slip, called him 'Berodach-baladan', and this form is found in the Authorised Version.)

MESHA, king of Moab, is noteworthy for being referred to both in the Old Testament and in a memorial inscription apparently erected at his own orders. The Old Testament reference comes in 2 Kings 3:4ff., which describes his rebellion against Israel and its gruesome conclusion, with the king offering his own son as a human sacrifice to the supposedly angry god. The 'Moabite Stone', as Mesha's inscription is usually called, was discovered in 1868 and is now in the Louvre in Paris. It describes a successful rebellion by the Moabites against Israel. The two accounts present some problems of historical reconciliation (e.g. the Old Testament speaks of the rebellion occurring after the death of Ahab (v. 5), whereas Mesha's inscription implies that Ahab was still alive), but far more important is the basic corroboration of the political situation and many similarities in religious thought between the Old Testament and the Moabite Stone.

METHUSELAH has given his name as a synonym for longevity, because of the 969-year lifespan with which he is credited (Gen. 5:27). All the pre-flood figures are given these vastly extended lifespans, but Methuselah's is the longest of all. The figures are perhaps best understood as one way of expressing the belief in a long-lost golden age; there is no evidence to suggest that at any time in his development man's expectation of life has greatly exceeded its present length. The Old Testament figures themselves are brief by comparison with those attributed to pre-historical Babylonian kings, whose reigns were measured in thousands of years. (The name Methushael, found in a different patriarchal list in Gen. 4:18, is a variant of Methuselah.)

MICAH and Micaiah are variant forms of the same name, with the meaning 'Who is like Yahweh?', and three quite distinct characters with this name are important in different parts of the Old Testament. Several lesser characters also bear the same name.

MICAH is described in Judg. 17-18 as a man of some substance, possessing a private sanctuary and dealing in considerable sums of money. The story begins in 17:1 as if Micah is to be its main character, but in fact it is really a story about the establishment of the sanctuary at Dan (18:29-31), and the references to Micah become increasingly allusive. Nothing else is known about him, and all that can be said is that he must have been the head of a powerful local clan in the 'hill-country of Ephraim' (a vague general description of the central Palestinian highlands) in about the eleventh century B.C., before Israel was firmly established as a nation.

MICAH of Moresheth-Gath, a prophet from Judah in the late eighth century B.C., was a contemporary of Isaiah, and his oracles have now been incorporated into one of the books of the 'minor prophets'. Little is known of his background and circumstances, but we learn from his book that he was active at the time when Samaria, the capital of the northern kingdom of Israel, was under threat from Assyria (1:6); the city fell in 722/1 B.C. But his main message was a word of doom against Jerusalem, and, in particular, its religious leaders (ch. 3 in particular). It was for this message that he was still remembered a century later, when Jeremiah had equally grim warnings to offer (Jer. 26:18f.). There were those who felt that Jeremiah should be put to death as a traitor, but the memory that Micah's harsh threats had gone unpunished helped to save Jeremiah's life.

The book of Micah is not, however, limited to threats. Two passages in particular stand out: first, the hope expressed in 5:2-4 for a new and better king to arise in the future, to come as David had from Bethlehem; the markedly optimistic tone has led many scholars to question whether this oracle is original to Micah, but it played an important part at a later date according to the story of the wise men in Matt. 2:5f., Herod's counsellors directing the wise men to Bethlehem to seek the promised Messiah on the basis of this oracle, which has, as a result, traditionally been used in Christian worship at the Christmas season. Second, and more probably from

103

Micah himself, is the section 6:6-8, where a series of wrong ways of approaching God is set out before the hearers are given a forceful reminder of what is really required of them: 'to do justice, and to love kindness, and to walk humbly with your God'. It could well serve as a summary of the message of Micah and of the other eighth-century prophets.

MICAIAH (the longer form of 'Micah'), the son of Imlah, is the central character in 1 Kings 22, a chapter of extreme interest and importance both for the development of prophetism and for the nature of Israel's belief in her god. The story tells how an anonymous Israelite king — in the present form of the narrative said to be Ahab, but this is probably an editiorial addition — seeks advice from the prophets of his court concerning his proposed military expedition to Ramoth-gilead. With one exception they assure him that he will be successful. The exception is Micaiah, who proclaims impending disaster — correctly, for Israel's army is routed and the king himself killed by a bow 'drawn at a venture'.

This story in 1 Kings 22 is of importance for our knowledge of ancient Israel in several respects. We learn that kings might maintain a corps of prophets on the royal staff, including those whose words, like those of Micaiah, were unfavourable. These prophets not only spoke but acted out the message they had received from God. The problem of contradictory messages is explained as deliberate deception by God rather than any insincerity on the prophets' part. On this view, therefore, 'false' prophecy was part of the divine plan rather than a testimony to human greed or incapacity. This understanding clearly poses problems, but is a vivid testimony to belief in the absolute sovereignty of God, pictured as supreme ruler over his court.

Nothing more is known of Micaiah, but v. 28 provides an interesting example of a wish to tie up loose ends. The phrase 'Hear, all you peoples', with which his words end, is quite irrelevant to the context. They have in fact been taken from the oracles of the eighth-century prophet Micah (see above) (Micah 1:2), by a later tradition which speculated that the two men of the same name were in fact identical.

MICHAEL is a name born by several human Old Testament characters, none of whom are more than part of a list of names. But the name was also given to a heavenly figure, who has come to be regarded as the archangel Michael.

During most of the Old Testament period divine messengers or 'angels' are mentioned, as having a role to play in conveying God's requirements to his people, but it is only at the very end of the Old Testament period that there is evidence of speculation about the role of angels, their names and particular duties. The earliest clear evidence comes from the book of Daniel, which reached its final form in the era of the struggle of Israel for independence against the Syrians, c. 165 B.C. The latter part of Daniel consists of a series of heavenly visions in which the true significance of events on earth was revealed, and in these visions Michael played an important part as the champion of God's people against their enemies (Dan. 10: 13, 21; 12:1). This warlike role is also attributed to Michael in the two New Testament references (Jude 9; Rev. 12:7), and in many of the non-biblical allusions to him. Speculation about angels and their role was a characteristic feature of Jewish writings of the post-biblical period, and Michael is often mentioned. This tradition has been continued within Christianity, where Michael is often represented as fighting for the Christian against the many evils that may attack him.

MICHAL, the daughter of Saul, was promised as wife to David on condition that he fulfilled an apparently impossible condition — the gift of a hundred Philistine foreskins (1 Sam. 18:20-29). The story combines various motifs — the fairy-tale element of a deed of heroic valour; the treacherous king hoping to trick his rival by proposing to him an impossible feat; the scorn felt by Israel for the Philistines, who did not practise circumcision. The story is continued in 1 Sam. 19, where Michal shows her love for her new husband by protecting him from her father's jealousy by a trick. It comes as something of a surprise, therefore, and as a reminder of the very limited rights of women, when she is given to another husband after David's final breach with Saul (1 Sam. 25:44).

After Saul's death David reclaimed Michal as one way of strengthening the legitimacy of his own claim to the throne (2 Sam. 3: 13-15). But the union was childless; when David brought the ark to Jerusalem it is likely that Michal was expected to perform a part in a ritual marriage as the climax of the ceremony. She refused to do so, and her barrenness was interpreted as punishment for this refusal (2 Sam. 6:16-23). Michal is also mentioned in some versions (e.g. the Authorised Version) at 2 Sam. 21:8, but this is probably an error for Merab, her sister (so Revised Standard Version, New English Bible).

MIRIAM, the sister of Moses, is described as a prophetess on account of the part she played in leading the ecstatic song of the women commemorating the deliverance from Egypt at the

105

Exodus (Exod. 15:20f.). She is linked with her other brother, Aaron, here, and again in Num. 12, where the two of them rebel against Moses' authority, and are seen as being punished for their presumption by being struck with a skin-disease which is healed by Moses' intercession. Her death is reported at Num. 20:1 as having taken place during the course of the people's wanderings in the wilderness. Two of these episodes are mentioned in later reflections upon Israel's sacred history: at Micah 6:4 her role, along with her brothers in the deliverance from Egypt; at Deut. 24:9 the example of her skin-disease is used as a warning.

Conventionally the well-known story of Moses in the bulrushes, watched by his sister who acts as a go-between with the Pharaoh's daughter, has also been related to Miriam, but her name is not mentioned in the story, and this point illustrates a sharp difference of opinion among modern scholars on this subject. Some suppose that all the allusions noted above are original; others take the view that a series of traditions, relating to quite different individuals in their original form, have been drawn together in their present form to speak of Miriam, Aaron and Moses as members of one family. The name Miriam is the Hebrew from which Greek Mariam, English Mary, has been derived.

MISHAEL.
See *Shadrach*.

MITHREDATH is the Hebrew form of the Persian name Mithradata, and two Persian officials with this name are mentioned in the book of Ezra. At 1:8 there is the treasurer who makes an inventory of the vessels to be returned to the Jerusalem temple. The story has often been regarded as a later idealisation, because according to 2 Kings 24:13 the vessels had already been destroyed, but there is no reason to doubt that this official had some part to play in making arrangements for re-furnishing the temple. The other occurrence is at 4:7, an extremely cryptic note, since reference is made to a letter being sent, but with no indication of its contents, and it is dated in the time of Artaxerxes (465-424 B.C.), whereas the outline structure of the chapter is concerned with events from the previous century.

MOAB is not a personal name, but that of the area east of the Dead Sea and its inhabitants, but it is included here by virtue of the story in Gen. 19:30-38, which tells how an original 'Moab' was born of an incestuous relation between Lot and his daughter. Moab and Israel were in constant conflict, and the tale here is a half-mocking, half-bitter attack upon Israel's enemy; the tone implied by the epithet 'bastard' today would be similar. In this case the point was strengthened by the fact that 'Moab' sounded similar to *me-abinu* ('from our father', v. 34) and this provided additional opportunity for speaking insultingly about the Moabites. A very different attitude is found in the book of Ruth, where the heroine is a Moabite and she is portrayed as the ancestress of the great Israelite hero David (Ruth 4:13-22).

MORDECAI was the counsellor whose sage advice was vital in ensuring the survival of his people in the story told by the book of Esther. First, he uncovers a plot against the life of King Xerxes, but is not immediately rewarded (Esther 2:21; 23); then he shows his loyalty to his religion by refusing to do obeisance to the king's adviser Haman (3:1-6). When a pogrom against the Jews is devised by Haman, Mordecai shows his cousin Esther, the queen, that only she can exert influence over the king sufficient to make him change his mind and spare the Jews (ch. 4). In the denouement, the king discovers that Mordecai had never been rewarded for his initial loyalty and prepares the special honours for him that Haman had hoped he himself might receive; Haman by contrast is hanged upon the gallows he had prepared for Mordecai (chs. 6-7). The story ends with Mordecai being given permission to alert the Jews to the threat they were under, so that they could take effective counter-measures, and Mordecai is promoted to be the king's chief minister (10:3).

Such a brief summary shows clearly that there is a certain fairy-tale element in the story, and it cannot be regarded as accurate history. Esther 2:6 describes how Mordecai was taken into exile in 597 B.C., yet the events of the book took place well over a century later, in the reign of Xerxes, king of Persia (486-465 B.C.). There are many details which seem to be unhistorical, though it may be that a particular threat against the Jews supplied the occasion for the story, and some of the detail may be true. It is noteworthy that the name Mordecai is the Hebrew equivalent of 'Marduk', the name of the chief Babylonian god, just as Esther is the equivalent of 'Ishtar', the name of a goddess. But if this story originated as a tale of the doings of gods and goddesses it has long since lost that element, and sets out in stark fashion the problem of anti-Semitism — a problem of antiquity which still remains with us.

MOSES has traditionally been regarded by both Jews and Christians as the author of the first five books of the Bible, Genesis to Deuteronomy, the Torah or Pentateuch, which for the

Jews forms the most sacred part of their Scripture. By contrast, one distinguished modern scholar has put forward the opinion that the only historically reliable tradition contained about him is that relating to his burial on the edge of Palestine. As is often the case, the truth is probably to be found somewhere between these two views.

A rapid outline of the Old Testament account may be given first. His birth is described in Exod. 2 as taking place in Egypt at a time when the Egyptians had decreed that all Israelite male children should be drowned. Escaping this fate through the sympathy of the Pharaoh's daughter, he was brought up at the royal court, but in manhood fled from Egypt after being involved in the murder of an Egyptian. It was while he was in exile from Egypt that he received the revelation of the divine nature at the burning bush (Exod. 3), and the assurance that God was going to lead his people out of Egypt into a 'land flowing with milk and honey'. In that Exodus Moses was to play the leading role; it was through his agency that various plagues were brought upon Egypt (Exod. 7-12), culminating in the death of all the Egyptian first-born, both human and animals. The Israelites escaped from Egypt, and when the Pharaoh, regretting his decision to let them go, pursued them, there followed the miraculous happening at the 'Red Sea' (more literally 'Sea of Reeds'), which completed the disaster that had struck the Egyptians. For the next forty years, Moses was the leader of the Israelites during their period of wandering through the wilderness, and it was during this time that the various laws of Exodus, Leviticus and Numbers, are described as being given to Israel during the sojourn at Mount Sinai. Eventually, Moses led the people to the edge of the promised land of Palestine, delivered the farewell sermons enshrined in the book of Deuteronomy, and was permitted by God to see the promised land from the heights of Pisgah east of Jordan, but not to enter the land itself, for he died on the mountain (Deut. 34).

Critical scholars for more than a century have reached the unanimous conclusion that much of this material comes from a date much later than that of Moses itself, and that it is only attributed to him as a kind of founding father of Israel and her religion. The laws, especially those dealing with religious practice, in Exodus, Leviticus and Numbers, reflect conditions after the people had settled in Palestine and established themselves as a settled community; the whole of Deuteronomy (written in a style markedly differing from the preceding books) is a later attempt to recreate the spirit of the pioneering days, when Israel was first a people. There are details, also, which have a legendary character; thus, the famous story of Moses as a baby in the bulrushes is paralleled by a similar story told of the founder king of Akkad (Babylonia), Sargon, from a date much earlier than Moses.

These later additions to the tradition have nevertheless left a body of historical events with which Moses can plausibly be associated. There can be little doubt that some at least of the groups who were to make up Israel had once been in Egypt, and Moses is a name of a type frequently found in Egypt. There it is usually combined with the name of a god, as with the Pharaohs, 'Thut-moses' or 'Ra-meses'; if Moses had once borne the name of an Egyptian god it is in any case scarcely to be expected that the Jews would have preserved that element in their sacred writings.

We may assume, therefore, that Moses really was involved in the deliverance of the people from Egypt; that his marriage into a family of semi-nomadic origin (Exod. 2:15-22) is an ancient tradition, and may be related to the stories about Israel wandering for many years in the wilderness. This was later interpreted as a punishment, but may in fact have been their natural habitat before they became a settled people. Later reflection then saw in Moses the ideal leader, and so came to glorify him as a prophet (Deut. 18:15), a priest (Ps. 99:6), and sometimes in terms reminiscent of those applied to kings (e.g. the account of him as supreme judge in Exod. 18). But there are curiously few references to him in the remainder of the Old Testament: the Exodus was of vital importance, but that was understood essentially as God's work, and the human agent was not often mentioned.

On one last question, scholarly opinion is sharply divided. Are the ten commandments in any sense Mosaic? Some have felt that this undoubtedly ancient collection of laws goes back to a unique experience undergone by Moses on Mount Sinai (whose precise location has never been established), but the more usually held view is that the commandments reflect conditions of life after Israel had settled in Canaan (e.g. the concern for a fixed day of rest characteristic of agricultural rather than nomadic people; the concern for the neighbour's house (Exod. 20:8, 17)), and that the commandments, like the more elaborate laws which follow, came at a later date to be associated with Moses. The truth of the matter is that it is notoriously difficult to separate historical nucleus from pious legend especially in the case of the founder of a religion, and there does seem to be a real sense in which Moses, as the one to whom the divine name was revealed (Exod. 3:14) was a founder of at least a great new development in religion.

R

NAAMAN, the Aramaean general whom Elisha cured of his disease, is known only from the story in 2 Kings 5. The story is of the type known as a 'prophetic legend', where all the interest focuses upon the three leading characters — Elisha, Naaman, and the prophet's greedy servant Gehazi. Only they are named; even the kings of the two countries, Israel and Aram, are anonymous, so that we have no means of dating the event.

The nature of Naaman's malady cannot be identified. Conventionally translated as 'leprosy', it was not Hansen's Disease, the true leprosy, but probably some form of skin-disease, perhaps eczema. The character of Naaman is used, in a way characteristic of prophetic legends, to illustrate various theological motifs: the folly of supposing that any foreign land could be better than Israel's 'promised land' (vv. 11-14); the foreigner acknowledging the power of Israel's God (v. 15); the continuing superstition that God could be better worshipped if a little Palestinian soil was taken to the foreign place of worship (vv. 17-19). Finally, it is noteworthy that Naaman is presented in a manner markedly more sympathetic than the description of the servant Gehazi, who ends by catching Naaman's disease as punishment for his own greed (vv. 20-27).

NABAL is the victim of one of the outlaw David's adventures in 1 Sam. 25. A prominent landowner in the far south, he refused David's demands for protection money to save his flocks from nomadic incursions. His churlish refusal was seen as sure to bring revenge from David, and so his wife Abigail, who seems to have had an eye for the main chance, quickly ingratiated herself with David, then, having assured herself of David's protection, told her husband of these developments while he was in his cups. The news brought on some form of seizure from which he died, leaving Abigail free to marry her protector. The story is told in part as an illustration of the way Nabal's character matched his name, which means 'fool'.

NABOTH plays an important part in the story of Elijah in his conflict with the king Ahab and his wife Jezebel. Nothing is known of Naboth save that he was the owner of a vineyard, probably in Samaria, which had recently become the capital of the northern kingdom of Israel. The likely background of the story in

1 Kings 21 is that the king wished to extend the amount of territory under direct royal control in the capital city, and Naboth's ancestral inheritance stood in his way. As the story is told, Ahab was prepared to accept this state of affairs, though reluctantly, but Jezebel engineered false charges against Naboth which led to his summary execution (1 Kings 21:14). The editors of the books of Kings stress the fact that both Elijah (1 Kings 21:20-29) and Elisha (2 Kings 9: 21-26) were motivated in their attacks upon the royal family by their conviction of the injustice done to Naboth.

NADAB is a name born by several Old Testament characters, three of whom are the subject of some personal detail.

NADAB, the oldest son of Aaron, might have been expected to succeed to the priesthood. He is indeed pictured as one of those privileged to join in the ceremony on Mount Sinai (Exod. 24) and is set aside as a priest (Exod. 28:1). But he and his brother Abihu were not to establish an acceptable priestly line and instead were put to death because of some unknown ritual offence (Lev. 10:1-5). The story probably comes from a period when great store was set by the proper priestly descent, and is a means of underlining the unacceptability of descent from Nadab and Abihu, who are always mentioned together.

NADAB, the son of Jeroboam, was the second king of the northern kingdom of Israel. His rule, dated about 900 B.C. was a brief one (1 Kings 15:25-31). The principle of dynastic succession had scarcely been established in Israel at that period, and his enemies took advantage of his commitment to a military campaign in one part of his territory to raise a rebellion elsewhere and bring about his violent death. The editor of 1 Kings clearly saw this as the fulfilment of the prophecy of disaster against the family of the arch-schismatic Jeroboam (1 Kings 14:10f.).

NADAB is mentioned in the apocryphal book of Tobit in two different contexts, which make it difficult to know whether the same individual is being referred to. In 11:18 he is mentioned along with Ahikar as a cousin of Tobit who came to share the merry-making at Tobit's marriage to Sarah. Then, at the very end of the book, reference is made in Tobit's dying speech to Nadab as a counsellor of the king of Assyria who had attempted to kill his kinsman Ahikar and fallen into his own trap. This curious allusion is dependent on the 'Tale of Ahikar', a widespread folk-tale in the ancient Near East, according to which Nadab had been adopted by Ahikar, but failed to show gratitude; instead he made false accusations about him to the king. Ahikar is miraculously released from prison before the death-sentence against him can be carried out, and Nadab is imprisoned and dies instead. It seems as if the book of Tobit was in part based on this story, and assumes knowledge of its characters.

NAHASH, king of the Ammonites, unwittingly played an important part in the establishment of the monarchy in Israel. He laid siege to Jabesh-gilead, a border-city whose possession was frequently disputed; the inhabitants summoned help, which came from Saul who scattered Nahash's army and was as a result acclaimed as king of Israel (1 Sam. 11). Nahash was Saul's enemy, and so it followed as a natural consequence that he would be David's friend (2 Sam. 10:1f.), a friendship which appears to have been sealed by a marriage-alliance and was of importance in the days when David was in danger from the rebellion of his son Absalom (2 Sam. 17: 25-27).

NAHOR is the name of two of Abraham's relations: his grandfather (Gen. 11:22-25), and his brother (Gen. 11:26-29). Of the former, nothing more is known, but more details are supplied concerning the younger Nahor. First, we are told that he married his niece Milcah (an unusual but not unknown practice in the Old Testament), and their children are listed in Gen. 22:20-22. It may be significant that there are twelve of them, this number being common in tribal lists, so that these twelve may in fact be the names of a confederation of tribes. Later, when Abraham is seeking a wife for his son Isaac, he sends his emissary to 'the city of Nahor' (Gen. 24: 10), and a marriage is eventually arranged with Rebekah, the granddaughter of Nahor. In due course Isaac's son Jacob concluded a covenant with Rebekah's brother Laban, and it is noteworthy that Laban swore by 'the God of Nahor' (Gen. 31:53), who was by this time regarded as the founding father of the clan. The detailed history underlying these incidents cannot now be reconstructed, but we are shown the tightly woven nature of these family and tribal structures.

NAHUM, the seventh of the twelve minor prophets, is known only from the book that bears his name. No precise date is possible, but since the main theme of the book is the downfall of the Assyrian Empire (whose capital, Nineveh, fell in 612 B.C.) we know the approximate time of his ministry. The bitter taunts against Nineveh in chs. 2-3 of the book of Nahum might be taken as a song of triumph that the city had already fallen, but it is more likely that they come from a time shortly before its final collapse, and are intended as a word from God designed to hasten that collapse.

This note of triumph in the defeat of his people's enemies, and the absence of any words of condemnation for Israel's own sin, makes Nahum stand somewhat apart from the majority of Old Testament prophets. It has even been suggested that he was one of the prophets of salvation for Israel whom Jeremiah attacked. More likely, he was basically a prophet of the same type as the others, but the particular emphasis of his message was that of woe to the foreign oppressor — a theme found also in many other prophetic books.

Of the prophet's own life nothing is known. His birthplace, Elkosh, is not mentioned elsewhere in the Old Testament, and the traditional identification of it with a site in south-western Palestine is based on very late traditions. It is likely that Nahum may have been involved with the Jerusalem temple in a professional capacity, since the type of prophetic oracle found in his book may well be that characteristic of the temple cult.

NAOMI, the mother-in-law of Ruth, is most attractively presented in the little story that comprises that book. Driven into exile by famine, she loses both her husband and her two sons, but her daughter-in-law remains faithful to her (ch. 1). At that point the outlook seemed 'bitter' (1:20), and she suggested that this should be her name instead of Naomi ('the pleasant one'). But through a mixture of guile and ingenuousness, God was seen still to favour Naomi and Ruth; and the child born to Ruth was counted as keeping Naomi's own name alive (4:14-17). Indeed, in the end her reputation was vastly enhanced, for she came to be remembered as the ancestress of David (4:17). This charming tale is best seen as a reflection upon the mysterious workings of divine providence.

NAPHTALI, like the other sons of Jacob, was originally a tribal name, treated by later tradition as an individual. The tribes of Naphtali and Dan seem to have been closely linked in status and geographical position, and this is expressed by describing them both as Jacob's sons by a slave-girl rather than by his wife (Gen. 30:4-8). Other traditions of the tribe's history speak of intermingling with the native Canaanite inhabitants of the land (Judg. 1:33), and — perhaps the most famous moment in their memory — the prominent part played by the men of Naphtali under their leader Barak in defeating the Canaanite army of Sisera (Judg. 4-5; esp. 4:6-10; 5:18). An echo of this great battle may be found in the victorious procession of Psalm 68:27. Other later references simply treat Naphtali as a geographical district, notably Isa. 9:1, referring to the

Assyrian invasion of the area as a prelude to the great hymn of God's true ruler, where 'The people who walked in darkness' may be the subjugated inhabitants of Naphtali. Matthew in his Gospel applied this to all the people before the advent of the true ruler — Jesus (Matt. 4:13-15).

NATHAN was the name of two different members of David's court. One was a son of David, mentioned in 2 Sam. 5:14 without further detail, but identified in 1 Chron. 3:5 as one of the sons of Bathsheba. This is curious, because the account of Solomon's birth is 2 Sam. 12:24 makes it very surprising that he should have had older brothers. The Gospel of Luke traces the genealogy of Jesus through this Nathan (Luke 3:31), whereas Matthew traces it through his brother Solomon.

Better known is the prophet Nathan, who appears in three incidents concerned with David. In 2 Sam. 7 it is he whom David consults concerning his plans to build a temple. Nathan at first approves, but subsequently says that David is not to build a house (temple) for God; rather God will establish a house (dynasty) for David. Secondly, it is Nathan who delivers the famous rebuke to David after the king has committed adultery with Bathsheba and arranged for the death of her husband (2 Sam. 12:1-14). Finally, Nathan is instrumental in establishing the succession of Solomon to the throne at a time when his half-brother Adonijah had attempted to seize power for himself by means of a pre-emptive strike (1 Kings 1). Though nothing else is known of Nathan this evidence is enough to show that not all prophets attached to royal courts were necessarily yes-men, prepared to speak only what their master wanted to hear. A later tradition made him the author of records dealing with David and Solomon (1 Chron. 29:29; 2 Chron. 9:29), but this is probably only an elaborate way of referring to our books of Samuel and Kings, and highlighting the important part played by religious figures at the royal court.

NEBUCHADNEZZAR was ruler of the Babylonian Empire from 605 B C. until his death in 562. The form of his name here given is that most commonly found in the Old Testament, but in Jeremiah (except chs. 27-29) he is called Nebuchadrezzar, and this form is closer to the original Babylonian Nabu-kudurri-usur.

He succeeded his father as king upon the latter's death in 605, and a series of campaigns in his early years enabled him to make Babylonia the leading power in the Near East, filling the gap left by the recent collapse of Assyria. Not all of these campaigns were successful, — we know of one defeat at the hands of Egypt — and so there were occasional risings against his power. Nevertheless he was able during the first ten years of his reign to remove all potential threats to his power. The discovery of the 'Babylonian Chronicle', a kind of official annal, now in the British Museum in London, has enabled scholars to reconstruct with considerable detail the early years of his reign. Unfortunately the Chronicle for the later years has not survived.

Much the most interesting statement in the Chronicle for the Old Testament reader is the statement of the capture of Jerusalem, which can now be dated precisely: "in the seventh year [Nebuchadnezzar] besieged the city of Judah, and on the second day of the month of Adar took the city and captured the king". This happened on 16 March 597 B.C. on our calendar. 2 Kings 24: 10-18 gives the Judahite account of the same event. One of the rebellions referred to above involved Judah, and as punishment Nebuchadnezzar sent his forces against Jerusalem again, captured it and on this occasion destroyed it and its principal buildings, including the temple. This event is not referred to in the Babylonian Chronicle, and so cannot be precisely dated; either 587 or 586 B.C. are possible.

Nebuchadnezzar is referred to in nine of the Old Testament books, most of the references being to the fact of his conquest of Judah. Jeremiah in particular sees the destruction as God's judgement upon his people, and in that sense Nebuchadnezzar is carrying out God's commands (Jer. 27:5f.). There are allusions to his later career in Ezekiel, who at first expected that he would be successful in his siege of Tyre (Ezek. 26:7), but later acknowledged that this prophecy had been mistaken and that Nebuchadnezzar would instead attack Egypt (29:17-21). It seems that in fact Tyre did come to an accommodation with Babylon, rather than being forced to surrender; and that Nebuchadnezzar did indeed invade Egypt in 568 B.C. Nothing is known in detail of the result of this campaign.

Perhaps the most familiar biblical references to Nebuchadnezzar are the stories in the book of Daniel, but unfortunately there is no means of telling how far they reflect accurate historical traditions. They were not set down in writing until some four hundred years after his death, and to some extent Nebuchadnezzar is used as a model of the foreign rulers of that period. Even in Daniel, however, it is noteworthy that most of the references are not hostile. Only in Dan. 4, where he is punished for his excessive pride, is he the direct subject of attack; elsewhere any injustices committed in his name are due to the pretensions of his servants.

NEBUZARADAN was in charge of the Babylonian forces involved in the final destruction of Jerusalem (587/6 B.C.).

In particular he is described in 2 Kings 25 and Jer. 52 as being responsible for deciding who should be deported to Babylon. It appears as if Jeremiah himself was given the option of accompanying the exiles or of remaining in Palestine; he chose the latter (Jer. 40). Nebuzaradan's title, translated 'captain of the guard' or the like in English versions, was literally 'chief of the slaughterers'; it is not known whether this was an official Babylonian title.

NECHO, Pharaoh of Egypt 609-593 B.C., played an important part at a crucial period in Judah's history. At the very beginning of his reign he led an army into Mesopotamia in an attempt to shore up the last remnants of the Assyrian Empire against the rising power of Babylon. Josiah king of Judah attempted to bar his progress and was killed at Megiddo (2 Kings 23:29). Necho then put his own nominee on the throne in Jerusalem in place of the son of Josiah whom the people had chosen and whom he exiled to Egypt (2 Kings 23:33-35). For all practical purposes Judah's independence was at an end.

For a time it seemed as if Egypt might emerge from its traditional isolationism to dominate the Near East, but a decisive defeat by the Babylonians at Carchemish in 605 put an end to such possibilities. The battle is evoked in vivid poetic language in Jer. 46:2-12. Thereafter Necho was able to prevent the Babylonians from extending their power into Egypt, but he made no further serious attempt to enlarge the traditional limits of Egyptian power.

NEHEMIAH played a major part in the re-establishment of Jerusalem and Judah after the exile. The temple was rebuilt in the sixth century, but thereafter little was done to restore Jerusalem for nearly another century. Then both Ezra and Nehemiah led important missions. Unfortunately there is no agreement among scholars as to the relation between them, or even as to which came first: the biblical account as it stands gives the priority to Ezra, placing his work in 458 B.C. (Ezra 7:7) and that of Nehemiah in 445 (Neh. 2:1). But while this date is generally accepted for Nehemiah, many feel that it is likely that Ezra should be placed later, perhaps in the reign of Artaxerxes II of Persia (398 B.C.).

Nehemiah's accomplishment is described in chs. 1-6 of the book named after him, in a first person account which might be a genuine memoir but is more likely a memorial written in his honour. His primary task was the restoration of the walls of Jerusalem, which had apparently lain desolate ever since their destruction by the Babylonians in 587 B.C., but he also played an important part in putting right various economic difficulties (Neh. 5), and in establishing the rights of Jerusalem as against the claims to the territory made by various rivals, notably Sanballat who was probably the governor of the adjoining province of Samaria (Neh. 2:10). Nehemiah was also zealous in enforcing the religious requirements of Judaism, especially those concerning the Sabbath (Neh.13:15-22, a section describing a second mission of Nehemiah). In later ages his memory came to be revered as one who had played a great part in restoring Jerusalem as a national and religious centre (2 Macc.1:18; Ecclus. 49:14).

The impression given by the account of his actions is that of a forceful and vigorous personality, yet his position as cup-bearer to the Persian king (Neh. 1:11) would usually have been held by a eunuch, and this might also be suggested by his being admitted to the queen's presence (Neh. 2:6). Certainty on this matter is impossible, but it is noteworthy that his adversaries never bring this charge against him. Alternatively, the traditional lethargy of eunuchs may have been overstated.

NICANOR was one of the generals of the Syrian forces which attempted to quell the rebellion of the Jews under Judas Maccabaeus. The assessment of his role is one of the differences between 1 and 2 Maccabees. In 1 Maccabees he is mentioned only incidentally (3:38), and the leading general is Gorgias, but in 2 Maccabees he is the chief enemy of the patriotic Jews (8:34). 2 Macc. 8 is devoted to a detailed account of the defeat of his army and his ignominious escape, probably in 165 B.C. A second attack on the Jews was planned after an attempt to win them over by a friendly policy had come to nothing. This battle is also described briefly in 1 Macc. 7:33-50, but in much greater detail in 2 Macc. 14 and 15, where it is the climax of the whole account, and the bringing of Nicanor's severed head and arm to Jerusalem leads to the observance of a festival, Nicanor's day, in conjunction with the established feast of Purim, which fell at the same season and was also strongly nationalistic in tone. This took place in 161 or 160 B.C.

Another Nicanor mentioned in 2 Macc. 12:8 as the chief of the Cypriot mercenaries in the Syrian army should probably not be identified with the general of the same name.

NIMROD, mentioned as a 'mighty hunter' in Gen. 10:8f., is not traceable as an historical figure, but was already for the compiler of the traditions in Genesis someone of proverbial antiquity as a warrior and one skilled in hunting.

NOAH, the hero of the biblical flood story (Gen. 6-9), has his counterparts in other versions of the universal flood known from other ancient near eastern literature. Thus the Sumerian

117

Ziusudra escapes the flood by building a boat, while in the Epic of Gilgamesh the actions of the hero Ut-napishtim have many details in common with those attributed to Noah: the carrying of animals in the boat, its grounding on a high mountain, the sending-out of birds to see if the water had abated, the offering of sacrifice after the flood. These parallels show that the Noah story is part of a widespread Mesopotamian tradition, though there is much that is unique in the biblical version. Among these elements are the name Noah and the stress on his rightness before God at a time of unique depravity (Gen. 6:9).

Quite a different tradition relating to Noah pictures him as engaged in viticulture and overcome by his own produce (Gen. 9:18-29). The main concern of this story is, however, not with Noah himself, but with the varied reactions of his three sons to the shame of their father. The sons are pictured as representatives of different races and judged accordingly.

Later biblical tradition uses Noah as an example of faith (Ezek. 14:14; Heb. 11:7), and mentions him also in connection with reflection upon the flood story, which was seen in contrasting ways. It might be used as a symbol of destruction (Matt. 24:37f.); as a reminder of God's gracious promise never again to destroy the world (Isa. 54:9); or, in the Christian church, as a symbol of those to be baptised (1 Peter 3:20).

Noah could also be a feminine name, and a woman of this name is mentioned several times in connection with a story concerning the rights of women to inheritance (Num. 27:1; 36:11).

OBADIAH, meaning 'servant of Yahweh', is a common Old Testament name. Most of its occurrences are in the genealogies in Chronicles or Nehemiah, and nothing is known in detail of the individuals concerned, but two earlier bearers of the name provide more detail.

OBADIAH, the confidant and steward of king Ahab of Israel (1 Kings 18:3-16), is presented as a devout Yahwist who stands in considerable awe of the prophet Elijah. It is significant that a fervent Yahwist should be in such a position of responsibility in Ahab's court, since it might appear from the remainder of 1 Kings 18, with its story of the prophets of Baal, that apostasy was rife there. This ambivalence is in keeping with the whole attitude of the books of Kings towards Ahab, who is sometimes praised (1 Kings 21:27-29) and sometimes regarded as the worst of sinners (1 Kings 16:30-33; 2 Kings 21:13).

OBADIAH the prophet, after whom is named the shortest book of the Old Testament. Nothing is known of this Obadiah, and it may not be a proper name; perhaps he was an anonymous 'servant of the Lord'. The book, much of which is paralleled in Jer. 49, is mainly concerned with God's anger against Edom, and probably dates from the sixth century B.C., when the Edomites apparently took advantage of the destruction of Jerusalem to advance their territorial claims. Ps. 137:7 shows a similar hatred of Edom and is probably from the same period.

OBED was the child born to Ruth following her marriage to Boaz after her adventures when she was left a widow by the death of her first husband (Ruth 4:13-17). A new dimension is given to the simple pastoral tale when it is revealed that this Obed was the father of Jesse, from whom came David and all the subsequent kings of Judah.

OBED-EDOM plays an important part in the account of David bringing the Ark to Jerusalem (2 Sam. 6:10-12). After the death of Uzzah, apparently caused by his touching the Ark, David — understandably nervous — refused to take the Ark into Jerusalem as he had planned. Instead he took it to the house of Obed-edom, whose reaction is not recorded. In fact rich blessing followed, and David was sufficiently encouraged to resume the procession into Jerusalem three months later. It is much disputed whether this story is an account of a single historical event, or whether it reflects some form of liturgical practice.

In 1 Chronicles Obed-edom's role is elaborated. His name ('servant of Edom') and home-town (the Philistine city of Gath) might seem to imply that he was a worshipper of a foreign god, but the Chronicler elaborates the references to him by supplying his name in a number of places to show that he had an important part in the temple ritual (1 Chron. 15:18, 21, 24; 16:5). For the Chronicler the supreme blessing from God was the privilege of being brought into the temple service.

OG, 'the king of Bashan', is referred to several times in different parts of the Old Testament, usually alongside Sihon king of the Amorites, as a typical example of the pre-Israelite rulers who were defeated by the incoming tribes. Bashan is the area east of Jordan noted for its fertility, and the account of Israelite penetration into Canaan implies an advance through that area (Num. 21:33-35; Deut. 3:1-11). Not enough detail is known of the history of the area to say more about Og, though most scholars are cautious of accepting his historicity. Such features as his 'sarcophagus of basalt' (the 'iron bedstead' of earlier translations of Deut. 3:11) and the use of his name in liturgical contexts (Ps. 135:11; 136:20), suggests that whatever historical core may once have underlain the traditions is now irrecoverable.

OHOLAH and Oholibah are not historical figures, but are the names given in Ezek. 23 to describe, in extremely blunt language, the two prostitute sisters, to whom Ezekiel likens the two kingdoms of Israel and Judah.

OMRI, king of Israel, is dismissed by the biblical account in very brief terms. In 1 Kings 16, vv. 16-22 describe the rebellion which led to his seizing the throne, and vv. 23-28 give a stereotyped and condemnatory account of his reign. The chronology is not clear, but his reign must be dated early in the ninth century B.C.

Even this brief account brings out the point that Omri was able to do what no previous northern king had achieved — set up a ruling dynasty which would last for more than one generation. The strength of Omri has, however, been shown by references to him in extra-biblical texts which make him the earliest biblical character to be clearly identifiable from other sources. The 'Moabite Stone', discovered more than a century ago, gives an account of his successful campaigns in Moab, and Assyrian records refer to Israel long after his death as 'the land of Omir'. He was also the first to establish a lasting capital, Samaria, and it may well be that his role in the northern kingdom was comparable to that of David in the south — though, of course, religiously less acceptable to the compilers of Old Testament tradition.

ONAN has the curious distinction of having had his name used in English for a practice quite unrelated to what is known of him. He was the second son of the patriarch Judah, and when his older brother died, the custom was that he should marry the widow so that she might bear children and keep her hisband's family in existence (Gen. 38:4-10). But Onan objected to the practice, and each time he had intercourse with his sister-in-law he engaged in *coitus interruptus*, to prevent her bearing children. It is this practice rather than masturbation which should logically be called onanism.

ONIAS was the name born by several high priests (and hence leaders of the Jewish community) in the third and second centuries B.C. Four different priests are known, all members of the same family which claimed to be able to trace its ancestry back to Zadok, the priest of the time of David.

ONIAS I is mentioned in 1 Macc. 12:7 as having corresponded with the contemporary ruler of the Spartans. Doubts have been cast upon the genuineness of this correspondence — it is difficult to think of reasons for diplomatic relations between two states whose interests were quite unconnected — but if it is genuine then Onias will have been high priest early in the third century B.C.

ONIAS II, the grandson of Onias I, is not mentioned in any biblical text, but is known from other sources to have been high priest about 250 B.C.

ONIAS III, grandson of Onias II, was high priest until his removal from office in 175 B.C. In the continual quarrels between Syria and Egypt for the control of Palestine, his earlier namesakes had supported Syria, but Onias III pursued a pro-Egyptian policy, and this led to his being deposed by the Syrian ruler Antiochus Epiphanes. 2 Macc. 1-4 depicts him in very sympathetic terms, as a just ruler unjustly deposed, and the story culminates in an account of the murder of Onias at the instigation of one of those who had been installed in his place (2 Macc. 4:30-38). The intrigues and accusations show the divided state of the community at the outset of the war against Antiochus Epiphanes. The reverence with which the author of 2 Maccabees regarded Onias may be seen from the account of his visionary appearance to Judas Maccabaeus, urging him to maintain his heroic fight. Onias is here even compared with the prophet Jeremiah (2 Macc. 15:12-16).

ONIAS IV, son of Onias III, is not mentioned in the Bible, but is known from other sources. Exiled from Jerusalem, he set up a rival Jewish sanctuary at Leontopolis in Egypt.

OREB and Zeeb are mentioned together as two Midianite chieftains who fought against Israel but were captured in Gideon's successful pursuit of the Midianites and put to death (Judg.

7:25-8:3). In later reflection upon the wars of the time of the judges, this triumph came to have a symbolic significance, as showing Yahweh's power over his enemies (Ps. 83:11; Isa. 10:26). However, the historicity of the names is suspect; both Oreb and Zeeb are Hebrew words, meaning 'raven' and 'wolf', and it is likely that the names originally attached to prominent natural features, perhaps from their unusual shape, and that they were only secondarily given to the enemies traditionally defeated at those places.

ORNAN.
See *Araunah*.

ORPAH was the wife of Chilion and sister-in-law to Ruth. After the death of her husband, both she and Ruth started to return with their mother-in-law Naomi to Judah from their native Moab. Naomi urged them to remain in their own homeland, and Orpah did so, and thereby passes out of the story, the remainder of which is concerned with Ruth's loyalty to her dead husband's family. There is no condemnation of Orpah; the whole interest of the story-teller focuses on her sister-in-law (Ruth 1:4-14).

OSNAPPER is mentioned in Ezra 4:10 as the Assyrian king who settled deportees from other parts of his empire in the province of Samaria. No known Assyrian king has such a name; the usual explanation is that this is a corruption of Assur-banipal (669-633 B.C.) or, according to another ancient tradition, of Shalmaneser (probably Shalmaneser V, 727-722 B.C.).

OTHNIEL is pictured in the books of Joshua and Judges as playing an important part in the history of Israel in the early days of the settlement in Canaan, in two somewhat contrasted ways. One tradition, found in Josh. 15:15-19 and Judge. 1:11-15, pictures the clan of Othniel as one of those which penetrated into southern Canaan from the desert fringes, and engaged in a marriage alliance with their neighbours. Here Othniel seems to stand for the whole clan.

The other tradition is found in Judg. 3:7-11, according to which he appears as judge over the whole of Israel, repelling its enemies. But the confusion of the two traditions and the improbability of some of the details in this second story (e.g. his enemy whose name Cushan-rishathaim menas 'Doubly-wicked Cushan') makes it likely that the first story preserves the older tradition, and that at a later date the local exploits of Othniel and his clan have been described as being of national significance.

PALTI(EL) forms the subject of one of the most pathetic little episodes in the Old Testament. David's wife Michal was taken away from him by her father Saul at the time of estrangement between the two men and married Paltiel (1 Sam. 25:44). When David gained power, Ishbosheth, Saul's son and successor as nominal ruler, tried to ingratiate himself with David by returning Michal to him. Paltiel, the hapless pawn in this political intrigue, followed her weeping until ordered to return home (2 Sam. 3:15).

PASHHUR is the name of three apparently different characters mentioned in the book of Jeremiah; it is uncertain whether they are in fact all distinct, or whether the same person may be referred to in different circumstances.

In ch. 20 Jeremiah falls foul of Pashhur the son of Immer, who appears to have been responsible for maintaining good order in the Jerusalem temple and was offended by Jeremiah's words of doom; he had Jeremiah flogged and put in the stocks, and thereby earned for himself a condemnation symbolised by a new name, Magor-missabib — 'terror let loose', and a warning about the inevitability of his punishment of exile and death in a foreign land.

In ch. 21 Pashhur son of Malchiah, apparently a contemporary of, but unrelated to the previous Pashhur, is one of those who was sent by the king to obtain an oracle from Jeremiah concerning the likely fate of the nation. Characteristically the word they received was of unrelieved gloom.

This Pashhur is mentioned again in 38:1 (and is also alluded to in the later priestly lists, Neh. 11:12), and that verse refers also to Gedaliah son of Pashhur; this Pashhur may be the same as the one who had Jeremiah punished in ch. 20.

PEKAH was ruler of the northern kingdom of Israel during the time of confusion shortly before the Assyrians overran the country and incorporated it into their own empire. The official Assyrian annals for the period make brief reference to him, but the Old Testament account enables us to fill in a more detailed picture.

The chronology is extremely confused. According to 2 Kings 15:27 Pekah ruled for twenty years, but it is clear from the Assyrian records that he cannot have ruled over the whole country for so

123

long a time. Either he had already claimed rule in one part of the country before the usurpation which brought him control of the capital and an official reign for a brief period, or the number 'twenty' is an error. (Chronological confusions abound in this part of 2 Kings, as can be seen from comparing the notes of Jotham's length of reign in 2 Kings 15:30 and 33.) It is likely that Pekah's rule over the whole country lasted for about five years, 737-732 B.C.

It was an extremely turbulent time. Pekah seized power by a conspiracy against Pekahiah (2 Kings 15:25), and it may be that he adopted his former master's name as a claim to legitimacy. Then, in the attempt to secure his position he joined with Rezin of Damascus in organising a coalition of all the small states of Syria and Palestine to withstand the Assyrian threat. But it was by no means generally agreed that such a policy of resistance was wise; Ahaz, king of Judah, preferred to seek terms from Assyria rather than join in a venture which he regarded as hopeless, and we have a vivid and scornful account in Isa. 7:1-9 of Isaiah's estimate of the success of the coalition. (Pekah is there referred to as 'the son of Ramaliah', vv. 4f., in an apparently slighting reference to his having adopted his former master's name.) Finally those elements in his own kingdom who opposed his policy conspired against him and a violent career ended with a violent death (2 Kings 15:30).

PEKAHIAH, who preceded Pekah on the throne of Israel and whose name as well as his throne Pekah may well have usurped, is otherwise unknown. It seems that he was never able to establish effective control of the kingdom, divided as it was by the threat of Assyrian power; his reign of 'two years' (2 Kings 15:25) may not imply more than a few months, since a reign which began in one year and ended in the next would be regarded as of two years' duration.

PELEG is mentioned in the 'table of nations' (Gen. 10), and other sources dependent on it, as one who lived at a time when 'the earth was divided' (Gen. 10:25; 1 Chron. 1:19). This is probably not a reference to an historical event, but an example of Hebrew delight in word-play, because the name Peleg means 'division'. The allusion might be to the custom of 'dividing' the land by building artificial watercourses or irrigation canals. The Peleg of Gen. 11:16-19 is identical with that of 1 Chron. 1:25, though the tradition has been preserved in a different form. In each case Peleg is presented as son of Eber, the supposed ancestor of the Hebrews, to whom he is said to have given his name.

124

PEREZ, the son of Judah by his daughter-in-law Tamar, was one of twin sons born to her, according to the account in Gen. 38:27-30. This story incorporates the widespread folklore motif of the younger of a pair of twins being accorded the priority; the same motif is found earlier in Gen. 25:21-26 with the story of the birth of Jacob and Esau. The account of Perez' birth also contains another popular Old Testament practice — the association of the personal name with a word of similar sound, in this case one meaning 'breach' (Gen. 38:29). It is likely that the historical circumstances giving rise to the story was the rivalry between different Judahite clans, Zerahites and Perezites (not to be confused with the Perizzites who are often (e.g. Gen. 13:7) listed among the pre-Israelite inhabitants of the land).

PHILIP is a Greek name, and so it is not surprising that the only use of this name comes from the Apocrypha, books which originate from the period of Greek contacts with Judaism. In 1 and 2 Maccabees four different figures named Philip are mentioned:

PHILIP II, king of Macedonia (359-336 B.C.) had set his country on its path to success in war before being succeeded by his more famous son, Alexander the Great. His rule provides the starting-point for 1 Macc. (1:1; cf. 6:2).

PHILIP V of Macedonia was a much less effective ruler than his forebear, and he is mentioned (1 Macc. 8:5) only as having been crushingly defeated by the Romans.

PHILIP THE 'FRIEND' (an official title) of Antiochus IV, the persecutor of the Jews, attempted to gain control of the Syrian state on the death of Antiochus (1 Macc. 6:14, 55-63). He was unsuccessful, though his attempted coup was of value to the Jews insofar as it divided their enemies. The Jewish historian Josephus says that he was killed by his rival, Lysias; but 2 Maccabees has two different traditions relating to him, one that he escaped to Egypt (2 Macc. 9:29), another that he went out of his mind (2 Macc. 13:23).

PHILIP the governor of Jerusalem appointed by Antiochus IV, was a Phrygian by origin (i.e. from modern Turkey) and his policy of Hellenisation was utterly alien to the author of 2 Maccabees (5:22; 6:11). Nothing is known of his subsequent fate.

125

PHINEHAS, the grandson of Aaron (Exod. 6:25), came to be regarded in late Old Testament times as the founder of one of the most important priestly families (1 Chron. 9:20; Ezra 8:2). As such he came to be greatly revered, and various stories about his zealous piety were told. To what extent these tales contain an ancient factual nucleus is disputed; it is clear that in their final form they are intended as an example for later generations, not necessarily to imitate his every action, but at least to show the same scrupulous zeal for the divine service. Num. 25:6-13 tells how he brought an end to a plague and was given the priesthood for killing an Israelite who consorted with a foreign woman; this episode is several times referred to in later traditions (Ps. 106:30f.; Ecclus. 45:23f.; 1 Macc. 2:26, 54). Num. 31:6 has him lead the people in holy war, and Josh. 22: 13-32 describes how his decision is vital in the proper allocation of territories to the different groups within Israel. Finally, in Judg. 20:27f., in an episode which should apparently have taken place centuries after the others, it is Phinehas who decides whether a battle may be fought with divine approval. All these matters were the concern of the priests and so stories relating to them are told of the 'model priest' Phinehas. Despite these late elaborations, the traditions about him may have an ancient element, for the form of his name is probably Egyptian.

PHINEHAS, son of Eli:
See *Hophni*.

POTIPHAR, the steward of the Egyptian Pharaoh, became the master of Joseph when he was sold into slavery in Egypt (Gen. 37:26; 39:1). The name is of a well-known Egyptian form, but is of a type otherwise only found in a period much later than Joseph's time. The Egyptian 'local colour' of the Joseph story, though genuine enough, may not therefore go back to the time of the events described. The story of 'Potiphar's wife' (Gen. 39) is a variant on a well-known folk-tale and it is noteworthy that in the story the woman's husband is never actually called Potiphar, but simply 'the Egyptian', suggesting that the link with Potiphar is a secondary one.

POTIPHERA was the father-in-law of Joseph (Gen. 41:45). The name is simply a variant of 'Potiphar' (q.v.), and poses the same difficulty, that is, that it is of a form only known in Egypt from much later times than Joseph, whose career is envisaged as taking place in the second millennium B.C. Potiphera is described as 'priest of On', that is, Heliopolis, the great centre of worship of the sun god Re, whose name forms the last syllable of Potiphera's name.

PTOLEMY was the family name of the rulers of Egypt from the death of Alexander the Great in the fourth century B.C. until its annexation by Rome three centuries later. During that time fourteen different rulers with this name governed Egypt, and it is not always possible to distinguish them in the ancient sources with complete confidence. Here only those who are specifically mentioned in the Apocrypha will be noted; there are no direct Old Testament references, but the various 'kings of the south' mentioned in the cryptic review of history in Dan. 11 were different Ptolemies: the second to the fifth rulers of the dynasty are alluded to in Dan. 11:5-18.

PTOLEMY VI was the king of Egypt (180-146 B.C.) while Antiochus IV Epiphanes, the villain of the books of Maccabees, ruled Syria. 1 Macc. 1:16-19 describes a victory by Antiochus over Ptolemy, an event also alluded to in Dan. 11:25-27. The Romans prevented Antiochus from assuming complete control over Egypt, so that Ptolemy retained his kingship and, at a later date, when Syria was weakened by rival claimants to the throne, Ptolemy favoured them each in turn when it seemed expedient to do so (1 Macc. 10:51-58; 11:1-13). But he overreached himself, was wounded in battle against his former ally Alexander Balas, and died of the wounds in 146 B.C. (1 Macc. 11:18) though not before he had seen the grisly fate of Alexander whose head was cut off and sent to him as a memento. (This ruler is also referred to at 2 Macc. 4:21 under the title of 'Philometor'.)

PTOLEMY VIII, the younger brother of Ptolemy VI, was associated with his brother on the throne and then remained as sole ruler until 117 B.C. He is mentioned in 1 Macc. 15:16 as the recipient of a letter from the Romans announcing their friendship with the Jews. Ptolemy's early hostility to the Jews seems to have lessened in his later years, and he is referred to in the Preface to Ecclesiasticus under his name Euergetes as the ruler under whom the translation of that book from Hebrew into Greek took place. The context suggests that the Jewish settlement in Egypt was not under any form of harassment at the time (about 132 B.C.).

Three other figures named Ptolemy (or the variant form Ptolemaeus) may be named; they are unconnected with each other, and with the Egyptian rulers already mentioned: one was the Syrian governor of Cyprus who tried to maintain friendlier relations with the Jews than official policy allowed, and was eventually driven to suicide as a result (1 Macc. 3:38; 2 Macc. 4:45f.; 8:8; 10:11-13); another became governor of Jericho at a slightly later date and was involved in the murder of Simon, the last of the Maccabee brothers (1 Macc. 16:11-22); the last is the bearer of the letter announcing the festival of Purim to the Jews in Egypt (Esther 11:1) – this last event occurring in the reign of another Ptolemy, whose identity cannot be certainly established.

PUL was the throne name of the Assyrian Emperor Tiglath-Pileser III (q.v.) (2 Kings 15:19). By the time of the writings of Chronicles, it seems that the fact that these were different names for the same person had been forgotten, and 1 Chron. 5:26 appears to treat Pul and Tilgath-Pilneser (as it renders the longer form) as two separate individuals.

QOHELETH is not a personal name, but is the Hebrew title of the book Ecclesiastes. This book is attributed to Solomon (Eccles. 1:1), but is actually a product of the late Old Testament period; the word *qoheleth* means 'spokesman in the (religious) assembly', which is not quite the same as the older English translation 'preacher'.

RABSHAKEH is not a personal name as might be inferred from the Authorised Version translation of 2 Kings 18-19 and Isa. 36-37, in which chapters the name occurs frequently. More appropriately it is rendered 'the rabshakeh' in some modern translations; the name was applied to a chief officer of the king of Assyria (and is so translated in the New English Bible). The names Rab-mag (Jer. 39:3) and Rab-saris (2 Kings 18:17; Jer. 39:3) are also titles rather than proper names.

RACHEL was the favoured wife of Jacob. Though he was tricked into marrying her elder sister Leah first, he willingly served his father-in-law Laban for seven extra years which "seemed to him but a few days because of the love that he had for her" (Gen. 29:20). Rachel was the mother of Joseph and Benjamin, in giving birth to whom she died (Gen. 35:19).

The story of Rachel contains characteristic folk-lore motifs — the deceit leading to the marriage with the wrong woman; the beautiful but infertile wife; the death of the mother in giving birth to the favoured son. It is impossible to decide whether there ever was a historical individual whose life formed the nucleus of these stories, but it is certain that the tribes identified as those of her sons — Joseph (subdivided into Ephraim and Manasseh) and Benjamin — were closely allied in Israel's later history. The particular tradition about Rachel which was known to later writings is that of 'Rachel weeping for her children', applied by Jeremiah to the exile (Jer. 31:15) and by Matthew to the slaughter of the innocents by Herod (Matt. 2:18).

RAHAB was the prostitute from Jericho whose historicity is difficult to establish, but about whom later traditions have developed with great richness. According to Josh. 2, when Joshua and the Israelite forces arrived near Jericho, they sent spies into the city; Rahab hid them, and tricked the city rulers into believing they had already left; then when the hunt for them was given up, she sent them away in safety. In return for all this she was promised immunity when the Israelites captured the city, a promise that was indeed fulfilled (Josh. 6:22-25). There are clear folk-tale elements in this account, which is in any case at variance with the main story of the capture of the city. According to this story, Rahab's house was on the wall, whereas Josh. 6 tells of the walls falling down. But attempts at harmonisation would be prosaic and useless; the various stories all reflect the people's delight in reflecting upon past prowess and victories gained with God's help.

Later both Jewish and Christian tradition made use of the figure of Rahab. In some Jewish stories she was one of the most beautiful women in the world; in the New Testament she is brought into the line of Jesus's ancestors (Matt. 1:5), and made an example both of

129

saving faith (Heb. 11:31) and of saving works (James 2:25).

The individual Rahab should not be confused with the Old Testament poetic usage of the word Rahab as the name of a mythological monster slain at the time of creation (e.g. Ps. 89:10) and as a derogatory description of Egypt (Isa. 30:7).

RAMESES II, Egyptian Pharaoh, is not mentioned by name in the Old Testament, but it is widely held that the Exodus of the Israelites from Egypt took place at about the time of his reign (1290-1223 B.C.). He may have been either the Pharaoh from whose anger Moses fled (Exod. 2:15), or, more probably, the next ruler under whom the Exodus itself took place. In either case there is no trace in Egyptian records of the plagues or of the actual Exodus events. The store city Raamses described in Exod. 1:11 will have been named after Rameses.

REBEKAH, the wife of Isaac, is prominent in four episodes in the patriarchal history. In the beautiful story of the journey to find a suitable wife (Gen. 24) she is the girl who guides Abraham's servant in his quest and in due course becomes Isaac's bride; for a long time she was barren (a regular motif in 'favourite wife' stories) but in due course bore twins — Esau and Jacob (Gen. 25:19-28). In the thrice-repeated story of the beautiful wife being passed off as a sister one version tells this story of Isaac and Rebekah (Gen. 26:6-11). Finally, a less attractive character is shown in her ruse to obtain Isaac's blessing for her favoured son Jacob rather than Esau (Gen. 27:5-17).

All these stories display a mixture of folk-lore motifs and traditions relating to the conflict between different styles of life, agricultural and nomadic, and it is impossible to discern any historical individual underlying them. This should not detract from their value of stories told to illustrate a belief in God's over-riding purpose for his people.

RECHAB.
See *Jonadab*.

REHOBOAM, the son of Solomon, was king of Judah in the late tenth century B.C. His father had ruled over both Israel and Judah, and Rehoboam's right to the throne was accepted in Judah, where the power of the Davidic line was considerable, but the people of Israel would only agree to accept his rule if he would accept their condition; his refusal led to the division of the two parts of the kingdom, which were never again united (1 Kings 12). The very fact that Rehoboam had to travel to the northern city of

Shechem to parley with 'all Israel' shows that the idea of automatic hereditary succession was not established.

Rehoboam's position as king of the tiny state of Judah was a weak one; he could not take any measure to regain control of the north (1 Kings 12:21-24), and the Egyptian Pharaoh Shoshenq (Biblical 'Shishak') carried out a devastating raid on his territory (1 Kings 14:25-28). The list of fortresses described in 2 Chron. 11:6-12 shows that Judah was reduced to an extremely limited area, with no access to the great trade routes, yet in the long run this proved a source of strength, for Judah was spared the depradations of the great powers which wrought havoc in the more prosperous northern kingdom of Israel. A variety of other notes on Rehoboam's religious policy (2 Chron. 11-12) seems to reflect the Chronicler's own religious viewpoint rather than the historical situation of Rehoboam's time.

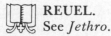 **REHUM** and Shimshai were Persian officials whose activity in Jerusalem is described in Ezra 4. They wrote a letter to the king Artaxerxes implying that the rebuilding of Jerusalem might endanger the security of the Persian Empire, and as a result the work was temporarily halted (Ezra 4:8-23). The events in this chapter are told out of chronological order and so cannot be dated, though the fifth century B.C. will have been the most likely period.

REUBEN is described as the first-born son of Jacob (Gen. 29: 32), but as with the other 'sons' of Jacob, the names seem to refer to tribal groupings rather than individuals. Reuben must therefore at some point have been an important group to be placed first in the various tribal lists (e.g. Num. 1:5), but in historical times the Reubenites were a relatively insignificant group, living east of the Jordan.

There are three episodes in Genesis relating to Reuben as an individual, which may reflect particular points in tribal history: the ensuring of fertility by the gift of mandrakes, a known aphrodisiac (30:14) — this may be linked with a festival at the time of harvest; incest with his father's concubine (35:22) — this may reflect an episode in which Reuben attempted in vain to increase its power; and the befriending of Joseph abandoned by his brothers (37:21f., 29f.; 42:22) — a more individual story, but still one which may reflect inter-tribal alliances when the different groups were settled in Palestine.

REUEL.
See *Jethro*.

REZIN was the ruler of the Aramaean kingdom of Damascus during the 730s B.C. He enters Old Testament history through his attempt, along with Pekah of Samaria, to establish a coalition of small states to check the advance of Assyria, of which, as is known from Assyrian records, he had previously been a vassal. A brief account of the attempt by Rezin and Pekah to enlist Ahaz of Judah in their coalition is found in 2 Kings 16:5-8; Isa. 7-8 supplement this by bringing together a number of prophetic oracles dealing with the same events. Isaiah dismisses Pekah and Rezin as a vain threat (7:4), and urges Ahaz to trust in the Lord. But Ahaz preferred to call in Assyrian power, and in the short run he was justified by retaining his independence whereas Rezin was executed (2 Kings 16:9) and Damascus incorporated into the Assyrian Empire.

REZON is described in 1 Kings 11:23 as an emeny of Solomon. He rebelled against him, threw off Israelite control of Damascus and set up a new kingdom there, which was to play an important part in Israel's history until both Damascus and Israel were overrun by the Assyrians. It is likely that both Rezon and Rezin (see preceding entry) were not personal names — the word means 'prince' — and that Rezon should be identified with Hezion, mentioned in 1 Kings 15:18 as the first king of Damascus. No extra-biblical records survive to throw light on the point.

RIZPAH is the heroine of a remarkable and poignant story in 2 Samuel. She was a concubine of Saul (2 Sam. 3:7), and as usual in such cases the Old Testament records this without moral overtones — it was expected that kings would have a harem. After Saul's death Abner, Saul's general, claimed her and thereby alienated himself from Saul's son Ishbosheth. She had borne two sons to Saul and David handed them over to Saul's enemies in the belief that this might bring to an end a famine that was then plaguing the country. The story is thus an interesting example of how what we should call superstition persisted then (as no doubt it often does today) alongside advanced religious concepts. Hearing of the fate of her children Rizpah kept vigil by the bodies to protect them from birds of prey and wild animals (2 Sam. 21:10). On hearing of Rizpah's loyalty David moved to ensure that Saul's body and that of Jonathan were given proper burial.

RUTH is the heroine of the book named after her. The book is a short story, without obvious polemic purposes, and it offers few clues as to its likely date of composition though it is set, very vaguely, in 'the days of the judges' (1:1). It can be briefly summarised: Ruth the Moabite, married to an Israelite and then widowed, renounces her own country to accompany her mother-in-law back to Bethlehem. After various adventures in which God's hand is clearly seen she marries Boaz, a wealthy landowner, and has a son by him, and so her loyalty to her mother-in-law and her first husband's kin is rewarded.

Historical speculations should be secondary to the tale itself, but there is evidence that they arose at an early date, and so in a kind of epilogue to the book, it is revealed that the child born to Ruth was the father of Jesse and so the grandfather of king David (Ruth 4:17-22). It is possible that this preserves a historical memory; perhaps more likely is the suggestion that the link was inspired by the note in 1 Sam. 22:3f. that David had taken refuge in Moab when he was being sought by Saul. Ruth is mentioned in the New Testament (Matt. 1:5) as an ancestress of David and therefore, in Matthew's genealogy, of Jesus himself.

SAMSON, the last of the major judges, is described in Judg. 13-16. He is, of course, primarily remembered in the English language as one of lengendary strength, and this is an important element in the biblical account, but he is the hero of several stories, and his strength is only one motif. Ch. 13 tells of his birth in unusual circumstances; in 14:1-15:8 we read of his intended marriage to an (unnamed) Philistine girl, and embedded in this story are the subsidiary tales of his slaughter of a lion within the carcass of which he later found a swarm of bees, the way in which he was tricked of his hoped-for bride, and the revenge that he took; 15:9-16:3 provides three more brief stories of his great strength, which is also used as an explanation of various physical features of the country; and then finally 16:4-31 tells of his love for another girl, probably also a Philistine, Delilah, and how she snares him into revealing the secret of his strength, by which she betrays him to her fellow-countrymen so that Samson is captured and taken to the city of Gaza. In the end, his strength is restored sufficiently for him to bring about his own death and that of his tormentors. Various episodes in the story have provided inspiration for artists of all kinds through the ages: one thinks of the famous painting by Rembrandt, of Handel's oratorio, of Milton's *Samson Agonistes,* or more recently, of Aldous Huxley's *Eyeless in Gaza.*

In the present form of the book of Judges Samson is part of the chronological structure which provides a series of rulers over Israel (15:20; 16:31), but it is generally agreed that this is part of the editorial structure of the book, and there is no indication that Samson was ever more than a local hero, at a time when his part of the country — the south-western area — was under some pressure from the Philistines, though Samson's penchant for Philistine women suggests that some measure of social intercourse took place. There is no reason to doubt that such circumstances did arise, or that an actual historical figure underlies some of Samson's exploits, but they have now become so elaborated by popular folk-legend that it is impossible to detect a historical core. At times certain affinities with solar mythology have been noted — Samson's name (Shimshon in Hebrew) is similar to the Hebrew word *shemesh* for 'sun', and the seven locks of his hair have been likened to the conventional depiction of the sun's rays (16:13); there are similarities with the exploits of Heracles (Hercules), for example, in the destruction of the pillars of the city (16:25-30); there are also many comic touches about the presentation of the story, perhaps attributable to the age-old delight of a subject people in seeing their oppressors discomfited. There is no suggestion of moral censure in any of the stories, even though much of Samson's behaviour might have seemed reprehensible; his treachery, his sexual promiscuity, his irresponsibility. Despite all these weaknesses, Samson is seen by the editors of the book of Judges as one of the deliverers of his people, and perhaps even more ironically, by the New Testament as a hero of faith (Heb. 11:32). No more valid example can be found of the way in which the biblical authors were able to transform popular folk-tales into an instrument of their purpose.

SAMUEL is the leading figure in 1 Sam. 1-16. The book begins with an account of his birth and divine calling (chs. 1-3); then, after an episode dealing with the ark, chs. 7-16 tell how Samuel was instrumental in establishing Saul as king, in announcing to him the withdrawal of divine favour, and in establishing David as the next king. The later chapters of 1 Samuel are mainly concerned with David's rise to power, and Samuel himself is scarcely mentioned, save for a brief note of his death (25:1), and the curious story of how his 'ghost' warned Saul of his coming fate (28:3-20).

These events will have taken place at the period when Israel was just establishing itself as a nation, probably in the eleventh century B.C., but it is very difficult to be certain of Samuel's own precise role. This is partly due to the fact that his reputation has been enriched by the addition of folklore motifs, such as the birth in unusual circumstances (1 Sam. 1), but also because different traditions appear to have understood his role in different ways. At times he is a prophetic figure (3:20), and even a member of one of the prophetic bands attached to local places of worship (19:19); at times he is a priest, as is illustrated by the first story of Saul's disobedience (13:1-18); elsewhere he appears as judge over Israel (7:15-17), charged with supervising the arrangements for establishing a monarchy (ch. 8). Even more confusingly, the story of Saul's search for his lost asses in ch. 9 seems to imply that Samuel was nothing more than an obscure village holy-man, whose favour might be won by means of a small gift, but it is likely that that story was originally told of an unnamed seer who was only later identified with Samuel.

The difficulty in establishing Samuel's precise role is compounded by our uncertainty as to the political structure of the country at the time. Some have seen him as the last of the line of judges, most of whom are described in the book of Judges, but it is doubtful whether they are all of a kind in the way implied, and their functions are in any case military rather than judicial; in only one story, and that almost certainly a late addition, is Samuel regarded as a military leader (7:7-14).

Because of these historical difficulties, Samuel provides a prime example of the way in which the biblical narrative is more important for the manner in which it presents God's dealings with his people — in this case at the crisis of establishing a monarchy — than for precise historical reconstruction. In later tradition Samuel was remembered primarily as an intercessor (Jer. 15:1; Ps. 99:6), and as the first in the great line of prophetic figures whose words pointed forward to Jesus (Acts 3:24). His words at 1 Sam. 15:22 are alluded to by Jesus in Mark 12:33, though with a certain irony in view of the fact that in the Old Testament account Samuel is then stated to have murdered the unsuspecting Agag.

SANBALLAT plays an important part in the book of Nehemiah as the principal opponent of Nehemiah's effort to restore the Jerusalem community. At first he and his friends jeered at Nehemiah's efforts (2:19), then they made an open attack (4:7), then by a variety of plots and denunciations to the imperial authorities they attempted to thwart Nehemiah's efforts (ch. 6). But all was in vain — not surprisingly, since the story is clearly told as a memorial of Nehemiah's achievement, setting him out as a heroic figure in the annals of Jersualem.

Sanballat's position is not stated in the book of Nehemiah, but papyri discovered at Elephantine in Egypt early this century referred to 'the sons of Sanballat the governor of Samaria'. These date from about 410 B.C., and seemed to fit well with the supposition that Nehemiah's mission, and Sanballat's opposition to it, had taken place in the twentieth year of the Persian Ruler Artaxerxes I, 445 B.C. (Neh. 2:1), and that by the time of the Elephantine papyri Sanballat was an old man with his sons carrying on the active rule. While this remains the most likely reconstruction, the position has been complicated by the discovery of further papyri, dating from about 380 B.C., referring to another Sanballat, who may have been a grandson of the Sanballat known from Elephantine, and it is possible that this was Nehemiah's enemy.

Sanballat is often referred to as a Samaritan, but this is misleading. The dispute between Jews and Samaritans was essentially religious, but Sanballat is never accused of religious malpractice; his own name is of Babylonian form, but the sons named in the Elephantine papyri had the good Israelite names Delaiah and Shelemaiah. The opposition between Nehemiah and Sanballat was essentially political; Nehemiah's work at Jerusalem, undertaken without reference to the authorities at Samaria, meant an important diminution of power and responsibility for the governor of Samaria.

SARAH, the wife of Abraham, is mentioned in many of the stories in Gen. 11-23. A central theme of those chapters is to show the way in which God would keep his promise that Abraham would have an heir; and eventually a child, Isaac, is born to the previously barren Sarah (Gen. 21:2). Much difficulty for those who wish to take every statement in the Bible literally has been caused by the assertion that Sarah was more than ninety years old at this time (Gen. 17:17). Much more significant is the way in which various motifs appropriate for the foundress of the race have been gathered around her: exceptional beauty (Gen. 12:11), distinguished descent (the name Sarah means 'princess'), and giving birth to a child by special divine favour. Less attractive, though understandable enough, is the episode, told twice in slightly differing forms, of her jealousy of Hagar her maid by whom Abraham had already had a child (Gen. 16:5f.; 21:9-13). The two names by which she is known, Sarai and Sarah, have no difference in meaning; the variation seems to be introduced simply to correspond with the change in her husband's name from Abram to Abraham.

Later Jewish tradition revered Sarah as the foundress of the race (Isa. 51:2), and in the New Testament she is honoured not only on this account (Rom. 9:9) but also as a model of faith (Heb. 11:11) and of wifely submissiveness (1 Peter 3:6).

SARAH is also the name of the heroine in the apocryphal book Tobit. Of her is told a version of the widespread folk-tale of the woman who had had many husbands, all of whom had died before the marriage could be consummated (Tob. 3:7-10). Eventually her prayers were answered, and with angelic assistance her cousin Tobias drove out the demon that had caused her misfortune and he married her (Tol. 8).

SARGON II, king of Assyria, is mentioned only once in the Old Testament (Isa. 20:1), but his influence was much greater than this might imply, for it was during his reign (722-705 B.C.) that Assyrian power in Palestine came to be firmly established. The capture of Samaria and the end of the northern kingdom of Israel as an independent state took place in his accession year, but neither Assyrian records nor the Old Testament (2 Kings 17:1-6) make it clear whether this was achieved under Sargon or under his predecessor Shalmaneser V. But it was certainly Sargon who was responsible for the deportation of many of the leading citizens of Israel (2 Kings 17:6): not, of course, the whole population as envisaged by the 'ten lost tribes' of later legend, but, according to his own annals, 27,000 people.

In about 711 B.C. Sargon crushed a rebellion of small Palestinian states fomented by Egypt, and the reference to him at Isa. 20:1 relates to this; the prophet's nakedness is a symbol of the folly of resistance to Assyrian power. At about the same time Sargon also put down the rebellious king of Babylon, Merodach-baladan. 2 Kings 20:12-19 alludes to the attempt by Merodach-baladan to gain the support of Judah in that rebellion, but Sargon's name is not mentioned.

SATAN may appropriately be mentioned here as a term that became a proper name, though of course not a human figure. In most Old Testament passages where the term is found it is a common noun meaning one who opposes or tests, and as such it is found in descriptions of the heavenly court (e.g. Zech. 3:1; Job. 1:6, where 'the Satan' would be the most appropriate rendering). Only in 1 Chron. 21:1 is Satan found without the definite article. In later Judaism the idea of a personal devil came to be accepted, and so references to Satan are frequent in both the Apocrypha and the New Testament, where a whole variety of other names descriptive of his functions is found.

137

SAUL, the first king of Israel, is one of the most enigmatic figures in the Old Testament. Even his age and the length of his reign are uncertain, for the original text of 1 Sam. 13:1 has been corrupted, and the various modern versions are in effect based on guesswork. All that can be said with confidence is that he ruled in the late eleventh or early tenth century B.C., at a time when Israel was becoming an organised and unified nation for the first time, and therefore local loyalties were gradually giving place to the recognition of the need for a more centralised and continuing form of government. This need was probably sharpened by the external threat from the Philistines, though estimates vary sharply as to the seriousness of this threat.

Saul's call to kingship is described in 1 Sam. 9:1-10:16, but quite different versions are provided in 10:17-27 and in ch. 11. As is commonly the case with great men assuming important positions, a variety of traditions survives describing the event; each group within the community treasures its own understanding of the past. A brief summary of Saul's achievements is found in 1 Sam. 14:47-52, and this implies a considerable measure of success, but virtually the whole of the rest of 1 Samuel is given over to an account of his decline. Two stories tell of his rejection by God and his earthly representative, Samuel (chs. 13 and 15), and the last half of the book tells of David's rise to power and favour, with the accompanying decline of Saul. Finally, Saul meets his death at the hands of the Philistines, and again there are two accounts of his end (1 Sam. 31; 2 Sam. 1). The biblical material relating to Saul ends with a moving lament over him and his son Jonathan attributed to his rival and successor David (2 Sam. 1:17-27).

It has been customary to interpret the 'evil spirit' which attacked Saul (1 Sam. 16:14) in psychological terms, and this has been the occasion both of many works of art and of attempts to describe the particular type of depressive mania from which he is said to have suffered. It is doubtful whether such an approach is justified by the evidence available. It would seem more appropriate to say that the books of Samuel were edited in circles which regarded David as God's chosen vessel, and were therefore likely to disparage his rival, Saul; and that the incontrovertible fact that Saul's reign ended with the shame of defeat at the hands of his enemies was a clear sign of the removal of divine favour. The pro-Davidic standpoint and the fact of Saul's failure would by themselves explain the picture of rejection and dereliction found in the last part of 1 Samuel.

SELEUCUS was the name of one of Alexander the Great's generals, who gained control of Syria and the Asiatic provinces of his empire after Alexander's death. He is not mentioned by name in the Old Testament, though Dan. 11:5 refers to him, but several of his successors took the same name, and it is one of these, Seleucus IV (187-175 B.C.) who is mentioned in 2 Maccabees, first as attempting to rob the Jerusalem temple of its treasures in order to pay his own debts (3:1-13), and then as having died, to be succeeded by his brother Antiochus IV Epiphanes, under whom the real persecution of the Jews began (4:7).

SENNACHERIB, king of Assyria (705-681 B.C.), provides one of the most important though disputed links between the Old Testament and other ancient Near Eastern evidence.

He succeeded his father Sargon and continued his aggressive policy, in particular in his campaign of 701 B.C. when be besieged Jerusalem. His own annals refer to this, describing the capture of forty-six walled cities, with great numbers of prisoners and spoil, and the siege of Hezekiah in Jerusalem 'like a caged bird'. He makes no claim to have captured Jerusalem, but states that Hezekiah was forced to acknowledge his suzerainty and to pay heavy tribute. This is confirmed by a brief biblical account (2 Kings 18:13-16), but seems to be at odds with the much longer stories of how Sennacherib besieged Jerusalem but had to withdraw, either because of the threat of an Egyptian army, or more dramatically, because the 'angel of the Lord' killed 185,000 of his troops (2 Kings 18:17-19:36).

Attempts have been made to maintain the historicity of this story, either by supposing that Sennacherib changed his mind after first being content with tribute and made an unsuccessful attempt to capture Jerusalem, or by positing a second campaign several years later, about which Assyrian annals are silent because a heavy defeat was involved. Both of these suggestions involve major historical and literary problems and it seems more likely that Sennacherib's willingness to accept tribute rather than to carry through the siege of a relatively insignificant city like Jerusalem came later to be interpreted as a victory, an example of divine protection of Jerusalem, and so elaborate legends describing the event were developed. (In modern times an analogous transformation has taken place with the events at Dunkirk in 1940.) The other biblical references in Isa. 36-37 and 2 Chron. 32 are dependent on the Kings account and add no fresh information. Both the Assyrian annals and the Old Testament agree that he met a violent end (2 Kings 19:37), though there are differences of detail in the accounts.

SERAIAH is a common Old Testament name; for reasons which are not now apparent this was particularly so in the seventh/sixth centuries B.C., when several individuals of this name are mentioned. Only those about whom some detail is provided are noted here, including one from a much earlier period.

SERAIAH was David's secretary in 2 Sam. 8:17. His precise status is not clear: 'scribe', 'adjutant-general' and 'executive officer' have all been suggested. His name is elsewhere found in differing forms: Sheva (2 Sam. 20:25), Shisha (1 Kings 4:3), and Shavsha (1 Chron. 18:16). This has led to suggestions that he may have been a foreigner, perhaps an Egyptian, brought in to add expertise at a time when Israel was first building up some form of civil service.

SERAIAH was the chief priest at the time of the destruction of the temple by Nebuchadnezzar in 586 B.C. (2 Kings 25:18; Jer. 52:24). Since the temple was regarded as a focus of opposition to the Babylonians, he and four fellow priests were killed. This is the Seraiah of whom Ezra is described as the son (Ezra 7:1), though he lived nearly two hundred years later. 'Son' here may mean 'descendant', or the author of the book of Ezra may be ignoring chronological niceties in order to stress Ezra's links with the exiles.

SERAIAH is the name of three other characters mentioned in the book of Jeremiah: a royal servant (36:26); a leader of one of the guerilla bands who continued resistance after the Babylonians had captured Jerusalem (40:8); and the brother of Baruch, Jeremiah's secretary (32:12; 51:59), who took an oracle of Jeremiah to Babylon, warning of that city's inevitable downfall.

SETH was the child born to Adam and Eve through whom, according to Genesis, the chosen line was to be established. One tradition (Gen. 4:25) pictures him as a divine gift to replace the murdered Abel; another (Gen. 5:3) seems to know nothing of Cain and Abel, and pictures Seth as Adam's first-born. These traditions are not historical, but are of great theological importance, as showing how the writers understood the working of God's grace in the chosen line.

SHADRACH, Meshach and Abednego are the names which were given to Daniel's three Jewish companions in exile with him. These were their Babylonian names; their Jewish names were Hananiah, Mishael and Azariah (Dan. 1:6-7), and it is possible that the forms given to the Babylonian names represent deliberate corruptions of known Babylonian names, so that, for example, the last is a parody of Abednebo, 'servant of (the Babylonian god) Nebo'.

They are always mentioned together, and it is likely that originally they were the heroes (perhaps anonymous) of a story which told of three servants of the true God being thrown into a fire and remaining unharmed. This has provided the nucleus of Dan. 3 and of its elaboration in the Apocryphal book known as the 'Prayer of Azariah' and the 'Song of the Three Young Men', part of which has passed into Christian liturgical use as the canticle *Benedicite, omnia opera*. Other traditions in Daniel which mention them seem to be editorial links to join them more closely to Daniel himself (2:17, 49), or, in the case of ch. 1, to provide a story which introduces all the main characters of the book together. The whole of Dan. 1-6 probably consists of popular stories which reached their present form in the second century B.C. when the Jews were being persecuted by Antiochus Epiphanes. Nothing is known of the origin of the stories.

SHALLUM is the name of fourteen different individuals in the Old Testament, but only two of these — both kings — are the subject of sufficient information to require notice here. One was king of Judah for a mere three months after the death of his father Josiah; he is called Shallum in Jer. 22:11; 1 Chron. 3:15, but is more usually known as Jehoahaz (q.v.).

The other king named Shallum had an even briefer period of power; just one month (2 Kings 15:13-15). After the death of Jeroboam II, whose reign had been long and successful, Israel was wracked by a series of conspiracies, possibly in part brought about by foreign pressure. Shallum came to the throne by a conspiracy and quickly perished in the same way, probably at some time in the 740s B.C.

SHALMANESER was the name of several Assyrian kings, of whom two were important for Israel. Of these, Shalmaneser III (858-824 B.C.) is not mentioned in the Old Testament, though he mentions Ahab of Israel in his annals. These list the kings who resisted his progress at the battle of Qarqar in 853 B.C., one of the earliest events relating to the Old Testament which can be dated with fair accuracy. Ahab was one of the largest contributors (10,000 infantry and 2,000 chariots) to the alliance against the Assyrians, and though Shalmaneser claimed a victory it seems as if his advance was halted. A few years later, however, he was able to impose tribute on Jehu, king of Israel, and the 'black obelisk' depicting this is in the British Museum in London.

The Shalmaneser of the Old Testament (2 Kings 17:3; 18:9) was Shalmaneser V (727-722 B.C.), who laid siege to Samaria when

141

its king rebelled agains him; neither the Assyrian records nor the Old Testament make it clear whether he or his brother and successor Sargon finally captured the city.

Shalman, mentioned in Hosea 10:14, could be a shortened form of the name of one of these kings, but the episode referred to is otherwise unknown.

SHAMGAR is the subject of two very obscure references in the book of Judges. In 3:31 he is described as a deliverer of Israel, and a heroic feat is then noted; in 5:6 his period of activity is categorised as a time when normal travel was impossible. The natural way to understand this would be to take Shamgar as one who oppressed Israel and so prevented normal life being carried on, but this is scarcely compatible with his being a judge of Israel. The only realistic course is to acknowledge that limited knowledge of the period prevents any confident decision being reached.

SHAPHAN played an important part in political and religious affairs in the last years of Judah's independent existence. The finding of the 'book of the law' is presented in 2 Kings 22 as occasioning a major religious reform in the time of Josiah, and Shaphan played a vital role as an intermediary between priest and king, and in advising the king as to the appropriate action to be taken (2 Kings 22:3, 8-14; the same events are described from a slightly different perspective in 2 Chron. 34). This 'book of the law' is commonly identified with some part of Deuteronomy, and it has been held that Shaphan and his immediate associates may actually have been responsible for the ordering of the book of Deuteronomy, or at least have been members of the 'deuteronomistic school' which played an important part in handing down and modifying older traditions in the seventh/sixth century.

Nothing more is heard of Shaphan himself, but various individuals described as 'son of Shaphan' are involved in the events of the last days of Judah, and the presumption must be that they are all sons of the same man. Thus Ahikam rescued Jeremiah from death at the hands of an angry mob (Jer. 26:24); Elasah took Jeremiah's letter of encouragement to those in exile (Jer. 29:3); and Gemariah was one of those who heard the scroll of Jeremiah's prophecies (Jer. 36:10-12). The family can probably be traced through one more generation, for Gedaliah, governor of Judah after the fall of Jerusalem, was a grandson of Shaphan (2 Kings 25:22; Jer. 39-43).

SHAVSHA.
See *Seraiah*.

SHEALTIEL.
See *Zerubbabel.*

SHEAR-JASHUB was one of two sons of the prophet Isaiah to whom symbolic names were given as part of the prophetic message (Isa. 7:3; cf. Isa. 8:18). The meaning of the name is 'A Remnant will return', and its original significance was probably to emphasise the overwhelming nature of the disaster which Judah could not escape. In later interpretation the emphasis shifted from 'only a remnant . . . ' to 'there will be a remnant . . . ', bringing out the hopeful rather than the threatening aspect. (See also *Maher-shalal-hash-baz.*)

SHEBA was a Benjaminite who led an unsuccessful rebellion against David (2 Sam. 20), apparently with some measure of success until he met a gruesome death at the hands of the inhabitants of Abel beth-Maacah (vv. 21f.). His rebellion is important as showing the measure of opposition to David, perhaps from those in Benjamin who remained loyal to the family (or at least the memory) of Saul; the editor of 2 Samuel makes his position clear from the outset by calling him a worthless fellow (v. 1) as any opponent of David might expect to be regarded. (It may help to avoid confusion by noting that this Sheba has no connection with the (unnamed and perhaps legendary) 'queen of Sheba' of 1 Kings 10. The word Sheba used of them both in English, in fact represents different Hebrew originals.

SHEBNA was a leading government official in Judah in the last years of the eighth century B.C., and as such played an important part in the negotiations with the Assyrian king whose army was besieging Jerusalem (2 Kings 19:19-19:7). It is difficult to decide upon an exact modern equivalent of his office — 'secretary', 'adjutant-general' and 'remembrancer' have all been suggested — but it is recorded that he and his fellow-officials could understand Aramaic, the language of international diplomacy, as well as their native Hebrew (2 Kings 18:26). It is likely that this is the same Shebna as the officer 'over the household', that is, the palace governor, condemned by Isaiah (Isa. 22:15-22). Less likely is the suggestion that a grave inscription excavated just outside Jerusalem referred to Shebna; the person interred had been a royal official, but the name has not survived, and the suggested identification was only made because of Isaiah's condemnation of Shebna for preparing a particular burial-place for himself (Isa. 22:15f.).

SHECHEM is described in several passages which imply that this was the name of an individual, notably in the story in Gen. 34 telling of his intended marriage with Dinah and the ruse by which the Israelites massacred Shechem's household. In fact Shechem is a place-name, and this story is told partly at least to cast aspersions on the legitimacy of the worship practised there. As such, this story was often told with various later elaborations in the last centuries B.C., when there was bitter hostility between the Jews of Jerusalem and the Samaritans of Shechem. It is most unlikely that there was an individual named Shechem.

SHEM was the son of Noah, who is described in two very different traditions. In Gen. 9:18-27 he and his brother Japhet show respect for their father Noah, lying drunk and naked, in contrast to the attitude of their brother Ham. This ancient tradition may well serve as a warning to the pastoral people of Israel against the danger of involvement in the viticulture of Canaan. There follows, in Gen. 10, the 'table of nations', a list of all the peoples of the known world popularly believed to be descended from Noah's sons. Those listed as descendants of Shem (10:21-31) cannot be equated by means of scientific ethnology with those whom we know as 'Semites', though it is from Shem that the name derives.

SHEMAIAH is the name borne by nearly thirty Old Testament characters; of only one do we know significant details concerning his role. This was a prophet, active at the time of the division of the kingdom, whose divine messages played an important part in determining the policy of Rehoboam. He is mentioned only once in 1 Kings, where it is appropriate that we find him, as the only southern prophet of whom we know between Nathan and Isaiah, playing a similar role in warning the king as to the appropriate action to take (12:22). In 2 Chron. this is elaborated to show Shemaiah as the mediator both of punishment and of forgiveness (12:5-7), and he is also described as the author of a history (2 Chron. 12:15). Nothing else is known of this, and it is likely that the reference is a way of claiming authenticity for the Chronicler's work rather than a survival of an ancient record.

SHEMER is stated in 1 Kings 16:24 to have been the owner of the site which later became the city of Samaria, but it is more likely that the name of the city lent itself to an imagined original owner.

SHENAZZAR.
See *Sheshbazzar*.

144

SHESHBAZZAR appears to have been a leading figure in the return of some Jews from Babylon to Jerusalem in the time of Cyrus (c. 539 B.C.). Ezra 1:8-11 calls him 'the ruler of Judah', and pictures him as being in control of the arrangements concerning the return of temple vessels; Ezra 5:14-16 is part of an Aramaic document describing Sheshbazzar as governor and crediting him with laying the foundation of the restored temple. The problem arises from the fact that elsewhere in Ezra and in the books of Haggai and Zechariah Zerubbabel is the Jewish leader carrying out the tasks here ascribed to Sheshbazzar.

Three possible solutions to the problem have been put forward. First, some have said that the Sheshbazzar traditions should be dismissed as totally unreliable. The objection to this is that it is difficult to envisage any plausible ground for the elaboration of such traditions. Secondly, Sheshbazzar might be an alternative name for Zerubbabel, or for Shenazzar, mentioned in 1 Chron. 3:18 as a son of the exiled king Jehoiachin. Suggestions of this kind are difficult to disprove, but must remain speculative. Sheshbazzar is never referred to as a member of the royal family, as is always done with the others mentioned. Most likely, therefore, is the suggestion that we have a variety of traditions from the period; that the events were already remote when they came to reach their final form; and that the author of Ezra (who was in no way a historian in the modern sense) was content to set down variant traditions side by side without attempting to reconcile them. We may reckon that Sheshbazzar was involved in the events of the period, without being confident as to his exact status or role.

SHEVA.
See *Seraiah*.

SHIMEI is a common Old Testament name, but only one person so called is more than a name to us. This was a member of Saul's family, the exact relationship not being stated, who saw in Absalom's apparently successful rebellion against David a sign of divine retribution (2 Sam. 16:5-13). When David put down the rebellion Shimei's life was spared after a grovelling apology (2 Sam. 19:16-23), but the episode was not forgotten, and Shimei's ultimate fate sheds an interesting light on royal morality. David pointed out to Solomon, his son and successor, that the pardon to Shimei only bound himself, David, and that Solomon need not be bound by it (1 Kings 2:8); and then Solomon waited three years for a pretext which enabled him to have Shimei killed for a trivial offence which broke the letter of his oath not to leave Jerusalem (1 Kings 2:36-46).

SHIMSHAI.
See *Rehum*.

SHISHAK is the biblical form of the name of the Egyptian Pharaoh Sheshonq or Shoshenq, a Libyan ruler who founded the twenty-second Egyptian dynasty and ruled c. 935-914 B.C. It is improbable that Shishak was the Pharaoh whose daughter Solomon married (1 Kings 3:1), but the note that he gave asylum to Jeroboam as a refugee from Solomon seems reliable (1 Kings 11:40), and provides perhaps the earliest cross-reference between the Bible and contemporary world politics. Egyptian pressure may have been involved in the division of Israel and Judah into separate kingdoms, though the Bible makes no reference to it. But clearly the Egyptians hoped to regain some influence in Palestine, and so Shishak carried out raids in the area; his own account has been discovered in an inscription at Thebes, and the Old Testament refers to the same events in 1 Kings 14:25-28, with further elaboration in 2 Chron. 12:1-12. The Old Testament accounts are concerned with Shishak's invasion of Judah, but Shishak's own account makes it clear that he also attacked the northern area.

SIHON was the Amorite king whose defeat was a major episode in the progress of the Israelites into Canaan. His kingdom was in trans-Jordan, centred upon Heshbon (Deut. 2:26-35), that is, east of the northern extremity of the Dead Sea. The accounts of the defeat of Sihon in the Old Testament are all from a much later period, and have elements of saga or folklore, so that it is difficult to establish the historical circumstances with any certainty. The account in Num. 21:21-31, for example, incorporates a poem which in fact is concerned with quite a different war, against Moab (vv. 27-30), and the other references to Sihon all occur in summaries of the great deeds wrought by Yahweh on behalf of his people. Sometimes these summaries appear to have a preaching context (Deut. 29:7; Judg. 11:19-21), sometimes they reflect liturgical usage (Pss. 135:11; 136:19). In nearly all of these later reflections, Sihon is linked with the neighbouring king, Og.

SIMEON, one of the sons of Jacob (Gen. 29:33) is pictured, like the other sons of Jacob, as the ancestor after whom the tribes of Israel were named. As with the other tribes, it is likely that the name of a tribal or clan grouping preceded the development of stories about an individual. Even in those stories which depict him as an individual, it may well be that some episode of clan history lies in the background and would, if known in greater detail, provide some explanation of the particular form which the story has taken. This is clearly the case in Gen. 34, where Simeon and Levi are the brothers who attempt to settle in Shechem and secure their position by a ruse, murdering the Shechemites before they had recovered from the effects of circumcision; it is less obvious in the incident which makes Simeon the brother detained in Egypt as a hostage by Joseph before he revealed himself to his unsuspecting brothers (Gen. 42:24).

In the later history Simeon appears as one of the smallest tribes, very much dependent on Judah (Judg. 1:3), and occupying an area in the far south of the land. In the tribal lists Simeon is usually placed second, reflecting the same tradition as that found in Gen. 29 of Simeon as the second-born son, but no other distinctive role can be traced.

SIMON, the high priest whose praises are sung in Ecclus. 50: 1-21, is probably to be identified with Simon II, high priest of the Jerusalem temple at the end of the third century B.C., and known in Jewish tradition as 'Simon the Just'. The portrait is remarkable in that it shows how the high priest had taken over many hitherto royal characteristics. Later Jewish tradition associated him with the conquests of Alexander the Great, alleging that the impression he made upon the conqueror led to the Jews being treated more favourably than their rivals, the Samaritans; but the chronology makes this story suspect, as well as some of its legendary details.

SIMON was the second of the five sons of Mattathias, the family which played so major a part in the war which enabled the Jews to establish their independence from Syrian rule. Little is known of his role in the earlier stage of the struggle, though his father's dying words speak of his expertise in counsel (1 Macc. 2:65). He first came to prominence during the rule of his brother Jonathan, and then eventually brought the struggle to a successful conclusion and himself became the ruler of the country (1 Macc. 13-16), and this represents the climax of the account in 1 Maccabees, which is written as an apologia for the Hasmonaean (Maccabee) family. From 141-136 B.C. Simon was the high priest and ruler of his people, supported by external allies (Rome and Sparta), and 1 Macc. 14:4-15 presents his time of rule as the golden age of his people's history.

SIRA/SIRACH. Explanation of the various names by which the book of Ecclesiasticus, in the Apocrypha, is known, is a somewhat complex matter. The book was originally written in Hebrew

147

early in the second century B.C., and its author, whose name is known to us only in its Greek form, was Jesus the son of Sirach (Ecclus. 50:27). Jesus is the Greek form of the Hebrew name Joshua, and Sirach is a Greek form of Hebrew Sira. The author's grandson later translated the book into Greek (Ecclus: Prologue), in about 130 B.C., and the book in our English Bibles is a translation of this Greek form; the Hebrew original seemed to have been lost without trace until A.D. 1896, when a fragment was found, and subsequently extensive parts of it have been recovered. Since the third century A.D. it has commonly been known as Ecclesiasticus, or 'the church book'. Its contents are mainly wisdom sayings, but the wisdom tradition is integrated more fully into Israel's distinctive religious self-understanding than had been the case with earlier wisdom books.

SISERA was the Canaanite general whose army was defeated in the battle described in Judg. 4-5. The first account is in prose, and presents Sisera as the commander of the army whose ruler was Jabin (Judg. 4:2), but in the poetic account in ch. 5 Jabin is not mentioned and Sisera appears as the effective ruler. His home base, Harosheth ha-goiim, is unidentified, and his name may indicate that he was a Philistine, or a member of one of the other 'sea peoples' who penetrated into Palestine in the twelfth/eleventh centuries B.C. In any case the poem takes a vivid delight in showing how the raging torrent of the river Kishon rendered Sisera's chariots useless; how he fled on foot and was murdered, in defiance of all the laws of hospitality, by Jael, who had given him refuge in her tent. The poem ends with a superbly ironic description of Sisera's court explaining the delay in his return by the time taken to gather the spoil. The poem has sometimes been taken as almost contemporary with the events it describes, but there is no real evidence for this, and it is more likely to come from a slightly later date; this would explain the many divergences in detail between the poetic and prose accounts of Sisera's defeat.

SO, king of Egypt, is said to have been involved in intrigue with the last king of Israel, Hoshea, which induced him to revolt against his Assyrian overlord, and so brought the downfall of Samaria and the end of the independent northern kingdom. The reference to So (2 Kings 17:4) has always been problematic, since no such Egyptian ruler is known, and it seems clear that the Old Testament tradition is mistaken. Either a place-name (perhaps Sais, in the Nile delta), as the New English Bible suggests, or a lesser Egyptian figure (perhaps Sibe, mentioned in Assyrian records as an Egyptian commander), may be meant.

SOLOMON, son of David, ruled over the united monarchy of Israel and Judah in the tenth century B.C. The Old Testament account makes it clear that his achievement was considerable, but caution is needed in its appraisal, since there are no extra-biblical references to him, and certain of the stories describing his reign have a folkloristic character. Such would include the account of his decision in the matter of the hariots' child (1 Kings 3:16-28). It is unlikely, too, that the statement that he ruled for forty years is to be taken literally (1 Kings 11:42); it is noteworthy that David is also credited with a forty-year rule. The sources of our knowledge are mainly 1 Kings 3-11, with some notes on his early years in 2 Samuel, and a further account, which may include a few independent traditions, in 2 Chron. 1-9.

Solomon was born to David and Bathsheba after the death of the child of their adulterous union (2 Sam. 12:24), and a second name, Jedidiah, is also mentioned; this may have been a personal name, with Solomon being a throne name. He seems not to have been involved in the often sordid intrigues as to who should succeed David, until — with David now senile — his mother and the prophet Nathan engineered a *coup d'état* on his behalf (1 Kings 1:5-53). When he succeeded to the throne, the account of the succession to David — perhaps a distinct literary entity within the books of Samuel and Kings — is rounded off by describing Solomon's often brutal measures to rid himself of all potential opponents (1 Kings 2:13-46).

The account of his reign in 1 Kings 3-11 is concerned with three main themes: his wisdom; his building of the temple; and his falling away from true worship. The material is thus arranged thematically rather than chronologically. His wisdom, insofar as it has a historical basis, appears to have consisted largely in organisational matters; he was not like David a hero-figure, relying upon the divine charisma to achieve success. Now Israel was a state among states, with its ruler engaging in treaties (1 Kings 5), marriage alliances (1 Kings 3:1; 11:1), and the establishment of a civil service (1 Kings 4:1-19), which imposed a royal establishment cutting across the older local and clan allegiances. The visit of the queen of Sheba (1 Kings 10:1-13) should probably also be seen in the context of establishing Solomon's kingdom as an important one in terms of the international trade of the day, though in this case the original tale has been subsequently embellished with all kinds of legendary accretions.

In one sense the temple building may also be seen as part of this display of ostentation, for it formed part of the royal complex of buildings (1 Kings 6:37-7:12). But it was, of course, far more than a royal chapel, and in 1 Kings 8 the later editors have constructed an elaborate theological reflection to draw out the significance of the

149

temple, which was in fact, as the details in chs. 6-7 make clear, physically a relatively insignificant building. But there can be no doubt that, alien as it may have been to older Israelite ideas of a god who dwelt with his people rather than in a building, it came to play an immensely important part in the religious life of Judaism.

The portrait of Solomon is not, however, an uncritical one. According to the editors of 1 Kings, his achievement was marred by his attachment to foreign women and his toleration of their religious cults. 1 Kings 11 ascribes the various misfortunes that befell the kingdom directly to this religious weakness, though a modern historical analysis would probably be more concerned with economic factors: the immense development had produced internal stresses which led both to inability to maintain the full extent of the empire (1 Kings 11:14-24) and to the division of the kingdom upon Solomon's death. Not all were convinced that strong central kingship in Jerusalem, with the apparatus of government, was to their own advantage; and it is widely held that the account of kingship given by Samuel in 1 Sam. 8 was in fact written with the depredations of Solomon in mind.

The final verdict on Solomon, therefore, has to be a mixed one. Nevertheless, it is indisputable that his great achievements caused his name to be long remembered. He was a builder of the temple and the 'patron' of the wisdom movement, so that books as diverse as Proverbs, Ecclesiastes, the Song of Songs and Wisdom of Solomon (the book in the Apocrypha, actually written in Greek!) came to be ascribed to him. Thus it was of Solomon that Jesus, wanting a picture of earthly glory, most naturally thought (Matt. 6:29; Luke 12:27).

SUSANNA is the heroine of the book named after her in the Apocrypha. The story has characteristic folk-tale motifs: the beautiful girl rejects the advances of the lustful elders, who then conspire against her, but are prevented from harming her by the skill of Daniel in showing the falsity of their statements. The tale has therefore been described as the first detective story, and as such is well worth reading; there is no serious likelihood of it being historical. It was probably originally composed in a Semitic language, but is now only known in Greek translation.

T

TABEEL is referred to in Isa. 7:6. The circumstances were the attempt of the kings of Damascus and Samaria to build up a coalition against the Assyrian threat. When Ahaz of Judah refused to join, they proposed setting up 'the son of Tabeel' as king in Jerusalem. The manner in which the story is told in Isaiah shows his contempt for the two kings; their conspiracy is bound to fail, and their candidate for the Jerusalem kingship is not even given his own name but simply referred to as 'son of a good-for-nothing' — which is the way in which the Hebrew text has deliberately misrepresented the name whose original meaning was 'God is good'.

TAHPENES is referred to in 1 Kings 11:19-20 in the account of the various enemies of Solomon as the Egyptian queen. But Egyptian records know of no such individual; and it is now widely held that Tahpenes is not a proper name, but a title for a female member of the royal family. In the Hebrew text the word 'queen' has been added as an explanation, and then the word Tahpenes came wrongly to be understood as a personal name.

TAMAR, meaning 'date-palm', and therefore a symbol of fertility and prosperity, is the name of several women mentioned in the Old Testament. The first was the wife of Judah's son Er, who was to be given after his death to his brother Onan; he refused to consummate the marriage, and when he in turn died Judah did not offer to Tamar the opportunity of marrying his third son, Shelah. In revenge for this Tamar disguised herself as a prostitute, and had intercourse with her father-in-law Judah, and had twin children by him (Gen. 38:6-30). The account acknowledges her innocence in this matter (v. 26), and her name is used in two later genealogies, in contexts where it was not necessary to mention the woman's name, thereby implying that Tamar's acts were regarded as praiseworthy. The first is Ruth 4:12; the second the genealogy of Jesus (Matt. 1:5).

TAMAR A second Tamar is also involved in a story telling of sexual intercourse. She was the beautiful daughter of David who was raped by Amnon, her half-brother (2 Sam. 13:1-14). Amnon then is filled with revulsion against her, and so Tamar is left, her virginity

151

violated but with no prospect of marriage. Her subsequent fate is not described, but her brother Absalom took revenge on Amnon and so furthered the quarrels which characterised David's family.

TAMAR A third Tamar is also mentioned in a passing note (2 Sam. 14:27) as a daughter of Absalom. Presumably she was named after her aunt, unless this is an alternative tradition according to which the woman raped by Amnon was Absalom's daughter rather than his sister.

TAMMUZ is mentioned by name in the Old Testament only at Ezek. 8:14. He was the Mesopotamian god of fertility, and the 'weeping' referred to by Ezekiel was part of an annual rite associated with dying and rising gods whose death and rebirth corresponded to the round of the agricultural year.

TERAH, the father of Abraham, is one of the many characters in the early Old Testament period who appear to us as a mixture of historical, geographical and clan traditions. A place-name corresponding to Terah is known from Mesopotamia; the account in Gen. 11:24-32 clearly implies a whole clan rather than a single family. Yet a later tradition (Josh. 24:2) shows that Terah was thought of as an individual, and somewhat surprisingly adds the note that he and his family worshipped 'other gods', thus betraying a recognition of the complex nature of Israel's forebears.

TIBNI is described in two equivocal verses (1 Kings 16:21f.) as one who attempted unsuccessfully to establish himself as king of Israel, the northern kingdom. Either there was a civil war, which Tibni lost, or he and Omri ruled over different parts of the country. The cryptic 'So Tibni died' might imply defeat in war, suicide, or even be a way of expressing his failure to establish himself as king.

TIGLATH-PILESER III, king of Assyria (745-727 B.C.), initiated the great resurgence of Assyrian power which led to the capture of Samaria and the end of the northern kingdom of Israel, and to the reduction of Judah to vassal status. His exploits are also vividly illustrated by the reliefs now in the British Museum in London. In the Old Testament direct references to him are few (2 Kings 15:19, 29; 16:7, 10, with the equivalent passages in Chronicles), but they show how the power of Assyria brought a swift end to the prosperity of Israel and Judah. In 2 Kings 15 we see Assyria interfering decisively in the political intrigues of Israel; 2 Kings 16 shows how Ahaz of Judah accepted a client role in political and religious matters as the price of keeping nominal independence, a course of action for which he is bitterly condemned by the editor of 2 Kings. In addition to these direct references, the rise of Assyria under Tiglath-pileser supplies the background to the prophetic messages of Hosea, Isaiah and Micah. He was also known by the throne name of Pul, whom the Chronicler (1 Chron. 5:26) seems to have taken to be a different individual. The Chronicler's version of the name, Tilgath-pilneser, also shows that the tradition of Assyrian names was foreign to Israel, just as many foreign names present problems in English today.

TIRHAKAH, Egyptian Pharaoh 689-664 B.C., was involved in the complicated events of Hezekiah's resistance to Assyria at the end of the eighth century. One version of the story tells that it was the threat of his Egyptian army that led the Assyrian king Sennacherib to withdraw from Jerusalem (2 Kings 19:8f.; Isa. 37:9). Many of the historical details of this story remain obscure, but the objection formerly raised, that Tirhakah would have been too young in 701 to have led an Egyptian army, is now usually thought to be invalid; Tirhakah was not yet Pharaoh, as the biblical text states, but he could have led an army.

TOBIAH played an important part in the opposition to Nehemiah when he attempted to restore the city of Jerusalem, probably in the fifth century B.C. His exact status is disputed; the New English Bible rendering of Neh. 2:10 calls him 'the slave Tobiah, an Ammonite', but it would be equally possible to regard 'slave' as a title for an imperial 'servant', and the Ammonite reference would mean that he was governor of the province of Ammon; his name is of Israelite formation. For the most part he is associated in the book of Nehemiah with the other opponent, Sanballat, but at the end his own status is brought out by the fact of his marital relation with the high priestly family and his position of privilege in the temple (Neh. 13:4-9). During later centuries one of the most important Jewish families was the Tobiads, and it is likely that the Tobiah of Nehemiah's time was their ancestor. (They are mentioned by Josephus, but not by any biblical source.)

TOBIAS and Tobit are the principal characters of the Apocryphal book Tobit. It is a popular folk-tale, written originally in Hebrew but surviving only in Greek, with many parallels in other folk-tales from the ancient world. The story is supposedly set in the Assyrian Empire, but it has a 'once upon a time' quality which is not linked with any particular historical or geographical setting. Essenti-

153

ally two stories are woven together; on the one hand, the pious Jew Tobit is visited by misfortunes, including blindness which is ultimately cured by the gall of a fish given to his long-lost son Tobias by an angel; on the other hand the wanderings of the son culminate in his breaking the spell cast by a demon on the beautiful Sarah, all of whose previous husbands have died before the marriage could be consummated. Such a bald summary makes the work sound trivial; in fact, it is eminently worth reading as a charming tale and a vehicle of a good deal of insight into the ways of God and men.

TOI/TOU was a king of Hamath in the north of Palestine who is described in 2 Sam. 8:9-11 and 1 Chron. 18:9f. as sending an embassy under his son to congratulate David on his successful campaigns. The note is important insofar as it shows the extent of David's influence, reaching far beyond the usual borders of Israel.

TOLA was one of the minor judges (Judg. 10:1f.), whose dwelling-place and period of rule are given, but no further details. It is thus impossible to decide from the extant tradition whether these minor judges were basically judicial figures, or warriors like the major judges. Tola appears to have been a name found in the tribe of Issachar, for the genealogies of that group make several other references to a Tola (Gen. 46:13; Num. 26:23; Chron. 7:1f.).

TRYPHO is one of the leading characters in 1 Macc. 11-15. One of the reasons for the success of the Jewish bid for independence under the Maccabees was the weakness of their enemies, and Trypho exemplifies this. He had been a Syrian general, but then took advantage of divisions in the capital, Antioch, to seize power for himself, and rule as a usurper for some four years (142-138 B.C.). Before that time he had the Jewish leader Jonathan killed (1 Macc. 12:39-53), as part of his attempt to rid himself of possible enemies, but in the end he was driven off his usurped throne (1 Macc. 15:10-37); non-biblical sources tell of his death soon afterwards, either by murder or suicide.

TUBAL-CAIN is described in Gen. 4:22 as the originator of metal-working. The note is not historical, but reflects the interest of the later biblical writers in the origins of practices known to them. It may be a variant of the same tradition which lists 'Tubal' in the table of nations (Gen. 10:2); there the reference appears to be a land famous for its metal-work.

URIAH is the name borne by five different Old Testament characters; in two cases they are no more than names in lists, but the other three are described more fully.

URIAH the Hittite was one of David's chosen group of warriors known as 'the thirty' (2 Sam. 23:39). The precise significance of 'Hittite' is not clear; at an earlier date there had been a Hittite Empire in Asia Minor, and it is possible that Hittite enclaves persisted in Palestine in David's time; alternatively it may simply be a general term denoting 'foreigner', though Uriah is itself an Israelite name. Uriah was the victim of a murder plot on account of his beautiful wife Bathsheba. In her husband's absence at the front she became pregnant by David. The king recalled Uriah hoping that he would have intercourse with his wife, and even got him drunk to bring this about; but Uriah refused, since this was forbidden to warriors on campaign. In order to rid himself of his embarrassment, David sent a message by Uriah's own hand to his commander to order his tactics so as to ensure the death of Uriah. The whole story is told in 2 Sam. 11, a masterly polemic against any view that kings had absolute power. Nathan's condemnation of David in 2 Sam. 12 is made more pointed by the way in which Bathsheba is always described as 'the wife of Uriah the Hittite', stressing the illicit nature of her relation with the king, and the story ends with the death of Bathsheba's child.

URIAH was the priest of the Jerusalem temple during the reign of Ahaz, probably around 735 B.C. Ahaz' submission to Assyrian domination was not a purely political matter, but involved acknowledgement of the suzerain's gods, and this is probably the significance of Ahaz' instructions to Uriah to reproduce in Jerusalem the religious practices of Damascus, where Ahaz was summoned by the Assyrian king (2 Kings 16:10-16). It is most probable that it was the same Uriah to whom passing reference is made in the book of Isaiah (8:2), as one who bore witness to a legal document.

URIAH was also the name of a prophet during the reign of Jehoiakim, who preached words of doom against Jerusalem and Judah, and thereby earned royal disfavour. He fled to Egypt, but Jehoiakim

155

was able to have him brought back to Jerusalem. We are not told whether this was a formal extradition or whether the political situation allowed raids of this kind. In any case Uriah was killed by the royal command (Jer. 26:20-23). The story is told as an illustration of the dangers facing Jeremiah, who preached a similar message of doom.

URIEL, one of the four chief angels along with Gabriel, Michael and Raphael, is mentioned by name in the Bible only in 2 Esdras, where he plays an important role as an intermediary, explaining to Ezra some of the mysteries of the divine action (2 Esd. 4:1, and frequently in the following chapters). He has a similar function in various non-biblical texts from the beginning of the Christian era.

UZZAH, the son of Abinadab, is known only because of the apparently bizarre circumstances of his death (2 Sam. 6:1-7). The story tells how he put out his hand to steady the ark of God when the oxen drawing it stumbled, and was struck dead. It is difficult to know whether this is an historical incident, in which Uzzah's sudden death subsequently came to be attributed to divine displeasure, or whether Uzzah may have played the role of the 'substitute king' whose brief period of power ended in his death; such a role is found elsewhere in the ancient Near East but not otherwise in the Old Testament.

UZZIAH, king of Judah in the eighth century B.C., is also known as Azariah. It is not clear why he is known by two different but closely related names, though the most commonly held explanation is that one was a personal and the other an official 'throne' name; nor is any ready explanation available of the usage of the different names in different Old Testament books — 'Uzziah' is found in the prophetic books (Isa. 1:1; 6:1; Hosea 1:1; Amos 1:1; Zech. 14:5) and in some of the references in Kings and Chronicles; 'Azariah' is confined to 2 Kings and one reference in Chronicles. His reign was a long one, though the fifty-two years mentioned in 2 Kings 15:1f. cannot be fitted in with the remaining chronology of the period, and a rule of some forty years (c. 783-743 B.C.) is usually proposed. It was a period of great success for Judah, temporarily free of pressure from the great powers, and this prosperity and the length of his reign may have contributed to the judgement that he 'did what was right in the eyes of the Lord' (2 Kings 15:3). The account of his reign in 2 Kings is very brief, but fuller detail is supplied by 2 Chron. 26, where the extent of his power is shown as reaching to the red Sea (v. 2), with local enemies defeated and

Jerusalem extensively rebuilt (vv. 6-15).

The account of Uzziah ends with the statement that he contracted leprosy (2 Kings 15:5), a fact which was interestingly illustrated by the discovery of a tablet from a later period with the words 'Here are laid the bones of Uzziah king of Judah: do not open'. The Chronicler has taken the theme of Uzziah's leprosy as the occasion to tell the story illustrating the danger of royal power when it usurps that which properly belongs to the priesthood (2 Chron. 26:16-23). This should be understood as an edifying tale rather than a statement of historical fact.

VASHTI was the wife of the Persian king Xerxes in the book of Esther (Esther 1:9-2:4). Her refusal to present herself to the king at his command occasioned the male chauvinist reaction that disaster would follow since all women would follow the example of her independence (Esther 1:16-18), leading to 'contempt and wrath in plenty', and in the longer term provided the occasion for Esther's introduction to the king. The incident with Vashti thus provides a dramatic beginning to the story, but is not to be confused with history; the wife of Xerxes was in fact called Amestris, and the incident described in the book of Esther seems to be a skilful fictional device.

XERXES, the Persian king (486-465 B.C.), is perhaps best known for his unsuccessful attacks on Greece which culminated in the sea battle at Salamis in 480 B.C.; to the Greeks he was, of course, an enemy to be described in unflattering terms. The Old Testament, however, is generally friendly to the Persian rulers, and this is true of the brief references to Xerxes, whose name in Hebrew is modified to Ahasuerus. He is mentioned in passing at Ezra 4:6, and plays a prominent part in the book of Esther, where he has a Jewish wife, Esther, and eventually realises how he has been duped by his leading anti-Jewish counsellor Haman. In Dan. 9:1 he is mentioned erroneously as the father of Darius; in fact Darius was father of Xerxes. Neither Esther nor Daniel can be regarded as reliable historically in their accounts of the Persian period.

ZADOK was the leading Jerusalemite priest at the time of David, and played an important part in the struggle for the succession after David's death. In subsequent centuries the concern for a properly authenticated priest in the Zadokite line of succession was an important motive in the struggles between different groups within Judaism.

Nothing is known for certain of Zadok's antecedents, but he is never mentioned before David's capture of Jerusalem, and this fact, together with the similarity between his name and that of other Jerusalemite names (e.g. Melchizedek, Gen. 14:17-20), has led many to suppose that he was a Jebusite priest whom David took into his service since he would be expert in matters pertaining to the proper worship of the Jerusalem sanctuary. The suggestion has even been made that he had been king, but this is very speculative. (The genealogy in 2 Sam. 8:17, which makes it appear that Zadok was descended from Eli, is textually corrupt, and is corrected in most modern versions.)

Zadok then is first introduced in a list of David's officials (2 Sam. 8:17); we subsequently see him and his family playing an important part in securing David's throne during Absalom's rebellion (2 Sam. 15-18); and in the last days of David Zadok's support was an important factor in ensuring that Solomon rather than Adonijah would succeed (1 Kings 1). Subsequent references to Zadok make it clear that in the struggle for the establishment of an acceptable priesthood, the claim to a Zadokite descent was important (1 Chron. 6: 3-15; Ezek. 43:19). The Dead Sea Scrolls, dating from the very last centuries B.C., make it clear that at that period the true priesthood could still be referred to as the 'sons of Zadok'. Indeed, a work discovered in the last century at Cairo and subsequently shown to have belonged to a group very similar to the Dead Sea Scrolls community was known as the 'Zadokite Fragment' because of its concern for the maintenance of a true Zadokite priesthood.

ZEBAH and Zalmunna were the two Midianite rulers killed by Gideon in his successful war (Judg. 8:4-21). It is difficult to be certain of the historicity of the underlying tradition; the names are Hebrew words meaning 'sacrifice' and 'protection withheld', and these names clearly reflect a later generation's understanding of their fate. But it is possible that these forms are corruptions of the Midianite originals, and that they were rulers — though scarcely kings — whose overthrow was remembered in popular tradition. The importance of their defeat is further illustrated by the way in which a reference to it has been woven into a liturgical account of God's acts in war (Ps. 83:11).

ZEBULUN is described both as an individual, one of the twelve sons of Jacob (Gen. 30:20), and as a tribe. It is generally agreed that the latter description is historically more reliable, and that the idea of eponymous ancestors of the tribes only developed later. No individual stories relating to Zebulun have been preserved.

Zebulun was one of the northerly groups, and therefore plays a small part in the Old Testament which for the most part enshrines southern traditions. An important exception is Judg. 5, the Song of Deborah, which emphasises the importance of Zebulun's role in the great victory over Sisera (Judg. 5:14, 18).

ZECHARIAH is one of the commonest of Old Testament names, more than thirty characters being so named, the vast majority of them simply in lists. Of some more detail is known:

ZECHARIAH son of Jehoiada. 2 Chron. 24:20 describes this Zechariah as denouncing the people in prophetic style for their sins; the result was that the king, Joash, egged the people on to kill Zechariah as denouncing the people in prophetic style for their Jehoiada. This episode is recalled in the New Testament; 2 Chronicles is the last book in the Bible in the Hebrew ordering, and so Jesus can refer to violence done to righteous men from Abel to Zechariah as taking in the whole Old Testament (Luke 11:51). The reference is complicated in Matthew by the erroneous description of Zechariah as 'son of Berachiah' (see below).

ZECHARIAH son of Jeroboam was a short-lived king of Israel in the troubled period in the mid eighth century B.C. when Assyrian power was first affecting Israel (2 Kings 15:8-12); no details of his brief reign are known.

ZECHARIAH son of Jeberechiah is used by Isaiah as a reliable witness of his signing of a document (Isa. 8:2). Nothing else is known of this Zechariah, but confusion has arisen, because his name 'son of Berechiah' has been applied both to the prophet Zechariah (see below) (Zech. 1:1, 7) and to the Zechariah referred to in the New Testament as an innocent martyr (see *Zechariah son of Jehoiada*) (Matt. 23:35). It is probably wrong to call these identifications mistakes; rather they emerge from a tendency traceable in later Judaism to identify different people with the same name. (See *Micah/Micaiah* for another example of the same tendency.)

ZECHARIAH son of Iddo the prophet. It is likely (see above) that the description of him as 'son of Berechiah' (Zech. 1:1-7) is erroneous; possibly his father's name was unknown, and he is remembered as a member of the larger clan of Iddo (Ezra 5:1; Neh. 12:16). He was active in the period when Judah was being re-established as a distinct province under Persian rule (c. 520 B.C.), and his particular concern, along with his contemporary Haggai, was to kindle anew the people's faith in the power of their God, to recognise their leaders, especially Joshua the priest, and to be active in rebuilding the temple. This message is expressed by means of a series of visions, whose exact significance is often obscure and which can be seen as marking a transitional stage in the development from prophecy to apocalyptic. It is generally agreed that only chs. 1-8 come from the prophet Zechariah; chs. 9-14 are a series of undated (and undatable) prophecies which were added to the words of Zechariah at a later date.

ZEDEKIAH was a prophet, apparently a member of the court staff of the king of Israel (1 Kings 22:11). He was the spokesman on behalf of a large group, who not only gave the king encouragement by means of a spoken message, but also acted out the context of that message by symbolic means. When his colleague Micaiah announced that Zedekiah's message was false, a feud broke out between the two prophets (1 Kings 22:24f.). The whole story is of great interest for the development of prophecy as an institution;

clearly there was a temptation for those, like Zedekiah, who were part of the royal entourage, to say what would be acceptable to the king; but the story also makes it clear that Zedekiah was not deliberately giving a false message.

ZEDEKIAH was also the name of the last ruler in Jerusalem before Judah was incorporated into the Babylonian Empire. According to 2 Kings 24:18 he was regarded as king in the same way as his predecessors had been, and the standard formula describing his reign is provided. This viewpoint is also found in Jeremiah, but the book of Ezekiel clearly regards Zedekiah's uncle, Jehoiachin, who was in exile in Babylon, as the true king, and the dates in that book correspond with the years of his reign.

Little detail of Zedekiah's reign is given by Kings or Chronicles, which pass rapidly on to the terrible climax of the destruction of the temple, but fuller information is provided in Jeremiah, where Zedekiah is pictured as a weak and vacillating figure, unable to control his subordinates who offered him advice which he knew to be unwise. On at least two occasions he sought the advice of Jeremiah, either through his officials (Jer. 21:1-7; 37:3-10) or privately (Jer. 37:17-21; 38:14-28) (in each case it seems that we have two accounts of the same incident), and we obtain a vivid impression of Zedekiah in the grip of forces which he could not control. He is characteristically remembered as abandoning Jeremiah to his enemies (Jer. 37:5), but then secretly ensuring that he was not abandoned to his fate. Driven into rebellion against Babylon, he attempted to escape from Jerusalem at the last, but was captured, saw his sons killed, and was then blinded and brought to Babylon (2 Kings 25:4-7). Nothing is known of his subsequent fate, but it seems improbable that he can long have survived such treatment. He was dealt with more severely than Jehoiachin, for the latter was regarded as a prisoner of war, whereas Zedekiah was rebelling against his suzerain.

ZEEB.
See *Oreb*.

ZELOPHEHAD is not known as an individual, but the example of his 'daughters' is twice used to establish an important point of legal practice (Num. 27 & 36). In the first case, it is stated that daughters might inherit if a man died leaving no son; in the second, they are required to marry within their own clan, so that ancestral property might not be dispersed. The stories are late, and provide a good example of making law by telling a story; the 'daughters' in fact appear originally to have been places.

ZEPHANIAH, the prophet, of whose oracles the ninth in the collection of twelve Minor Prophets is composed, was active during the reign of Josiah, king of Judah (640-609 B.C.) (Zeph. 1:1). Nothing is known of him save what can be deduced from his book. The listing of his ancestors for four generations has led some to speculate that this was because his great-grandfather was king Hezekiah. The over-riding impression given by the book of Zephaniah is that the prophet belonged to the tradition of those who were convinced of the inevitability of God's judgement upon his people — a theme best illustrated by the oracle on the 'day of the Lord' (Zeph. 1:15ff.), which came to be used by the Catholic Church in the Middle Ages as the hymn 'Dies irae' used in the Mass of Requiem for the Dead.

ZEPHANIAH the priest was one of the leading officials of the Jerusalem temple at the time of its destruction by the Babylonians (587/6 B.C.). He is mentioned several times in the book of Jeremiah, and appears to have been one of those who was sympathetic toward that often persecuted prophet; for example, he showed Jeremiah a letter severely criticising him rather than put Jeremiah in custody, as the letter suggested (Jer. 29:25-32). But he was regarded by the Babylonians as one of the leaders of resistance to them, perhaps because the temple was as much a political as a religious symbol, and so when the city fell he was one of those executed by the victorious Babylonians (Jer. 52:24-27; 2 Kings 25:18-21).

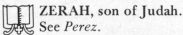

ZERAH, son of Judah.
See *Perez.*

ZERAH the Ethiopian provides a classic illustration of the problem posed for the historian by the books of Chronicles. 2 Chron. 14:8-15 describes him as an Egyptian king whose attack on Judah with a million men was overcome by the power of prayer alone. Few moderns accept the account as it stands. Some are prepared to envisage a historical nucleus, with a less dramatic outcome than the biblical story implies. Here the difficulty is that Egyptian records allow for no ruler who could plausibly have been known as Zerah in Hebrew. It is probably wise, therefore, to accept that we can know nothing of the historicity of this episode and see in it rather an illustration of the writer's theological purpose, of showing how effectively God responds to prayer.

162

ZERUBBABEL played a major part in re-establishing Judah and Jerusalem when Persian rule was first established in the area in the sixth century B.C. His achievement is described in Ezra, Haggai and Zechariah, with incidental references elsewhere; and though the broad picture is clear enough, a number of details remain obscure.

He was a descendant of David, and as such may well have served as a focus of the aspirations of those who were eager to see an independant monarchy restored. 1 Chron. 3:19 says he was the son of Pedaiah, but all other references name him 'son of Shealtiel'; in either case he was a grandson of the exiled king Jehoiachin. A further complication is caused by the fact that his achievement and that of Sheshbazzar seem largely to have overlapped (cf. Ezra 1 and 3); no satisfactory explanation of their relation has been achieved.

The date of Zerubbabel's appointment is unknown but by 520 B.C. it is clear that he was the effective leader of the Jerusalem community. Much of the book of Haggai is concerned with the importance of his task, and the book ends with a description of Zerubbabel in messianic terms (Hag. 2:23). He has a less prominent part in the book of Zechariah, Haggai's contemporary, and some have suggested that this was due to the Persian authorities' concern that he was proving too great a focus of nationalist hopes. But he clearly played a leading part in organising the rebuilding of the temple (Ezra 5:2), and was much esteemed by later Jewish tradition for the vital role he had played in re-establishing the community (Ecclus. 49:11); a good example is provided by the story of the competition of the three guardsmen in 1 Esdras, in which the winner, expatiating on the virtue of women and truth as strongest of all, is quite unexpectedly identified as Zerubbabel (1 Esd. 4:13).

ZERUIAH indirectly plays a part of great importance in the stormy history of the succession to David, for her sons, Joab, Abishai and Asahel, are always referred to by their mother's name. This may have been because she was a sister of David (1 Chron. 2:16), though the reliability of this information is not certain, since an earlier source, 2 Sam. 17:25, gives what appears to be a different genealogy.

ZIBA is a minor but vividly depicted character in the account of the succession to David. Three separate episodes portray his role; in 2 Sam. 9:1-13 he acts as an intermediary between David and Saul's surviving grandson Mephibosheth, and is installed as personal attendant to Mephibosheth; in 2 Sam. 16:1-4, at the time of Absalom's rebellion he shows his loyalty to David and implies that

163

Mephibosheth had been disloyal; in 2 Sam. 19:17-30 he is rewarded by being given half of Mephibosheth's estate, despite Mephibosheth's protestations of loyalty.

ZILPAH, like Bilhah, was given to Jacob by her mistress, and bore him two sons, Gad and Asher (Gen. 30:9f.). It is impossible to establish any historical circumstances underlying this, but the slighting designation of these as 'handmaid tribes' may reflect the later historical development.

ZIMRI was the name of two Old Testament characters, both of whom are condemned. In the book of Numbers an account is given of the development of the practice of sexual intercourse between Israelite men and Midianite women, and of the spread of plague; the first is regarded as the cause of the second. In particular, a flagrant offender, Zimri, brought his partner into the holiest part of the camp — fertility rites may be implied — and both of them were immediately killed by the priest Phinehas, whose action brought an end to the plague (Num. 25:1-18). Phinehas' action was later regarded as a model of piety (Ps. 106:30f.; 1 Macc. 2:26).

ZIMRI attempted to seize the throne in Israel in the ninth century B.C., but his coup was unsuccessful (1 Kings 16:9-26). He was an army commander who hoped — in vain — for support from the troops at large. His bloody rebellion was recalled at the downfall of the next dynasty as part of the 'last words' of Jezebel (2 Kings 9:31).

ZIPPORAH, the wife of Moses, is actually named at three passages in Exodus (2:21; 4:25; 18:2), and it is not clear whether references to an unnamed wife of Moses (e.g. Num. 12:1) are to the same woman or not. The references to Zipporah show the links between Israelites and other semi-nomadic groups inhabiting the desert fringes. Undoubtedly the most mysterious reference is that in Exod. 4:24-26, where the description of Zipporah circumcising her son to avert imminent danger seems to be a half-remembered tradition of great antiquity.

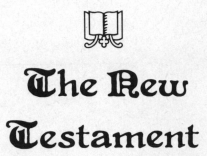

The New Testament

AGABUS is twice mentioned (Acts 11-28; 21:10) as a Christian prophet, apparently from Jerusalem. The existence of such a group in the early Church is well attested; their exact function and significance remains obscure.

AGRIPPA was the name of two members of the Herod family. Of these the father is simply called Herod (q.v.) in the New Testament; when the name Agrippa is found it is the son who is being referred to (Acts 25-26). Allowed the title of king by the Romans, to whom he always remained loyal, he was able gradually from about A.D. 50 to increase the area of Palestine over which he ruled. Unlike many of his family he lived to an old age, dying about A.D. 100. He was widely suspected of living in an incestuous relationship with his sister Bernice.

ALEXANDER. Three references to men named Alexander in the New Testament have occasionally been supposed to be to one person only; but the name was a common one in the ancient world, and it is unlikely that they were the same person. In the riot at Ephesus (Acts 19:33) Alexander appears to be a Jew and possibly one of the city's craftsmen; in 1 Tim. 1:20 a false teacher is condemned; and in 2 Tim. 4:14 an 'Alexander the coppersmith' is condemned for the harm he has done, but it is not specified whether this is some form of personal injury or false teaching. The problem of identification is made more acute by the difficulty of knowing the authorship and date of the epistles to Timothy (see under *Paul*).

ALPHAEUS is not referred to directly in the New Testament, but someone of this name is mentioned as the father both of Levi (Mark 2:14) and of James (Mark 3:18), and a further complication is added by the fact that Matt. 9:9 and Luke 5:27 tell the same story but name the person called by Jesus as Matthew rather than Levi. It is impossible to know whether more than one individual is involved, or whether traditions have become confused.

ANANIAS. Three very different characters named Ananias are mentioned in the Acts of the Apostles. In ch. 5 a story is told of how an early disciple, Ananias, with his wife Sapphira, pretended

167

to follow the example of other Christians in Jerusalem by selling their property and handing the proceeds over to the church; the sudden death of each of them when their plot was found out was regarded as a clear sign of God's displeasure. In ch. 9 a Jewish disciple named Ananias, living in Damascus, played an important part in the conversion of Paul, welcoming him to the Christian community in Damascus which he had set out to persecute. In chs. 23-24 the Jewish high priest at Paul's trial is also named Ananias. This last is mentioned in other sources, where he appears in just as unfavourable a light as in Acts; the first two are not known from any other reliable traditions.

ANDREW is included in all the lists of the twelve disciples as one of the close followers of Jesus. Similarly, all the traditions state or imply that he was the brother of Simon Peter, son of John or Jonah, and a Galilean fisherman by upbringing. A reference in Mark 13:3 might imply that he was one of the leaders within the group; otherwise all the references to Andrew as an individual are found in the fourth Gospel. There is very sharp disagreement among scholars as to the historical reliability of traditions found only in this Gospel, some arguing that early traditions are enshrined here, others pointing to the similarity with the later apocryphal stories that grew up around Jesus and his followers, and concluding that reference found only in John should not be regarded as historical.

In the fourth Gospel Andrew is represented as coming from Bethsaida (John 1:44), and as being responsible for his brother Peter coming to Jesus (1:40-42), a tradition which has led to the linking of Andrew with missionary work in the Christian chruch. In this Gospel also he is singled out in connection with the feeding of the five thousand (6:5-9) and the bringing of Greek enquirers to Jesus (12:20-22). Nothing is known of his later life.

ANNA is mentioned in Luke 2:36-8 as one of those who gave thanks for the coming of Jesus. She is described as a prophetess; this probably implies a gift of inspired speech rather than membership of a distinct order.

ANNAS was the Jewish high priest A.D. 6-15 when he was deposed. Apparently he remained an influential figure, for he is mentioned along with Caiaphas his son-in-law at Luke 3:2, and both in Acts (4:6) and in the account of the trial of Jesus in the fourth Gospel the natural sense of the words is that he was still acting as high priest (John 18:12-22, esp. v. 19). We cannot be certain whether this is a misunderstanding, or whether the title continued to be accorded to former high priests.

ANTIPAS.
See *Herod.*

APOLLOS was clearly a leading figure in the early Christian church but unfortunately our knowledge about him is very fragmentary. The primary source of information is 1 Corinthians, from which it appears that he — like Paul, though at a later date — had worked as an evangelist in Corinth, and that the church there had divided into rival factions, one of which might be regarded as an 'Apollos party'. But we know nothing of the exact cause of this division, or the characteristic features of the Apollos party. There is no clear indication of personal rivalry between Paul and Apollos, though this has often been suggested. Supplementary information is provided by Acts 18:24-28, which describes Apollos' Egyptian origin and a possible link with John the Baptist. Despite his eloquence as a preacher, he needed fuller instruction in the Christian way. It has been argued, but on inadequate grounds, that he was the author of the Epistle to the Hebrews.

AQUILA.
See *Priscilla.*

ARCHELAUS is mentioned only in the New Testament, and that in an allusive way (Matt. 2:22), but his rule was important because of the change of forms of government in Judah which took place during the lifetime of Jesus. Archelaus was the son of Herod the Great (q.v.), and succeeded him as ruler from 4 B.C. to A.D. 6; he was never given the title of king, and the troubles during his time of office led the Romans to add Judah and Jerusalem to the Roman province of Syria. Archelaus was banished and a system of Roman prefects (of whom the best known is Pontius Pilate) set up.

ARETAS was the ruler of the Nabataean Arab kingdom from 9 B.C. to A.D. 39, and exercised wide-ranging rule under general Roman suzerainty. The New Testament gives what appear to be two slightly differing accounts of the same incident involving a dramatic escape by Paul from potential arrest; the earlier, in 2 Cor. 11:32-33 is more likely to be reliable than that in Acts 9:24-25. The exact role of Aretas, particularly in the Roman city of Damascus, remains obscure.

ARISTARCHUS is mentioned several times in Acts as a companion (and on one occasion fellow-prisoner, Acts 19-20) of Paul. It is probable that the same individual is referred to in Col. 4:10 and Philemon 24. He was a Gentile, from Macedonia, and there

169

is no suggestion in his case, as there is with other of Paul's companions, that he ever let his master down.

AUGUSTUS the first Roman Emperor was the ruler of the Mediterranean world at the time of the birth of Jesus. Born in 63 B.C., he played a major part in the disputes following the death of Julius Caesar, and was eventually given the title Augustus by the Roman senate in 27 B.C.; his family name, by which he was previously known, was Octavian. His rule inaugurated a time of peace and prosperity for Rome and her empire. He died in A.D. 14. The only direct reference to him in the New Testament is at Luke 2:1, which appears to imply a universal census for the whole Roman Empire. There is no evidence to support this, though local censuses became an important feature of the administrative machinery of the Empire from this time. (Other apparent references to Augustus in the Authorised Version, e.g. Acts 25:25, are in fact to the ruling emperor of the time, as modern translations make clear.)

BARABBAS All four Gospels are agreed that during the trial of Jesus before Pontius Pilate, the crowd persuaded him to release a criminal named Barabbas, though Pilate himself would have been willing to release Jesus. There are parallels for Roman magistrates granting pardons to particular individuals, but the Gospel-writers are probably going beyond the evidence when they state that this was an annual custom (Mark 15:6-9). The name Barabbas is curious, since it means 'son of the father', and is not otherwise attested, but some manuscripts of Matthew suggest that his name may have been 'Jesus Barabbas' (Matt. 27:16, New English Bible; this would have added point to Pilate's question in the following verse). Nothing else is known about Barabbas, though later legends grew up around his name.

BAR-JESUS.
See *Elymas.*

BAR-JONA.
See *Peter.*

BARNABAS plays a prominent part, particularly as a companion of Paul, in the account of the growth of the early church in Acts 4-15, and is also mentioned by Paul himself in some of his epistles (Gal. 2 and 1 Cor. 9). Like Paul, Barnabas came from one of the many Jewish colonies scattered all over the Mediterranean world — in this instance Cyprus. He seems to have been one of the first Christian leaders at Antioch, and in a number of references in Acts he is named ahead of Paul, as if he were, on occasions at least, the leader (e.g. Acts 14:14, where he is identified with Jupiter, the chief of the gods). Eventually a rift developed between Barnabas and Paul, attributed by Acts 15 to division as to whether John Mark was a suitable helper after his earlier defection, but by Paul himself to Barnabas' insufficiently welcoming attitude toward Gentiles (Gal. 2:13).

Nothing is known of Barnabas' subsequent history, though a much later tradition described his martyrdom in Cyprus. One of the earliest non-biblical Christian writings, the 'Epistle of Barnabas' is named after him but is most unlikely to have any direct connection with him.

BARTHOLOMEW is listed as one of the twelve disciples of Jesus, but not mentioned in the Gospel of John. He plays no part as an individual in any story, though later tradition described him as the writer of a gospel, as a missionary and as a martyr; none of this has any historical value. The lack of reference in John has led to the theory that Bartholomew should be identified with Nathanael, who is mentioned only there; this view is widely accepted, but has little substantial basis (see also *Nathanael*).

BAR-TIMAEUS was the blind beggar healed by Jesus near Jericho (Mk. 10:46 ff.). The event is described in considerable detail, which has led some scholars to conclude that the memory of an eye-witness underlies the account, and others to suspect later elaboration of the story.

The 'BELOVED DISCIPLE' There are several references in the Gospel of John (e.g. 13:23; 19:26) to an unnamed 'disciple whom Jesus loved'. Church tradition from an early date, and the still widely held popular view, identifies this disciple with John, son of Zebedee, also traditionally regarded as the author of the Gospel, but there is little support in the Gospel itself for such a view, and the

171

identification becomes even less likely when it is no longer held that John, son of Zebedee, was the actual author of the Gospel. Various other suggested identifications have been put forward, but it is likely that the figure is intended to be mysterious and anonymous.

BERNICE, referred to in Acts 25-26, was the sister of Herod Agrippa II, before whom Paul was on trial, and was widely suspected of living in an incestuous relationship with her brother. See *Agrippa*.

CAESAR was a personal name in the case of Julius Caesar, who is not referred to in the Bible or Apocrypha, but it was used as a title by successive Roman Emperors, so that its New Testament usage refers to the emperor of the time rather than an individual. In the letters of Paul, in particular, uncertainties about dating prevent us from knowing which emperor may be referred to.

CAIAPHAS was the Jewish high priest at the time of the trial of Jesus. Sources outside the New Testament attest his existence, but it is only from the Gospels that we gain any detailed knowledge of him. Even there his position is problematic, for John 18:13 implies — wrongly — that the high priesthood was an annual appointment, and other passages seem to refer to Annas, who was apparently his father-in-law, as the high priest. The gospel tradition in this respect is much less clear than that which identifies the Roman governor before whom Jesus was tried as Pontius Pilate.

CANDACE, referred to in Acts 8:27, as 'the queen of the Ethiopians', was a title rather than a proper name (as is made clear by the New English Bible translation). It is not possible to identify the particular queen whom the eunuch of the story served.

CEPHAS is a Greek transliteration of an Aramaic word meaning 'Rock', for which the Greek equivalent is 'Petros'. It is thus an alternative name for Peter (q.v.).

172

CHLOE is referred to only once, and that indirectly (1 Cor. 1:11), but it was through her 'people' (presumably members of her household) that Paul learnt of the serious divisions among the Corinthian Christians, and their report may well have influenced Paul's reaction.

CHRIST has come to be popularly regarded as a personal name, but it is in fact the Greek word *Christos* used as a title. The word means 'the Anointed one' and is the equivalent of the Hebrew word 'Messiah'. In the New Testament there is a distinction of usage not always observed by English translations: sometimes the texts speak of 'Jesus the Christ'; elsewhere 'Jesus Christ' or simply 'Christ' is used as if it were a proper name. See *Jesus*.

CHUZA had a Christian wife, Joanna, and was 'Herod's steward' (Luke 8:3). The 'Herod' in question here is Antipas, son of Herod the Great, and ruler of Galilee during the time of Jesus' ministry there (see *Herod*).

CLAUDIUS, Roman Emperor A.D. 41-54, is directly referred to in the New Testament only twice: once in connection with an (otherwise unattested) universal famine (Acts 11:28), and again as requiring all Jews to leave Rome (Acts 18:2). There is some external literary evidence to support this statement, though it is not clear whether any distinction was made at that date between Jews and Christians.

CLEMENT is mentioned in Phil. 4:3 as a fellow-worker with Paul, and there was also a Clement who was Bishop of Rome and writer of an important Epistle at the end of the first century. Attempts have been made to identify the two, but the name was very common, and it is probable that there was no such connection.

CLEOPAS and Clopas are both referred to as followers of Jesus, but it is not certain whether these are variant forms of the same name, so that only one disciple would be meant. Cleopas is one of the two disciples who accompanied Jesus on the journey to Emmaus (Luke 24:18); Clopas' wife Mary (q.v.) was one of those standing near the cross of Jesus at the time of the crucifixion in the account given in the fourth Gospel (John 19:25), which is different from that in the other Gospels.

CORNELIUS, a Roman centurion (the rank might be regarded as that of a warrant-officer) has an important encounter with

173

Peter, fully described in Acts 10. He is presented as typical of the widespread group of those sometimes called 'god-fearers', who were sympathetic to Judaism without accepting its ritual requirements. His conversion and acceptance by the church represents for the author of Acts a major development in the mission to the Gentiles which the book describes. Nothing else is known of Cornelius, and the episode poses considerable historical problems in view of subsequent disputes about the admission of Gentiles to the church in Acts 15, and Paul's account of Peter's role in Gal. 2.

CRISPUS is mentioned by Paul (1 Cor. 1:14) as one of those whom he personally had baptised. It is presumably the same Crispus who is mentioned in Acts (18:8) as the ruler of the synagogue at Corinth, though the note in that verse that others were also baptised is not entirely consistent with Paul's statement limiting the number of those whom he himself had baptised.

DEMAS, a colleague of Paul, is favourably spoken of in Col. 4:14 and Philemon 24, but at 2 Tim. 4:10 he is said to have deserted Paul. It is often held that the present form of 2 Timothy consists of genuine Pauline excerpts within a later context; if this view is taken, the reference to Demas would be one of the genuine fragments.

DIDYMUS is a name meaning 'the twin' which is sometimes applied to Thomas (q.v.).

DIONYSIUS is mentioned only once in the New Testament (Acts 17:34) and we know nothing of him from any other reliable source. His title 'Areopagite' implies that he was a member of the governing council of the court which met on the Areopagus hill. A much later tradition held that Dionysius became the first Bishop of Athens and in the fifth or sixth century an extensive literature grew up, attributed to him, which was held in much veneration during the Middle Ages before the realisation that it was spurious.

DIVES is treated as a proper name in some versions of the parable in Luke 16:19-31, but the story properly understood simply tells of an anonymous rich man.

DOMITIAN was Emperor of Rome, A.D. 81-96, and has traditionally been regarded as a persecutor of the early Christian community. The evidence for such persecution on any systematic scale is, however, extremely slight, and it may well be that Domitian has been depicted unduly harshly by church historians. It is possible that the threat of persecution accounts for the hostile attitude to the Roman state underlying the book of Revelation.

DYSMAS. This name, given by tradition to the thief crucified with Jesus who, in the tradition enshrined by Luke, acknowledged the justice of his treatment (Luke 23:39-43), has no authority in the biblical account.

ELIZABETH is the Greek form of the Hebrew name Elisheba. The Hebrew name was that of the wife of Aaron the priest; its Greek form is that of the wife of Zechariah the priest and mother of John the Baptist. She is mentioned only in Luke 1, and is said to have been a relative of Mary the mother of Jesus — the exact relationship is unspecified. The story of the conception of John contains the very common biblical motif of the child born to aged and hitherto barren parents (cf. Abraham and Sarah), of exemplary piety. The 'Magnificat', the Song of Mary (Luke 1:46-55) is ascribed by some ancient traditions to Elizabeth (see the footnote at this point in the New English Bible).

ELYMAS is mentioned in Acts 13:6-11 as a Jewish magician living in Cyprus who apparently exercised some influence over the Roman proconsul of the island, Sergius Paulus. His resistance to Barnabas and Saul led to his being struck blind. The little story is instructive in several respects: it shows the widespread belief in magical power, from which the author of Acts was himself not wholly immune; it illustrates a major theme of Acts — the friend-liness of Romans towards the spreading Christian movement when not hindered by false Jewish claims; and it introduces the change from 'Saul' to 'Paul' in the terminology of Acts. Elymas is also called Bar-jesus, which the author claims to be a name with the same meaning, but this is not so, and the relation between the two names, or whether one or two traditions have survived here, has puzzled commentators ever since.

EPAPHRAS is mentioned in Colossians (1:7; 4:12) and Philemon (23) as one of the founders and leaders of the church at Colossae, in Asia Minor. There is no evidence that Paul himself ever visited Colossae, so that Epaphras may have acted as his agent, and is praised accordingly. From Philemon 23 it would appear that he was imprisoned with Paul, though the circumstances and the charges are unknown.

EPAPHRODITUS is another form of the name Epaphras, but it seems likely that the references to this name imply a differ-ent colleague of Paul, who, to judge from the presence in his name of the goddess Aphrodite, probably came from a pagan background. He is mentioned only in Philippians (2:25) and the description there shows the high esteem in which Paul held him as a leader of the church at Philippi.

FELIX is mentioned in Acts, in the Jewish historian Josephus and in various Roman sources as the prefect of Judea and his date of holding office can be estimated with fair certainty at A.D. 52-60. In Acts he is mentioned only in connection with Paul's trial (23:24-24:27), of which we have no knowledge from Paul's own letters or any other source. Opinion among scholars as to the his-torical reliability of Acts is sharply divided, but — though no doubt some of the details are the author's own — there seems no reason to doubt the basic facts.

FESTUS succeeded Felix (see above) as prefect (60-62 A.D.) and we know of him from Josephus and Acts with its vivid account of the legal processes involving Paul (24:27-26:32). As with Felix, the account in Acts has no support elsewhere, and opinions about its reliability will depend upon the general view taken of the historicity of Acts, a matter on which there is no agreement.

GABRIEL. The idea of a hierarchy of angels only developed very late in the Old Testament period, possibly under Persian religious influence. Part of this development was the giving of names and distinctive roles to certain of the angels, the most prominent being Gabriel. He is first mentioned in Daniel (8:16; 9:21), where his function is to explain hidden mysteries to Daniel. In the New Testament he plays a major role in the Lucan version of Jesus' birth, revealing secrets and bringing reassurance to both Elizabeth, the mother of John the Baptist, and to Mary, the mother of Jesus (Luke 1:19, 26). There are no other biblical references, but Gabriel plays a prominent part in non-canonical writings, both Jewish and Christian.

GALLIO is mentioned in the New Testament only at Acts 18:12-16, as the proconsul of Achaia (a substantial part of modern Greece), before whom the Jews of Corinth attempted to bring Paul to trial, only to have their case dismissed as not being within his competence. His importance lies in the fact that he is several times mentioned in contemporary Latin authors, and that an inscription has been discovered indicating that he was proconsul in either A.D. 51 or 52. This is a clear indication that the author of Acts had access to reliable sources of information, and gives useful indications of the chronology of the book.

GAMALIEL is mentioned twice in Acts; first, as a member of the supreme Jewish council, the Sanhedrin, who advised against any attempt to take harsh measures against the early Christians

(Acts 5:34-39); secondly, as the mentor of Paul (Acts 22:3). Jewish sources also speak of him as one of the most highly esteemed of the early rabbis, though there is some confusion between him and his grandson who bore the same name.

The New Testament references are not without problems. The speech in Acts 5 refers to one Theudas, whose rebellion was actually later than the alleged date of Gamaliel's speech, while the statement that Paul sat at his feet is entirely without support in Paul's letters, either by way of specific reference or in terms of teaching method. It is noteworthy also that Paul before his conversion appears to have been much less tolerant than Gamaliel.

HEROD. Various members of the Herod family are mentioned in the New Testament, often in a way which can confuse the unwary reader. Whether at times the New Testament writers were themselves unsure of the different relationships is a matter of dispute.

The Herod family probably originated from Edom (or, in its Greek form, Idumea) though it has also been suggested that they were in fact Jewish and that the Edomite origin is a hostile legend, since Edomites and Jews were traditional enemies. The family first rose to prominence in the first century B.C., and as far as the New Testament is concerned the first important figure to be mentioned is Herod the Great, king of Judea 37-4 B.C. Despite the considerable achievement of holding his kingdom together, his title 'the Great' has often been questioned because of his brutality (he had several of his ten wives and fifteen children murdered) and the hostility of many of his subjects, who continued to regard him as a foreigner.

This is the Herod under whose rule the birth of Jesus is placed by Matthew (2:1) and Luke (1:5); in other words, if this dating is correct, the conventional division into 'B.C.' and 'A.D.' has been wrongly calculated. There is no corroboration of the story of the wise men and the murder of the innocents (Matt. 2) outside the Bible, but the latter is certainly in accordance with what is known of Herod's character.

After his death, Herod was succeeded by Archelaus (q.v.) as ruler of Judah, and by another son, also called Herod, in Galilee. (In non-biblical sources he is given the distinguishing name 'Antipas'.) This is the Herod who was ruler (called 'king' by Mark 6:14, but Matthew (14:1) and Luke (9:7) correctly have 'tetrarch') at the time of Jesus' ministry, and who was responsible for having John the Baptist put to death. Little is told us of Jesus' relations with Herod, though Luke does indicate that Herod's household contained some links with the followers of Jesus (8:3) and that Herod had some minor part in the events leading up to Jesus' death (23:7-12). This Herod eventually fell out of favour with the Roman authorities, and was deposed in about A.D. 39. Yet another son of Herod the Great, Philip (q.v.) ruled over part of his territory, and confusion is increased by the fact that he is referred to also as 'Herod' in some sources (not the New Testament).

The remaining members of the family who are mentioned in the New Testament come from a slightly later date. Herod Agrippa I was a grandson of Herod the Great, who had been brought up in Rome as a hostage for the good behaviour of other members of his family, and he was granted the title of king as a form of government different from that of the Roman prefects. Little is known of his brief rule (A.D. 41-44), but Acts 12:1-23 pictures him as hostile to the early Christians, and as meeting an unpleasant death. His son, also called Agrippa (q.v.) was also given the title of king, over an area which was gradually extended during his long life.

HERODIAS was a grand-daughter of Herod the Great, and she married successively two sons of Herod the Great by different wives; that is, she married two of her father's half-brothers. Such incestuous relationships appear to have been not uncommon within the Herod family, and it is this which appears to have led to John the Baptist's condemnation (Mark 6:17). Her second husband was Herod Antipas (q.v.); her first husband is called Philip in the New Testament (Mark 6:17), but other sources suggest that he was also called Herod, to add still more to the confusion of names. It was the daughter of Herodias — unnamed in the Bible but called Salome in other sources — whose dance (allegedly the 'dance of the seven veils') pleased Herod Antipas and enabled Herodias to demand the death of her enemy John the Baptist as a reward. After the banishment of her husband Herod Antipas, Herodias remained loyal to him and accompanied him into exile.

HYMENAEUS is mentioned in both 1 and 2 Timothy as a false teacher. 2 Tim. 2:17 indicates that he was associated with Philetus (otherwise unknown) in giving false teaching about resurrection; 1 Tim. 1:20 states that he has been 'handed over to the power of Satan', which probably implies excommunication from the church. The historical circumstances and the nature of the doctrines involved are unknown, because of uncertainties about the date and background of the letters to Timothy; but it is probable that the situation was one of the growth of various kinds of heresy, perhaps at the end of the first century, in churches which Paul had been associated with.

IMMANUEL is a name applied to Jesus in Matt. 1:23, where his birth is associated with the prophecy of Isa. 7:14. (See also the Old Testament section.)

JAIRUS is the name given at Luke 8:41 to the synagogue official whose daughter Jesus raised from death. (The name is also found in most texts and translations at Mark 5:22, recounting the same incident, but it may well be that this is dependent on the tradition found in Luke.) His role will have involved him in the maintenance of good order at the synagogue rather than a specific function in its worship as a teacher or rabbi. Jairus was clearly sympathetic to Jesus' teaching, unlike the other, anonymous, synagogue official mentioned by Luke (13:14).

JAMES, the English form of Greek Jakobos, was as common a name in the ancient world as it is today. Five different men of this name are mentioned in the New Testament, as well as the author of the Epistle of James, and it is unlikely that any two or more of them should be identified with one another, though attempts to do so have been numerous.

180

JAMES son of Zebedee is included in all lists of the twelve disciples who appear to have formed the immediate circle of Jesus' followers, and within that circle James formed an inner group along with his brother John, and Peter. On several occasions these three are summoned by Jesus to witness some particularly significant event in his life and ministry: the raising of Jairus' daughter from death (Mark 5:37); the transfiguration on the mountain (Mark 9:2); and the agony in the garden of Gethsemane on the night before Jesus' death (Mark 14:33). The same three disciples, together with Peter's brother Andrew, are also pictured in Mark 13:3 as questioning Jesus about his understanding of future events. On two occasions James and his brother John are singled out for rebuke as displaying all-too-human emotions, unworthy of committed followers; at Luke 9:54 they invoke a curse upon a village which will not offer them hospitality, and at Mark 10:35-41 they fall foul both of Jesus and of the other ten disciples because of their request for a special place of honour. In this episode it is noteworthy that Matthew's Gospel, perhaps out of respect for the memory of the disciples, suggests that the wrong request originated with their mother (Matt. 20:20).

Of the twelve disciples, James in the only one whose death is described in the New Testament; he was martyred in about A.D. 43 by the hostility of king Herod Agrippa I (Acts 12:2), but no further details are known. In the Middle Ages a tradition developed that he was buried in Spain, and a pilgrimage centre developed at the site, Santiago de Compostela.

JAMES the son of Alphaeus is included in some lists of the twelve immediate disciples of Jesus (Mark 3:18), but elsewhere it is Levi who is described as the son of Alphaeus, and it is impossible to be certain whether these traditions refer to one or two men. No details are given of this James, who in later church tradition was known as 'James the Less' as against James son of Zebedee who was James the Great.

JAMES Two others named James are also mentioned, without personal details: one of the women present at the crucifixion of Jesus had a son named James (Mark 15:40; 16:1); and a disciple called Judas is said to be the son of James (Luke 6:16). These two are probably unrelated to one another, or to any of the others so named. Confusingly the Authorised Version called the first of these 'James the Less', but this is not the same as the church tradition mentioned in the entry above, but may refer to his stature or youthfulness.

JAMES the brother of the Lord. There are incidental references to this James in the Gospels (Mark 6:3; Matt. 13:55). But it is only in Acts, 1 Corinthians and Galatians that he plays a significant role. It is natural to suppose that 'brother' should be understood literally and in its natural sense, but the church doctrine of the perpetual virginity of Mary led to suggestions that James was either a son of Joseph by an earlier marriage or a cousin of Jesus; such interpretations have no historical basis.

Nothing is known of James during Jesus' lifetime, but he evidently became a prominent Christian leader in the very earliest community. He is listed as a witness to Jesus' resurrection (1 Corinthians 15:7), and both Acts and Galatians regard him as a leader of the Jerusalem Christians. His mission was to the Jews, whereas that of Paul was to the Gentiles (Gal. 2:9). Peter was also commissioned to preach to Jews, a situation which led to tension between James, Peter and Paul, as described in Gal. 2 and Acts 15; in particular Galatians reports the difficulties that arose over the question of circumcision, which some (apparently including James, v. 12) regarded as essential for entry to the church. Acts 15:13-21 presents James' views as much more sympathetic to those of his colleagues, and it is disputed how far Acts, as a later composition, has glossed over real differences.

The tradition in Acts that James was the leader of the Jerusalem Christians certainly seems trustworthy, though it may be anachronistic to call him 'bishop of Jerusalem'. No doubt his kinship with Jesus gave him greater authority among his fellow-Christians, but it also exposed him to greater risks, and there are strong traditions (not found in the New Testament) that he was killed by the Jewish priestly authorities at a time when relations between Jews and Christians had sharply deteriorated, probably in the 60s.

JAMES, the author of the Epistle of James. James 1:1 describes its author as 'James, a servant of God and of the Lord Jesus Christ'. It is unlikely that the letter was actually written by any of the James already listed, but probably the author was presenting his letter as if it came from James the Lord's brother (see above). This device of pseudonymity was quite common in the ancient world, and was not then, as it would be now, a matter for moral obloquy. Though described as a letter, it is not addressed to any identifiable body of recipients, and it is rather a general treatise on the Christian life, perhaps concerned to guard against an exaggeration of the Pauline doctrine of justification by faith by insisting on the need for good works (ch. 2). There is no agreement among scholars as to the circumstances, place and date of composition, and the epistle itself gives very few clues as to its origin.

JANNES and Jambres are named in 2 Tim. 3:8 as the Egyptian magicians who attempted to emulate Moses at the time of the plagues of Egypt described in Exodus. The reference is an interesting example of the way in which the New Testament writer (perhaps Paul, but more probably a later disciple) elaborates on the Old Testament traditions, where the Egyptian magicians are unnamed. This tendency was very characteristic of Jewish literature of the period in which several other references to Jannes and Jambres are found.

JESUS of Nazareth is the central figure of the New Testament. Among both believers and non-believers, the figure of Jesus has continued to bring about passionate loyalty and violent argument; wars have been fought both by and among his followers, and there is no sign of any agreement as to the significance of his person. A new twist has been given to the last verse of the fourth Gospel; of people's thoughts of Jesus 'were every one of them to be written, I suppose that the world itself could not contain the books that would be written' (John 21:25). All that can be attempted here is a brief outline of what can be known of his life and some indication of the particular ways in which the New Testament writers understood his significance. Here, more than anywhere else in this book, it will be understood that virtually every statement could be disputed.

His name

Jesus is the Greek form of the common Hebrew name Joshua, meaning 'the Lord saves', and presumably this was the name by which he was known in his lifetime. But no trace of this has survived in our records, for the New Testament books are all written in Greek. 'Christ', which is often treated as if it were a proper name, is in fact the Greek word *Christos* meaning 'the anointed one' or 'Messiah', used as a title and it would be more accurate to speak of 'Jesus *the* Christ' rather than omit the definite article as is now the usual way.

Sources of our knowledge

For practical purposes these are confined to the books of the New Testament, and because of this the view has occasionally been put forward that Jesus did not exist. There can be no irrefutable proof, but it is now generally agreed, even by those with no Christian involvement, that the evidence for the existence of Jesus is stronger than that for virtually any other figure in the ancient world. It may be added that there are references to Jesus in non-Christian sources, such as the Roman historian Tacitus or the Jewish writer Josephus, but these are purely incidental and give no detailed information.

The basic source of our knowledge of Jesus, then, is the New Testament, and for centuries Christians have been content to accept its testimony at face value. The development of scientific historical study during the last two centuries has, however, forced a re-appraisal of the nature of the New Testament evidence. Two particular difficulties must be mentioned.

First, it is apparent even at a cursory reading that the four Gospels, which are our main sources of knowledge, display considerable differences. In particular, the understanding of Jesus in the first three Gospels is quite different from that found in the fourth. The first three — the synoptics, as they are commonly called — have a picture of a wandering teacher and healer, whose ministry was spent mainly in Galilee, in northern Palestine, and who came to Jerusalem only shortly before his death. His teaching is given in short, often epigrammatic form, and the Gospels intersperse the sayings of Jesus himself with a good deal of narrative describing his movements, the reactions of the crowd, and the like. The fourth Gospel, by contrast, is set largely in Jerusalem, and the vivid narratives and brief sayings have given way to extended discourses on the part of Jesus, in which it is often difficult to decide where Jesus' own speech ends and the reflections of the writer begin. It is hardly possible to give equal credit to both types of tradition, and the usual modern view has been to concentrate on the Synoptics (Matthew, Mark and Luke) for our understanding of Jesus. Some scholars have also been willing to accept traditions found only in the fourth Gospel, but this is a much-debated issue. It is generally agreed that the fourth Gospel was the last to be written, and that its author was attempting to explain the significance of Jesus for the church situation of his own day.

The second difficulty to which reference has been made causes even sharper differences of opinion. The early Christians were unanimous in believing that God had raised Jesus from death. For them, therefore, he was not a dead figure from the past, but a living contemporary. In the parts of the New Testament that were written first, especially Paul's letters, this is very clear: to be 'in Christ' for Paul meant a communion with a living Jesus, not a recollection of a past figure. Paul shows little interest in the earthly life and ministry of Jesus. Such an interest only emerges with the writing of the Gospels in the last third of the first century A.D.

Because of this time-lapse of thirty or forty years from the death of Jesus to the setting-down of the Gospels in writing, and the fact that this committal to writing took place in places far removed from Palestine, and in Greek rather than Jesus' own Aramaic, doubts have often been expressed about the reliability of the traditions.

For the most part it is probable that this difficulty can be overcome, or at least minimised, by taking into account the retentiveness of the ancient world's oral traditions and by making allowance for earlier sources behind our written Gospels. In some ways an even greater problem is caused by the fact that many of the acts and teachings ascribed to Jesus might be derived by the earliest Christian communities, not from memories of the Jesus who had lived in Palestine, but from their experience of the Jesus who was still alive in Heaven, continuing to guide his followers. If this were to be so, many sayings ascribed to Jesus in the Gospels would humanly speaking have to be considered as creations of the early church, convinced that it was inspired by its living Lord. No solution of these problems can here be put forward; but they should be borne in mind as helping to explain the very different views held by scholars concerning the reliability of the Gospel traditions.

The Gospels mentioned here are, of course, the four Gospels of the New Testament. From the second century onwards several other 'gospels' were composed, which elaborated various aspects of the story of Jesus, usually stressing his miraculous powers and creating a generally fantastic or magical atmosphere. Some originated from various heretical groups; others seem simply to have delighted in elaborating stories, but none of them is likely to contain further genuine information about Jesus' earthly life.

His birth and infancy

Accounts of Jesus' birth are given in Matthew and Luke, which differ considerably in detail, but are agreed that it took place at Bethlehem and that his mother Mary was a virgin, the baby having been miraculously conceived by the action of the Holy Spirit. Though the biblical accounts are much more sober and undramatic than the manner in which they are often presented in nativity plays, there is still here an element of elaboration of the account of the birth of the hero characteristic of the later 'gospels'. Both the central affirmations have therefore been challenged. Jesus is always spoken of as coming from Nazareth, and the earliest tradition (Mark) knows nothing of Bethlehem (Mark 1:9) and it is therefore possible that the Bethlehem tradition grew because it was believed that the saviour-Messiah would be born at Bethlehem as king David had been (Matt. 2:5f.). With regard to the virgin birth, it is again alleged that a miraculous birth of this kind was more appropriate for the saviour than the normal birth-processes, and it is indeed difficult to envisage how accurate historical memories could have been preserved of the events recorded in Luke 1-2.

His ministry

It is in any case clear that the birth stories are no more than a kind of prologue to the Gospels; in each case the bulk of their story is devoted to his ministry. But what kind of ministry was it? Here each Gospel provides its own distinct emphasis, though there is much material common to all the synoptics. The earliest, Mark, lays especial stress on the miracles performed by Jesus; for the most part of healing, but also those that show command over nature, such as the stilling of the storm (Mark 4:35-41) or the ability to feed vast numbers with meagre provisions (Mark 6:35-44; 8:1-9). In Matthew the emphasis is to a greater extent on the teaching of Jesus to his disciples: the sermon on the mount, chs. 5-7, is one of five great blocks of teaching material distributed through that Gospel. Among the particular characteristics of Luke are the parables found only there — for example the Good Samaritan (10:29-37) or the Two Sons (15:11-32), and this has led to suggestions that Jesus should be regarded either as a prophet, comparable to one of the Old Testament prophets or as a rabbi, as the Jewish teachers of a slightly later age were called. By the time that the Gospels came to be written, Jesus was regarded by his followers as having fulfilled all these roles, and it is very difficult to be certain which of them were primary, or in what particular way he understood his own mission.

These differences of emphasis are all based on the evidence of the New Testament itself. The suggestion has been put forward in recent years that the reality of Jesus' role was somewhat different, and is largely, but not totally, obscured by the New Testament documents. Jesus has been regarded as a political agitator, and it is noted that he included among his immediate followers a member of the Zealots, the extreme revolutionary group within Judaism (Mark 5:15), and that he was put to death by the Roman authorities, apparently on charges of insurrection. Such a view cannot be disproved, but it is contrary to the main body of available evidence, and has usually been put forward by those with their own contemporary political views to propagate.

His trial and death

Whatever doubts there may be about the exact nature of Jesus' ministry, one fact that is beyond any serious question is that he met his death by crucifixion at the hands of the Roman authorities. 'Crucified under Pontius Pilate' has been recited countless times as part of the Church's creed. The Gospels all mention Pontius Pilate, yet their main emphasis in the accounts of Jesus' last hours is with the various trials before the Jewish authorities, and there appears to be an increasing tendency to maintain that the responsibility for

Jesus' death lay on Jewish shoulders. This reaches a climax at Matt. 27:25, a verse which has given rise to much anti-semitic feeling and activity in later Christian circles, but is also found in the other Gospels and passages like Acts 3:13-15. It seems clear that by the time the New Testament was written there was deep animosity between Christians and Jews, as well as a desire to present Christianity in a sympathetic light to the Romans.

On one other point all the Gospels are agreed: that an important part was played by one of Jesus' own followers, Judas Iscariot, in betraying Jesus to the Jewish leaders. We may speculate as to the reasons for this action of Judas, but the New Testament will not help us here; for its writers Judas was simply the embodiment of evil, the traitor, whose every action is suspect.

That Jesus died on a Friday is agreed by all witnesses, and that it took place at the Passover season is also agreed. But there is a difference in the exact relation to Passover which makes precise dating impossible. The synoptic Gospels regard the last supper eaten with the disciples as being the Passover meal (Mark 14:12-26), whereas the fourth Gospel, which does not describe the supper itself, implies that Jesus died at the time that the lambs were being killed ready to be cooked for the Passover meal that evening (John 19:31). In other words, this dating implies that the Passover was a day later than is implied by the synoptic dating, and we have no means of deciding which is right, though the generally greater reliability of the synoptic testimony may make that date preferable.

The Resurrection

Of the historicity of the events just described there should be no real doubt, even though there are differences of detail. The accounts of Jesus' resurrection present problems of quite a different order. It is a basic tenet of Christian belief, underlying the whole New Testament, that on the third day after he had been crucified, Jesus was raised from the dead by God. Each of the Gospels ends with accounts of appearances of the risen Jesus to various disciples, but these seem to be told as stories illustrating an existing faith rather than as explanations of the origin of that faith. The earliest summary account of such appearances is found in 1 Cor. 15:5-7. In this and all the other accounts it is taken for granted that Jesus appeared only to disciples or potential disciples. We might wish to ask whether a by-stander could have seen the risen Jesus, but the New Testament, written as it is for believers, is not interested in such questions, and indeed stresses that the appearances were not for the world at large (Acts 10:41). It remains a point at issue among contemporary Christians to what extent the reality of the Resurrection of Jesus

187

depends upon empirically verifiable facts such as the emptiness of the tomb in which he had been buried.

Two other points may briefly be noted. First, all the New Testament writers agree that the resurrection was an act of God; they never imply that Jesus himself had the power to 'stop being dead', as it were; and the actual resurrection is never described. Secondly, there is a difference with regard to the subsequent chronology which has had great effects upon our calendars ever since. Only Luke, in his Gospel and Acts, pictures a forty-day period of appearances followed by an Ascension and then the gift of the Holy Spirit at the Jewish festival of Pentecost (the Christian Whitsun) ten days later; the other Gospels have no such chronological structure, and it would be impossible to fit their accounts into such a structure. But the Lukan version has become normative, and so the churches regularly observe Ascensiontide and Whitsun as festivals quite distinct from Easter, though it might be truer to the main New Testament understanding if Resurrection, Ascension and gift of the Holy Spirit were all seen as parts of one great whole.

The New Testament understanding of Jesus

Much has been written on Christology, that is to say, the role or status to be accorded to Jesus, and in particular the sense in which he has been understood as both God and man. It may seem curious to modern readers that in the earliest Christian centuries it was the reality of his manhood rather than that of his godhead which was liable to be called into question, and the opening verses of 1 John, for example, are clearly concerned to stress that Jesus really was fully human. The later doctrine of the Trinity, though consistent with one interpretation of the New Testament, is not present there in any organised fashion. Many titles were, however, applied to Jesus as expressing the way different Christian groups understood his significance.

Some of these titles, such as *logos*, 'word', link Jesus with a long line of ideas in the Greek and Hellenistic worlds, though found also in Judaism; this term is found only in the Johannine writings (e.g. John 1:14). For the most part the terms used are more directly linked with the Old Testament. For example, Jesus himself apparently favoured the term 'son of man', probably based on Dan. 7:13f. This expression seems sometimes simply to mean a human being, but more often it denotes one who comes down from God to bring judgement to the world (e.g. Mark 14:62). Again, the prophecies in Isaiah (esp. ch. 53) of a 'suffering servant' are applied to Jesus, especially in the Lukan writings and 1 Peter; and the hope expressed in Deuteronomy (18:15) of a prophet to arise in the last days is also applied to Jesus (e.g. Acts 3:22f.). The title *Christos*, 'Christ', is the Greek equivalent of the Hebrew word 'messiah' or 'anointed one', expressive of the hoped-for ruler of the line of David who would come to save his people from oppression.

These are but a few of the titles applied to Jesus in the New Testament. Through out its history the church has continued to develop new ways of assessing the person and significance of Jesus. There is no reason to suppose that this process is likely to cease.

JOANNA is mentioned twice in the New Testament (Luke 8:3; 24:10 — there is no reason to doubt that the two references are to the same woman) as one of the group of apparently well-to-do women who ministered to the needs of Jesus and his disciples. Her husband was the steward of Herod Antipas, the tetrarch (q.v. under *Herod*), but this office may not have implied direct membership of his household — it may be that he was manager of one of Herod's estates.

JOHN is the English form of the Hebrew name Johanan and of Greek Ioannes, both being common biblical names. Joanna (see above) is the feminine equivalent, but Jonathan is a different name, though confusion with Johanan or Ioannes is occasionally found. For Johanan see the Old Testament section.

Of the various New Testament figures named John, John the Baptist and John son of Zebedee are dealt with below; for John Mark see under *Mark*. In John 21:15, 17 Simon Peter's father is said to have been called John, but other and more probably reliable traditions give the name as Jonah. In Acts 4:6 one of the priests, of whom nothing else is known, is called John, and this is one of the cases where a variant tradition gives the name Jonathan.

JOHN the Baptist is mentioned in all four Gospels as a predecessor of Jesus, the special characteristic of whose work was the baptising in the River Jordan of those who came to acknowledge their sin. There is a reference to him in the Jewish historian Josephus, who mentions his practice of baptising and states that he was widely respected, and then describes his death at the hands of Herod Antipas, who feared that John's influence over the people might lead to a popular uprising.

The discovery of the Dead Sea Scrolls has made it possible to see John as part of a larger movement within Judaism, keeping away from the main centres of population and proclaiming the need for baptism after repentance to bring about the remission of sins and so be prepared for the imminent in-breaking of the kingdom of God.

This is not to say that John was himself a member of the Dead Sea community at Qumran, for of such a link we know nothing; but simply to note the similarities between the movements.

There is clear agreement among the New Testament writers that John's mission represents the 'beginning of the Gospel'. It is portrayed in this way in the opening verses of Mark, the earliest Gospel, and again in the prologue to John (John 1:6); and in the summaries of the gospel-message in Acts John is once again the starting-point (Acts 1:22; 10:36). Even in Matthew and Luke, where stories about Jesus' birth have been added, the beginning of Jesus' ministry is his baptism by John.

It seems that the fact of Jesus being baptised was something of an embarrassment by the time that the Gospels were set down in writing, for John's baptism was for sinners, and Jesus was regarded as sinless. Matt. 3:14f. clearly reflects an early attempt to resolve this problem. But there were deeper differences between John and his followers and those of Jesus, which have received different types of explanation in the Gospels. In Matthew explicitly (11:14; 17:11-13) and in Mark implicitly, John's mission is identified with that of Elijah who was widely expected to return at the end of time to announce the coming of the Messiah. But the tradition in the fourth Gospel flatly contradicts this (John 1:21), and the stress there is entirely on the preliminary nature of John's ministry which John himself is said to have accepted (John 3:30).

This particular stress may be due to the fact that some of John's followers refused to accept that Jesus was his legitimate successor, and continued to regard John as God's unique agent. Acts knows of those who had been baptised by John and had reached Ephesus in the furthest part of Asia Minor (Acts 19:1-7); these joined the Christian movement but presumably there were others who may not have done so. Rivalry between followers of John and of Jesus is the most natural explanation for those passages in the Gospels which stress how much greater Jesus is than John (Matt. 11:11, to show the merely human character of John's ministry), including self-depreciatory words put into John's own mouth (Matt. 3:11; John 1:15).

There are two main strands to John's preaching as presented in the Gospels. Since his baptism was closely linked with the need for repentance, it is natural that his preaching should stress the need for such repentance, sometimes in strongly denunciatory terms ('You brood of vipers', Matt. 3:7), sometimes with more specific ethical demands upon particular classes (Luke 3:10-14), some of which are reminiscent of Jesus' own teaching. Alongside this is the other strand, which emphasises John's preparatory role and envisages his preaching as mainly a making-ready for Jesus (e.g. Mark 1:7f.; John 1:19-34). The two elements are not necessarily incompatible with one another, but the great elaboration of the preparatory role in the fourth Gospel passage shows that this side of John's ministry was especially emphasised in the Christian church.

There is an account of John's birth in Luke 1:5-24, 57-80, interwoven with the account of Jesus' conception which would imply that John and Jesus were related. As with the stories of Jesus' birth, there is much dispute whether this story is historical or an idealisation from a later period. The account of his death, by contrast, is well documented both in the Gospels and Josephus, even if the details of 'Salome' (a name from later tradition) dancing and the Baptist's head being brought on a dish (Mark 6:14-29) may be later elaborations, as is the motif — popular in folk-tales — of the extravagant vow which cannot be broken. But there is no real doubt that Herod had John beheaded, probably for what we should call political reasons, since he feared the possibility of insurrection if John's preaching gained too firm a hold. The place of John's death is not mentioned in the Gospels, but according to Josephus was Machaerus, a fortress-palace near the Dead Sea.

JOHN son of Zebedee is one of the New Testament characters concerning whom scholarly and popular views show great discrepancies. Church traditions from the second or third century A.D. have regarded John as being the 'beloved disciple' mentioned in the fourth Gospel, maintaining that he used the title as a self-designation since he also wrote that Gospel, as well as the Johannine epistles and Revelation. These writings were thought to be the product of his old age, when he was bishop of Ephesus. The consensus of modern scholarly opinion would be to doubt, and usually to reject, the historicity of all these statements. Before considering the reasons for this, it may be helpful first to note what would generally be agreed about John.

Matthew, Mark and Luke all describe how Jesus demanded — no weaker word will do — that John should leave his everyday occupation of fishing and follow him, along with his brother James, and two other fishermen, Andrew and Peter. No indication is given why these particular men should have been chosen, or whether Jesus already knew them. Only the detail of 'hired servants' (Mark 1:20) might suggest that John's father Zebedee was a man of some substance. Thereafter John always appears in lists of the twelve followers of Jesus, and he along with James and Peter appear to have been an inner group within the twelve. The title 'sons of thunder' (Mark 3:17), together with their suggestion of destroying a Samaritan

191

village with fire because of its inhospitable behaviour (Luke 9:54) seem to imply that James and John were both fierily aggressive disciples who wanted the highest rewards in return for their loyal service (Mark 10:35-41). There are scattered references to John in Acts and Paul mentions him once, in Gal. 2:9, as a 'pillar' of the church in Jerusalem.

The picture thus given is a somewhat shadowy one, and the question arises whether it is legitimate to accept the later traditions that have filled out this outline in the way already mentioned. These later developments fall into two groups; those concerned with his authorship of certain New Testament books, and incidents from his later life.

It has been generally believed from the second century A.D. that the John whom we are here considering wrote the fourth Gospel, but this view has increasingly been challenged in recent years. This gospel appears to be a late reflection upon the significance of Jesus, wherein the traditions enshrined in the first three Gospels can be taken for granted, and their real importance drawn out. Both the late date and the theological profundity of the writing tell against any direct association with John the son of Zebedee, the character briefly discussed above. Again, the long discourses attributed to Jesus in this Gospel are very different from his manner of speaking in the other Gospels. On a number of historical details, furthermore, there seem to be inaccuracies which make apostolic authorship very difficult to defend — most notably the relation of the death of Jesus to the Jewish feast of Passover. (In this Gospel Jesus' death is made to coincide with the killing of the Passover lambs, whereas the older tradition has it that the last supper eaten the previous evening had already been the Passover meal.) The gospel itself makes no statement about authorship, and it seems best to accept this anonymity, noting only that the first epistle of John almost certainly came from the same author, or someone closely in touch with his patterns of thought. (2 and 3 John are too brief for useful conclusions about authorship to be drawn.)

The book of Revelation stands apart from the other Johannine writings, not only because of its different literary form and subject-matter, but also because of the very different quality of its Greek. It is difficult to suppose that it can have come from the same source as the Gospel, and the name John (Rev. 1:1, 4) may be introduced either as a pseudonym for the apostle John or may refer to some other John, known to his readers but not to us.

When we turn to the question of additional biographical material, this is of two kinds. In the fourth Gospel there are several references to 'the beloved disciple', (John 13:23 is the first), whose identity has remained a puzzle ever since. It is noteworthy that there are no references to John son of Zebedee in the book, and so popular belief has long identified the two figures, being encouraged to do so by the ascription of the gospel to 'John' and by the statement in 21:24 that the 'beloved disciple' was its author. Unfortunately, ch. 21 is now almost universally regarded as a postscript, and not part of the main body of the Gospel, and so its theory of authorship may itself have been intended to answer questions that were already current. The only other individual of whom it is said that Jesus loved him in this Gospel is Lazarus (11:5) and it has been suggested that he was the 'beloved disciple'. Otherwise, his identity must remain a mystery.

With regard to the tradition that John reached a great old age as Bishop of Ephesus, the difficulty here is to disentangle this tradition from beliefs about the origin of the gospel. Certainty on matters of this kind is impossible; some have felt that the statement of Jesus at Mark 10:39, that both James and John would be martyred, would only have been included in the Gospel if this had in fact happened, while others have given greater credence to the Ephesian links of John, which are first clearly attested in the writings of Irenaeus (about A.D. 180).

JONAH was the father of Simon Peter; this form of his name (Matt. 16:17) is more probable than the 'John' of John 21: 15, 17. The name is only used as an alternative way of speaking of Peter, and no biographical details are provided. In general, the Gospel writers assume that the identity of the leading characters will be known to the first readers and rarely provide any background information. (Other New Testament references to Jonah are to the prophet, for whom see the Old Testament section.)

JOSEPH. There are several New Testament figures with this name; the exact number is not entirely clear, because in several cases variant forms have been preserved. Thus the Authorised Version list of the ancestors of Jesus (Luke 3:23-38) contains four so named, but probably there are only three, as indicated in most modern translations (vv. 23f. 30). Again, variants are found between Joseph and Joses as the name of a brother of Jesus (Matt. 13:55), as another name for Barnabas (q.v.) (Acts 4:36) and as the name of the son of the woman who watched by the cross of Jesus in his last hours (Matt. 27:56 has 'Joseph'; Mark 15:40, 47 have 'Joses'). Of Joseph/Joses the brother of Jesus nothing else is known, and there is no reason to doubt the New Testament tradition which would imply that he was Jesus' natural brother. Only at a later date did church traditions concerning the perpetual virginity of Mary suggest other explanations for this relationship.

Joseph is clearly attested as the name of one of the disciples (Acts 1:23) who was considered as a candidate to fill the place of Judas Iscariot. When lots were drawn, the other candidate, Matthias, was chosen, and nothing more is heard of Joseph.

There remain two more about whose name there is no doubt: **JOSEPH** the carpenter of Nazareth, and Joseph of Arimathaea. Of these the first is mentioned by name in the stories of Jesus' birth (Matt. 1-2; Luke 1-3) with three other incidental references in the Gospels. That he was a carpenter is known only by inference (Matt. 13:55), but there is no grounds for doubting the tradition. Luke states that his home town was Nazareth (Luke 2:4), whereas Matthew seems to imply (2:23) that he only settled in Nazareth after the birth of Jesus. The former seems more likely, and it is possible that the link with Bethlehem is a late development of the tradition which wanted to stress the descent of Jesus from David, who had been a Bethlehemite. Joseph is several times called the father of Jesus (John 1:45; 6:42), and it is possible that this is a tradition which knew nothing of the virgin birth of Jesus. It is also possible that these passages simply reflect a desire to avoid the use of such awkward expressions as 'Jesus the son [as was supposed] of Joseph' (Luke 3:23). Belief in the truth or otherwise of the virgin birth of Jesus is scarcely likely to be affected by such ambiguous evidence as this.

Nothing is known of Joseph after the events described in the stories of Jesus' birth, and the absence of any reference to him in such a passage as Mark 3:31-35 might imply that he had already died. Only with the later apocryphal Gospels is a renewed and quite unhistorical interest developed in Joseph.

JOSEPH of Arimathaea is mentioned in all four Gospels as a member of the central Jewish council, the Sanhedrin, who provided a tomb for the burial of Jesus after his crucifixion (Mark 15:43, etc.). His home town Arimathaea, is possibly the same as Ramathaim (mentioned in 1 Macc. 11:34), north-west of Jerusalem, but the basic element of the name, *Rama*, means 'height', so many other sites are possible in hilly Palestine. We know nothing of Joseph's motivation, but the incident suggests that relations between Jesus and other pious Jews were not as strained as a superficial reading of the Gospels might imply.

JUDAS is the Greek form of the Hebrew name Judah, which was originally a geographical area, but came to be associated first with a particular tribal group within Israel, and then, in effect, became an alternative name for Israel. It was a popular personal name in New Testament times, and it may be no coincidence that several of those who bore it were associated with a strong sense of Jewish nationalism: Judas Maccabaeus, from the Apocrypha; Judas of Galilee (see below); and possibly Judas Iscariot.

JUDAS of Galilee is mentioned in Acts 5:37 as one who had led an uprising against the Roman authority. This Judas is probably the same as the figure described in the writings of the Jewish historian Josephus, who mentions a Judas the Galilean as one of the first of those who attempted to resist Roman power by violent means. This would link him with the brigand groups (or freedom-fighters?) later known as Zealots or *sicarii*.

JUDAS the brother of the Lord is mentioned in Matt. 13:55 (= Mark 6:3). It is unlikely that he can historically be identified with any-one else who bore this name in the New Testament, thoug it seems that the author of the Epistle of Jude is either claiming this position or that it was attributed to him by later tradition (see below: *Jude*). As with others who are called 'brothers' of Jesus, it is natural and now fairly usual to take the relationship in its ordinary sense, and to regard attempts to claim that the word 'brothers' really means half-brothers or cousins as motivated by the later belief in the perpetual virginity of Mary the mother of Jesus.

JUDAS BARSABBAS was one of those commissioned by the meeting of apostles in Jerusalem to take to Antioch a letter summarising the decisions they had reached (Acts 15:22, 32). Judas is described as a prophet, and this is one of a number of references to such a role in Acts; it seems as if 'prophets' played an important part in the earliest Christian communities, but that they disappeared as a more formal structure of Church order emerged. It is possible, though not proven, that this Judas was related to Joseph Barsabbas who is mentioned at Acts 1:23.

JUDAS ISCARIOT has rightly been called 'the most enigmatic person in the gospel story'. The one fact which penetrates to the deepest level of tradition and is reiterated whenever his name is mentioned, is that he was a follower of Jesus who betrayed his master to the authorities, a course of action which led directly to Jesus' crucifixion. The circumstances and motivation of this betrayal have been endlessly discussed, and we are no nearer to an answer to the enigma.

That Judas was a member of the group of twelve followers who accompanied Jesus during his ministry appears to be beyond doubt. The meaning of the word Iscariot is still disputed and may well not have been known to the Gospel-writers themselves. If he already bore the name during Jesus' lifetime, the explanation 'man of Kerioth', Kerioth being his home-village, seems most likely; if it was a name of condemnation given him later, many suggestions are possible (e.g. the false one or liar, based on an Aramaic word of similar sound to Iscariot). The tradition that Judas was the one who had the money box containing such offerings as the group received is found only in the fourth Gospel, and may be a later invention from the time when all evils were attributed to him — in this case the fact that he was a thief (John 12:6).

More recent views, which see in Jesus a man subject to human error like others, have to some extent eased the problem which used to be felt when it was assumed that Jesus was the possessor of perfect knowledge. If he knew everything, why did he choose as a follower one whom he knew would betray him? Such a question is not usually posed now in that sharp form, and attention has turned rather to psychological theories, which suggest that Judas was one of those who are capable of great deeds whether for good or evil, and that it was in the hope of eliciting the former that Jesus chose him.

The only real motive implied in the Gospels for Judas' betrayal is greed (Matt. 26:14f.), and this seems scarcely credible as an adequate explanation for his act. Instead, it looks like an early stage in the process of vilification of Judas that developed in much early Christian literature. Another example of this tendency in the New Testament is to be found in the two accounts of his death, which can scarcely be reconciled with one another. According to Matt. 27:3-10, he hanged himself (and this tradition has much to do with the condemnation of suicide in subsequent Christian thinking), whereas Acts 1:18-20 gives a vivid but somewhat imprecise account of his bowels 'gushing out' in the field which he had bought with the reward for his treachery. Each account links Judas' fate with an Old Testament condemnation of treachery, which suggests that no reliable early traditions of Judas' death survived, and the biblical writers drew their evidence from the Old Testament. Thus Judas' end is as greatly shrouded in mystery as his life.

JUDAS 'NOT ISCARIOT' is so called in John 14:22 to distinguish him from the traitor. He may be the same as the 'Judas son of James' mentioned in the list of Jesus' twelve followers in Luke 6:16 and Acts 1:13. But traditions about the more obscure of the twelve are very uncertain, and in Matthew and Mark the equivalent place is occupied by one named Thaddaeus or Lebbaeus. These may be alternative names for Judas, but it is likely that different traditions have been handed down. Nothing is known of any personal details of the life or character of any of these men. Later tradition sometimes regarded this Judas as the writer of the Epistle of Jude, and linked him with Simon the Zealot in church observance (Sts. Simon and Jude).

JUDE is an alternative form of the name Judas, and replaces it in some translations of the Bible. For the most part, however, this form is confined to the last but one book of the New Testament, the Epistle of Jude. This is a brief letter encouraging its readers to stand firm in the faith they had received against contemporary heresies. It is ascribed to 'Jude . . . the brother of James' (v. 1), which may be an attempt to identify the author with one of the brothers of Jesus (Mark 6:3). Such an ascription cannot be disproved, but is unlikely to be genuine, and may be regarded as an attempt to gain greater authority for the work. The author is either using this name as a pseudonym or is an otherwise unknown Jude.

JULIUS, a common name throughout the Roman Empire, is attested in the New Testament only as the name of the centurion detailed to accompany Paul to Rome to be tried there (Acts 27:1, 3). Nothing else is known of this Julius; the sympathetic account of his action in Acts 27 (vv. 3 and 43) is in line with the author's usual custom of showing how there was no friction between the Christians and the Roman authorities, a practice which may have been part of his purpose in writing.

JUNIAS is known only as one in a list of names (Rom. 16:7). Nevertheless, this person has been the subject of some controversy. The form Junias is masculine, but some manuscripts of the epistle have the feminine name Junia, a form found, for example, in the Authorised Version, which would be remarkable in view of the fact that (s)he is then described as an apostle. Modern scholars are generally agreed that the form Junias is the more likely.

JUSTUS is the name given to three different members of the early Christian community; they appear to be unrelated to one another. In Acts 1:21-26 lots are drawn to decide upon a replacement for Judas Iscariot; the unsuccessful candidate, Joseph Barsabbas, has the additional (Roman) name of Justus. In Acts 18:7-11 Paul, driven out of the Jewish synagogue, stays in the adjacent house of

197

Titius (or Titus) Justus, and it would appear that the Corinthian 'house church' was established there. In Col. 4:11 Jesus Justus is mentioned among the companions who remained loyal to Paul.

Ll

LAZARUS is mentioned as an historical character only in the fourth Gospel. In the parable of Jesus in Luke 16:19-31 one of the characters, the poor man, is — most unusually in such a context — specifically named as Lazarus. Many scholars have taken the view that the story of Jesus' raising of Lazarus (John 11) originated, not in any historical event, but in the allusion in the parable to one being raised from the dead (Luke 16:31). However that may be, there are formidable difficulties about taking the story in John 11 as historical. It is unmentioned in the other Gospels; the note that Lazarus had already been dead for four days (John 11:39) is the kind of detail added to heighten the reader's wonder at the miracle which only poses additional difficulties for modern men. As with the other miracles of Jesus, belief or non-belief in their possibility will scarcely depend upon a weighing of the balance of detailed argument in each particular case.

Peculiar to the fourth Gospel also is the tradition that Martha and Mary had a brother; and the other references in that Gospel all occur in connection with the account of his being raised to life (John 12: 1-17). The note that 'Jesus loved . . . Lazarus' (John 11:5, and cf. v. 36) has sometimes been taken as grounds for identifying Lazarus with the enigmatic figure, mentioned only in the fourth Gospel, of 'the beloved disciple'; but this can be no more than conjecture.

LEBBAEUS is mentioned in the Authorised Version at Matt. 10:3 as one of the twelve disciples of Jesus, but most modern translations of the New Testament prefer the reading 'Thaddaeus' found in other Greek manuscripts. This uncertainty, coupled with the variation of names found in other lists, suggests that some of the twelve were not well-known figures by the time that the Gospels came to be set down in writing.

LEGION is the name used in Mark 5:9 by the demon cast out by Jesus from the Gerasene demoniac. The name is used to indicate both the power and the number of the demons who were tormenting the sufferer, for the name legion was that of the main unit of the Roman army, the most efficient military machine known to the world of the first century.

LEVI, the son of Alphaeus, was called by Jesus to follow him while engaged in his work as a tax-farmer (Mark 2:14). The story illustrates two important points in the ministry of Jesus; the suddenness and abruptness of his demand, which snatches men away in the midst of their ordinary occupations; and the outreach to the social group most despised by their fellows (for tax-farmers were widely regarded as traitors to their people, both because of the extortionate methods they often adopted and because of their co-operation with the Roman authorities). Luke elaborates the story by telling how Jesus attended a feast in Levi's home (Luke 5:27-32).

It is unusual that Mark should describe the call of Levi in such detail, for he is never mentioned as a member of the twelve, and this has led to some confusion of identity. The same story is told in Matthew's Gospel of the call of Matthew (Matt. 9:9) who is in Matthew (not Mark) described as a tax-collector. Mark and Matthew both include in their lists of the twelve disciples 'James the son of Alphaeus' (Mark 3:18; Matt. 10:3), who may be understood as the brother of Levi, or (as is implied by some manuscripts of Mark) they may have regarded Levi and James as different names of the same person.

LINUS is mentioned in 2 Tim. 4:21 as one of those who sends greetings to the recipient; the dating of the letter is uncertain, since its Pauline authorship is doubtful, and it may well be that Linus should simply be regarded as one in a list of names. However, there is an ancient tradition of the church of Rome that the first Bishop there after the apostles Peter and Paul was named Linus, and a tradition dating back to the second century identifies this Linus with the Chrsitian mentioned in 2 Timothy.

LUCIUS, a common Roman name, is found twice in the New Testament: in Acts 13:1, of a Christian from Cyrene in Africa; and in Rom. 16:21, of a colleague of Paul. The name Luke (see next entry) is a variant form of Lucius, but there is no ground for identifying him with either of these men, as has on occasion been suggested. Nor is it very likely that the two references to Lucius are both to the same individual.

LUKE is known to us from the New Testament as a fellow-worker with Paul (Philemon 24), and is described (Col. 4:14) as one of the few who remained loyal during a time of stress, a point also emphasised at 2 Tim. 4:11, which may be a genuine Pauline fragment even if the letter as a whole comes from a later period. Luke is distinguished from the others listed in these greetings at the end of letters as 'the beloved physician'. Not much is known of the role of physicians in the world of the New Testament, and the main reference is distinctly unflattering (Mark 5:26), but however limited Luke's skill may have been, he was clearly highly regarded by Paul for his personal qualities.

Church tradition since the second century has identified this Luke with the author of the third Gospel and Acts, and this may well be correct, since Luke was certainly not a prominent figure in the early church around whom traditions would naturally accumulate. At the same time, it is perfectly possible that an originally anonymous work was subsequently attributed to Luke, the companion of Paul. The use of the pronoun 'we' in much of Acts required that the author had been with Paul, and the tradition of Luke's faithfulness, noted above, might have led to the spread of the view that he was the author. One argument formerly used to identify the Luke of Colossians with the author of Luke-Acts is now generally recognised as having no real weight — there is no ground for detecting in Luke-Acts any special knowledge of medical terminology. Indeed, the fact that Luke-Acts is written in good Greek should not lead us to supose that his author was probably a professional man such as a doctor — the physician was by no means so highly regarded as this might imply. While it remains probable, therefore, that the 'beloved physician' was also the author of Luke-Acts, the measure of doubt that exists has made it seem more appropriate to deal with the author in a separate article.

LUKE, the author of the third Gospel and Acts, may well have been the companion of Paul mentioned in Philemon 24 and Col. 4:14 (see previous entry); if not, we have no means of knowing whether Luke was actually the evangelist's name, or whether it was applied to the author of a previously anonymous writing.

The introduction to Acts (1:1f.) makes it clear that its author regarded it as a sequel to the Gospel of Luke (cf. Luke 1:1-4), though in all surviving traditions they are separated by the Gospel of John as in our present Bibles. The two books are written in good Greek, and it is often supposed that their author may have been a Gentile rather than a Jew, but there is insufficient evidence to be certain. In Acts there are numerous passages, the first being at 16:10, which are expressed in the first person plural, and these 'we' passages have often been taken as evidence that the author was a colleague of Paul. The ending of Acts is curious, since it leaves Paul awaiting trial, and this has led to speculation about its date and the author's purpose. Was it written before the trial had begun, perhaps as a plea to the authorities to show that Paul was innocent of any charge that might be brought against him? Did the author originally intend a third volume? Opinion remains sharply divided on these points, and on the dating, on which suggestions ranging from A.D. 65 to the mid-second century have been put forward.

By comparison with the other Gospel writers Luke takes particular care to correlate the events he describes with the secular history of the period, and, though some references remain dubious, he was clearly in general well informed. It seems also to have been his concern to write a 'life of Jesus', bringing out his humanity, introducing such familiar parables as the Two Sons and the Good Samaritan, and thereby justifying the remark of the French writer Renan that Luke's Gospel remains the most beautiful story ever written. Nowhere else is Jesus' universal concern, extending to those who were liable to be the outcasts of society, so vividly portrayed.

LYDIA is a personal name (Acts 16:14), but it may also have denoted a place of origin, for the woman so named came from Thyatira in the district of Lydia in Asia Minor. Thyatira was known as a centre of the dyeing industry, and it was such dyed goods that Lydia will have been selling in Philippi. She is described as a 'worshipper of God', which may imply that she was one of the class of 'god-fearers' — Gentiles who were sufficiently attracted by Judaism to be involved with the local synagogue. The baptism of herself and her household (v.15) may have been an important impetus in the establishment of a Christian congregation at Philippi, though she is nowhere mentioned in Paul's letters.

LYSANIAS is mentioned only once in the New Testament (Luke 3:1), but this allusion has become a notorious historical crux. He is mentioned by Luke as part of an elaborate chronological 'fix' for the beginning of Jesus' ministry, as being the ruler of Abilene, a somewhat obscure area north of Palestine. It is not clear why Luke should have used an otherwise unknown ruler of so distant a region to link Jesus' ministry to known historical events, and the only known reference to a Lysanias in other ancient sources refers to a ruler who was put to death by the Roman authorities c. 36 B.C. Either Luke has made a chronological error, or there was another ruler of this same name of whom we know nothing save this one biblical allusion.

CLAUDIUS LYSIAS is mentioned by name only once in the New Testament: at Acts 23:26, where his letter to the governor Felix is prefaced by the mention of the writer's name, as was customary in letters of the period. But in fact he plays an important part in the account in Acts of Paul's confrontation with the authorities which ends with his being brought to Rome, for he is the 'tribune' mentioned several times in Acts 21-23. He was apparently the commander of the Roman garrison in Jerusalem, and as such was involved in protecting Paul from the hostile crowd (21:30-40), in arranging the trial before the Jewish council (22:29f.), and in sending Paul to the governor under proper escort (23:16-35).

MALCHUS is the name given in John 18:10 to the servant whose ear was cut off by Peter at the time of Jesus' arrest. The detail has been interpreted in two contrasting ways. It is generally agreed that there was some kind of scuffle when Jesus was arrested and all the Gospels mention that the high priest's servant had his ear cut off (Mark 14:47 is the earliest account). Some scholars have felt that the detail of the name, found only in John, points to that Gospel having access to an independent source of historical tradition. Others have taken the view that the increasing detail found in the later Gospels is to be regarded rather as the addition of legendary accretions. Such details are the note that it was the *right* ear and that Jesus immediately restored it (Luke 22:50), and the mention of a personal name.

MANAEN is mentioned only at Acts 13:1 as a member of the church at Antioch. The interest in the incidental reference lies in the fact that he is described as a member of Herod's entourage. Herod Antipas (q.v.) the son of Herod the Great, is alluded to frequently in Luke and Acts, and several of these references show him taking some interest in earliest Christianity, though not usually of a sympathetic or informed kind (Luke 8:3; 15:31; 23:7-12).

MARK (Marcus) was probably the commonest name of all in the early Roman Empire. This at once poses a problem when the various New Testament characters bearing this name are considered. Have we to do with one or many individuals? Christian tradition has usually tended to welcome the tying together of loose ends and to identify characters of the same name when a plausible (and sometimes not so plausible) argument for doing so could be mounted; in fact there is little secure basis for such identifications. It may therefore be better to note the different references and to leave open the question whether some or all are speaking of the one man.

The New Testament contains three types of reference: the name is found in the lists of greetings at the end of several epistles; a John Mark plays a role in the missionary work of the church in Acts 12-15; and the second, and probably earliest, of the Gospels, is ascribed to Mark.

A Mark is mentioned in the closing greetings of four of the epistles. In Colossians (4:10) and Philemon the reference is clearly to the same person, since those two epistles are very closely related. From Colossians we learn that this Mark was related to Barnabas, which links him with the Mark referred to in Acts. We do not know what the instructions referred to in Colossians may have been. In 2 Timothy 4:11 Mark is referred to as being useful to the writer in his work of service. It is usually thought unlikely that 2 Timothy as a whole was written by Paul, but it may have included Pauline fragments, of which this could well be one. If so, it would suggest that Mark was now in a much happier relation to Paul than had been described in Acts. Finally in this category, 1 Peter 5:13 refers to 'my son Mark'. There is really no ground save the identity of name for taking this Mark to be the same as any of the others, though it might well be that the link with Peter here expressed led to the tradition that this Mark was the author of the Gospel, which was early understood as incorporating the reminiscences of Peter.

The second set of references is found in Acts. Here he is called John Mark. It was at the house of his mother (the fact being thus put probably implying that she was a widow) that the disciples were gathered during Peter's arrest and miraculous release (Acts 12:12), and his name appears to serve as a link to the next episode, the undertaking of a missionary journey by Barnabas and Saul, with John Mark as their assistant (Acts 12:25). But he soon returned home, for reasons unknown (Acts 13:13), so that when a further journey was proposed Paul (as Saul was now generally called) refused to have John Mark as his assistant (Acts 15:37). He therefore accompanied Barnabas instead (v. 39), and we hear nothing more of him, since all the remaining interest of Acts is focussed upon Paul. These events in Acts involve considerable problems if they are to be taken as straightforward history, but there is no reason to doubt their general reliability, and the reference in Colossians to Mark as Barnabas' cousin may throw some light on the situation.

Finally, there is Mark the gospel writer. Who this may have been remains completely unknown. That the writer was indeed called Mark is likely to be a reliable tradition, even though it is nowhere stated in the Gospel itself. It dates back certainly as far as the middle of the second century, and there would be no reason for attributing the writing to an unknown disciple unless reliable tradition underlay it. Various attempts have been made to identify this Mark more precisely; in the ancient world this involved the identification with the disciple(s) called Mark mentioned elsewhere in the New Testament; other suggestions have been that he was a follower of Peter, or that he was the unknown young man who fled away naked the night before Jesus was crucified (Mark 14:50f.). But the first view, though it has been popular since questions about the Gospels began to be asked, seems to be contradicted by the modern study of their transmission, which stresses the important role of the early Christian communities rather than personal 'memoirs'; and the second is no more than ingenious speculation. Authorship may not matter too much in Gospel study; we must be content to say that Mark was probably the first to compose this unique form of literature, perhaps about A.D. 70, and possibly in Rome (though the place of origin is as uncertain as the identity of the author).

MARTHA is mentioned in Luke and John as a follower of Jesus, at whose home he was welcomed. The context in Luke would lead one to suppose that this home was in Galilee, but John, who sets much more of Jesus' ministry in the south, identifies it as at Bethany, just outside Jerusalem. Luke 10:38-42 shows Martha as the householder, concerned that Jesus should be properly looked after; the slight rebuke not to be over-concerned with such practical details must not be exaggerated into a condemnation. As the margins of most modern translations show, Jesus' exact words at 10:42 are very uncertain, and cannot be built upon as forming a sharp contrast between ways of life exemplified by the two sisters.

The other reference to Martha comes in John 11-12, where the central concern of the story is the raising to life of her brother Lazarus (whose existence is not mentioned or even implied in Luke). Both this episode and that of the supper in John 12:1-8 present Martha in a way similar to that already found in Luke: concerned, practical, perhaps a little lacking in the larger vision. Characteristically the fourth Gospel uses her partial understanding as an opportunity to present a fuller truth, for it is in answer to Martha's statement of belief in the resurrection of her brother at the last day that Jesus makes the arresting and enigmatic pronouncement, 'I am the resurrection and the Life' (John 11:24f.). This Gospel also provides the basic statement of Jesus' affection for the whole family: 'Jesus loved Martha and her sister and Lazarus' (John 11:5).

MARY is the name borne by several women in the New Testament; as will be seen below, the exact number is much disputed. It does not appear to have been a particularly common name in the Greek world, but is a Greek form of the Hebrew name Miriam (q.v. in the Old Testament section). In what follows the account of Mary the mother of Jesus will be considered first, and then the various other people with this name in the Gospels and Acts.

There need be no doubt that the mother of Jesus was called Mary. Almost every other statement that can be made about her, however, might be the subject of doubt or criticism from one direction or another. In addition to the difficulties surrounding investigation of all biblical characters, the mass of later traditions and legends relating to Mary raises many additional complications. In one sense the basic difficulty can be very simply put: it is the question whether or not this legendary expansion has already taken place within the New Testament itself, or whether the biblical material has preserved accounts which are free from such accretions. On the one hand may be put the point that many, perhaps the overwhelming majority of, people in the present day will reject immediately the very possibility of virginal conception; on the other hand may be noted the sobriety and lack of elaboration which characterises the gospel material by comparison with the later legends. Here it will be possible only to point out some of the difficulties that have been raised, and to attempt to give some indication of which traditions may probably be regarded as reliable.

In our earliest Gospel, Mark, Mary is mentioned only once by name, at 6:3. In such a context the lack of reference to her husband Joseph is more likely to have been caused by his having already died than by any question relating to the virgin birth; and there is no ground for supposing that the brothers of Jesus, whose names follow, are anything other than true brothers. They are most probably understood as younger sons of Mary and Joseph. Mary and the other brothers are also alluded to at 3:31-35, but the story there is told in such a way as to point to its climax in the saying of Jesus in v. 35, and gives no clue as to why they should have sought Jesus. Their motives could have been either sympathetic or hostile.

There is no account of Jesus' birth in Mark, but the later Gospels, Matthew and Luke, each supply one. No clear indication of Mary's ancestry is given, the descent from king David being through Joseph, but since she is said to have been a kinswoman of Elizabeth (the mother of John the Baptist) who was of priestly family (Luke 1: 36 and 5), Mary may also have been of priestly family. Both Matthew and Luke stress that human intervention had played no part in the conception of Jesus, and beliefs about this are clearly not susceptible to any kind of proof. (It is observable that whereas in the early part of this century, belief in the virgin birth of Jesus was an extremely important criterion of Christian orthodoxy, in more recent years it has come to be almost incidental, though it is of course affirmed in the main Christian creeds.)

Another matter on which certainty is impossible is the place of Jesus' birth. Matthew and Luke both state that it was Bethlehem, but this appears to be motivated by a desire to see in his birth a fulfilment of Old Testament prophecy, and the tradition represented by Mark (1:9) that Jesus came from Nazareth and had probably been born there may be more reliable.

Little is known of Mary during the lifetime of Jesus. Luke 2 gives some indications that her role was already beginning to be a matter of speculation within the Christian community, with its cryptic statements, "Mary kept all these things, pondering them in her heart" (v. 19) and "his mother kept all these things in her heart" (v. 51). Only in the fourth Gospel, with the story of the wedding at Cana in Galilee (John 2:1-11), is Mary at all involved with Jesus' ministry. Her confidence in her son's powers, despite an apparent rebuff, show the esteem in which she was held in the early church, for it is unlikely that this incident, unmentioned elsewhere, is a historical reminiscence.

The earlier traditions relating to the death of Jesus make no mention of Mary (e.g. Mark 15:40); but again the fourth Gospel reflects the increasing interest in the role of Mary, and here she is pictured as standing by Jesus' cross in his last hours (John 19:25-27). This Gospel presents Jesus as if he were in entire command of all that was going on, despite his agony, and it is entirely in keeping with this that he commends his mother and the unknown 'beloved disciple' to each other's care. The final note concerning her in the New Testament is provided by Acts 1:14; which associates her with the disciples in the earliest Christian community after the resurrection.

This very slight and restrained picture soon came to be elaborated, as the early Church devised a rich variety of legends concerning

Mary's ancestry, the circumstances of her own conception and her death and subsequent raising to Heaven, together with many intervening details. Two of these picturesque legends have come to be of especial importance for many Christians, since belief in her Immaculate Conception (that is, her freedom from all sin from the time of her conception) and her bodily Assumption into Heaven after her death are required articles of belief for Roman Catholics.

A number of other women named Mary are mentioned in the Gospels and Acts, and it is very difficult to be certain in some instances whether the same or different people are being referred to. The five separate entries given below must not, therefore, be regarded as more than one possible way of interpreting the evidence. The Gospel-writers were writing for an audience some of whom would know who was being referred to without further reference; on other occasions the Gospel-writers themselves may not have been sure of the identity of the minor characters.

MARY of Magdala (Mary Magdalene) is the best known of these other Marys. Mark mentions her in his account of the death of Jesus without previous explanation, as if she would be quite well-known to his readers (Mark 15:40), and this sets the scene for her most important function in all four Gospels — as a witness to the resurrection of Jesus. She remained near the cross till Jesus had died and saw where he was buried (Mark 15:47), and on the third morning she prepared spices for the customary anointing rites (Mark 16:1). She thus became the first to discover that Jesus' tomb was empty. In the other Gospels, written later than Mark, her role was elaborated as speculation about Jesus' resurrection increased. In Matthew (28:1-10) Mary and her companion are met first by an angel and then by the risen Jesus himself; Luke has two angels and adds the detail that the male disciples refused to believe women's testimony (Luke 24:1-11); while John adds a scene of a personal appearance of Jesus to Mary, in which she at first mistakes him for a gardener and only after hearing his voice does she recognise him as her Lord (John 20:11-18). These attractive stories allow us to see something of the early church at work, in its endeavour to put the mystery of the resurrection in terms that could be readily understood.

Only Luke provides an earlier reference to this Mary; a cryptic note that 'seven demons' had been driven out of her (8:2), presumably by Jesus, though this is not stated, nor is any further detail offered. Even her home village, Magdala, is not otherwise mentioned in the New Testament, though we know of it from a reference in the first-century Jewish writer Josephus. Later Christian traditions have usually identified this Mary as being both the sister of Martha and the unnamed 'woman of the city who was a sinner' referred to in Luke 7:36-50. Attractive though such speculations may be, they say more about the constant fascination of the 'prostitute with the heart of gold' theme than about historical likelihood.

MARY of Bethany, sister of Martha, is known only from the stories relating to Martha (q.v.). Both Luke and John emphasise Mary's devotion to Jesus; Luke has her listening to his teaching and being commended despite the consequent neglect of the menial tasks of the household (Luke 10:38-40), and John stresses her devotion to her dead brother Lazarus and her conviction of Jesus' power to conquer death (John 11:31f.).

The sequel to this story of the raising of Lazarus poses another problem of identification, for John 12:1-8 has the story of Mary anointing the feet of Jesus as a preparation for his burial. This story is so close to the account in Mark 14:3-9 that it must surely be a variant of the same account, but in Mark (the earlier writing) the event takes place in 'the house of Simon the Leper', and is performed by an unnamed woman. It may well be that the link supplied by the place-name Bethany led to this incident being associated with Mary at a late stage in the tradition. As with Mary of Magdala, there is an obvious link here with the story of anointing placed at an earlier point in the Gospel by Luke (7:36-50).

MARY the mother of James and Joses is mentioned only in connection with the burial and resurrection of Jesus. All the first three Gospels mention her as present at the crucifixion (Mark 15:40; Matt. 27:56) or as expecting to minister at the tomb of Jesus on the Sunday (Mark 16:1; Matt. 28:1; Luke 24:10), but no other personal details are supplied.

MARY the wife of Clopas is mentioned only in the fourth Gospel (John 19:25). Taken literally the Greek (and some English translations) could mean that this Mary was the sister of Jesus' mother; but since she was also called Mary this is unlikely, and the phrase 'his mother's sister, Mary the wife of Clopas' should be taken as referring to two different women. This Mary seems to be the equivalent of the Mary the mother of James and Joses (see previous entry), and may be the same person. In this case the fourth Gospel would have preserved her husband's name; the three other Gospels would have referred to her by the names of her sons who may have been well-known early Christians.

MARY the mother of John Mark is mentioned in Acts. 12:12. Again this matter of referring to her may be due to the fact that her son (concerning whose identity see under *Mark*) was a well-known figure in the early church.

MATTHEW is listed four times (Mark 3:18; Matt. 10:3; Luke 6:15; Acts 1:13) as one of the twelve disciples of Jesus. In Christian tradition he is also regarded as the author of the first Gospel. Both of these assertions pose considerable difficulties, a solution to which is by no means agreed.

Probably in the earliest traditions, represented by Mark 3:18, Matthew was a member of the group of twelve disciples, about whom nothing else was known. At a later stage the story of the tax-collector called by Jesus 'from the receipt of custom' (Mark 2:14), whose name was apparently Levi, came to be transferred to Matthew, to solve the obvious problem that there was no Levi among the twelve. It is not impossible that Matthew was a name later given to Levi, or that he had two names; but it is much more likely that a transfer of tradition has taken place, and that we can know nothing of the original Matthew.

For different reasons difficulties are now felt in accepting the traditions that this Matthew was the author of the first Gospel. Church tradition has long explained its close links with Mark by supposing Mark to be dependent on Matthew; but it is the almost unanimous verdict of modern scholarship that the dependence is in the other direction, and that Mark is the earliest of our Gospels. If this is so, it seems most improbable that one of the twelve, a close companion of Jesus, would have been dependent upon the writings of someone unknown in the earliest Christian community.

It seems more probable, therefore, that the Gospel of Matthew was written in the last quarter of the first century, using Mark as its basis, but incorporating much more of the teaching of Jesus, which was available to the author from another source. This teaching was arranged in five blocks within the book, the most familiar being the 'sermon on the mount', in which material found scattered in different contexts in other Gospels has been brought together as one great sermon (chs. 5-7). The exact circumstances of the writings of the Gospel are not known, but it shows a particular interest in Jesus as the fulfilment of the expectations of the Old Testament, and it is likely that it was aimed at a Christian community whose roots were in Judaism, and who may have been involved in controversy with contemporary Jews. This may best explain the opposition to the 'scribes and Pharisees' (ch. 23), and the stress on the Jewish responsibility for the killing of Jesus (Matt. 27:25 — a verse which has had most deplorable results in fanning anti-semitic feelings ever since). Despite this anti-Jewish feeling, there are also very positive aspects of Matthew's presentation of Jesus, culminating in the final command to make converts in every nation and bring them to Jesus through baptism (28:19f.). Scholars have often doubted whether these words were original to Jesus himself, but they have certainly exercised a powerful effect on the church through the ages.

MATTHIAS is known to us from one episode only, which is found in Acts 1:15-26. This describes Peter's assertion that the number of the twelve disciples must be maintained despite the treachery of Judas Iscariot, and so after prayer and the casting of lots Matthias is chosen for this role. The conditions laid down imply that Matthias must have been a follower of Jesus during his earthly life, but he is never mentioned in the Gospels, nor do we hear of him again in Acts. Though there are no reasons for doubting the historicity of the story, it remains without parallel in the New Testament. When other members of the twelve were killed they were not replaced as such (e.g. James: Acts 11:2), and, indeed, little more is heard of 'the twelve' as a special group in the church. Later Christian tradition tended to regard Paul rather than Matthias as the one who made up the number of the twelve.

MELCHIZEDEK. One of the aims of the author of the Epistle to the Hebrews was to present the ministry of Jesus in priestly terms, and to do this he used the Old Testament traditions relating to 'Melchizedek, king of Salem' (Heb. 5-7). Little was known of this mysterious figure, and the author of Hebrews uses this very fact to stress the awesome, mysterious character of Jesus' ministry, which is different from, and far above, all earthly forms of priesthood. Such a mode of argument seems baffling to modern men, but it well illustrates the variety of ways in which the early followers of Jesus tried to understand his work for them and to communicate it to others in the thought-forms of their day (see also the Old Testament section).

MNASON was a Cypriot, one of the early (this is the probable meaning of 'old', found in some English versions) disciples, with whom Paul lodged on his last visit to Jerusalem (Acts 21:16). Most of the Greek texts of Acts imply that he lived in Jerusalem, but some place him in an unnamed village between Caesarea and Jerusalem.

NATHANAEL, a disciple of Jesus, is mentioned only in the fourth Gospel, which here as on many occasions includes traditions unknown to the first three. An allusion to him in John 21:2 gives his home as Cana, where, according to the same Gospel Jesus had performed his first sign; but the more detailed story is in John 1:45-51, where he is brought to Jesus by Philip. The account is extremely terse, and is clearly as much a confession of faith as a statement of historical event. In it, Jesus speaks of Nathanael's sincerity, thereby showing his own ability to discern men's true nature, and Nathanael confesses Jesus as 'son of God' and 'king of Israel', terms whose real meaning will be elucidated during much of the remainder of the Gospel. The scene ends with a promise of greater visions for Nathanael, picturing a vision to be revealed to him in terms reminiscent of Jacob's dream (Gen. 28:12). Like so much in the fourth Gospel, it is a mysterious, allusive episode.

The lack of all other reference to Nathanael has led to widespread but entirely baseless speculation that this might be another name of a disciple better known by a different name. Bartholomew has often been suggested for this dual role, which is pure guesswork.

NERO is not mentioned by name in the New Testament, but it was while he was Roman Emperor A.D. 54-68 that developments of great importance for the Christian church took place. The most dramatic event was the fire of Rome in 64, for which Nero put the blame on the Christians. The tradition of the later Roman church held that in the subsequent persecution both Peter and Paul were put to death, and it has been suggested that one result of the crisis for the Roman Christians was the writing of the earliest Gospel by Mark.

It is possible that other New Testament books which refer to persecution (e.g. 1 Peter) may also have Nero in mind, but the passage most commonly held to allude to Nero is Rev. 13:18, with its mysterious reference to the 'number of the beast' being 666. No agreed solution to this puzzle has ever been found, but a popular theory is that it corresponds to the words 'Nero Caesar', which in the letters of the Hebrew alphabet (which were given a numerical as well as a literal value) add up to 666. Whether the author of Revelation or his readers know Hebrew remains uncertain, and prevents the general acceptance of the theory.

211

NICODEMUS plays an important part in the Gospel of John (the only New Testament book in which he is mentioned), as symbolising the possibility of a sympathetic Jewish reaction to the teaching of Jesus. In John 3 he is presented as an important Jewish teacher who comes to Jesus to question him, but fails to grasp the real importance of Jesus' person and work; in this he stands for the whole Jewish nation as presented by John. But whereas others turned decisively against Jesus, Nicodemus remained sympathetic and fell foul of his own colleagues, who rejected Jesus out of hand (John 7:50-52). So after Jesus' death Nicodemus is willing to assist in the rites for a proper burial (John 19:39). No indication is, however, given that this sympathy was translated into full commitment, though at a much later date a legendary 'Gospel of Nicodemus' was composed.

NICOLAS (or more accurately Nicolaus, as in most modern translations) was one of the seven believers appointed in Acts 6 to help the apostles in their ministry. He is described as coming from Antioch, in Syria, and as being a proselyte, that is, one who had been converted to Judaism from paganism. It seems that many such became Christians, especially in the areas away from Palestine.

In the book of Revelation there are two references to a group called Nicolaitans, who were apparently an heretical sect, to be avoided by orthodox Christians (Rev. 2:6, 15). Such a group will probably have taken its name from a founder or prominent member called Nicolaus, and ever since the second century the suggestion has been made that this was the Nicolaus of Acts 6. This can only be a guess, for there is no known link save that of the identical, and not uncommon, name.

ONESIMUS is mentioned in the greetings at the end of the Epistle to the Colossians (Col. 4:9), but this brief allusion comes to life in the letter to Philemon, which shows us that Onesimus was a slave who had in some way wronged his master, Philemon, had become a Christian, and was now with Paul, who was in prison.

Paul hopes that Philemon will let Onesimus minister to him a little longer, for he is very useful — a play on the meaning of the word Onesimus which means 'useful' (Philemon 11).

An interesting but speculative view is that this Onesimus should be identified with the Onesimus who was bishop of Ephesus c. A.D. 110, and that the reason for the brief and insignificant letter to Philemon being preserved is that it was due to the initiative of Onesimus who, on this view, would have played a major part in gathering the Pauline letters together (and even, according to some scholars, himself composing that to the Ephesians).

ONESIPHORUS is mentioned twice in 2 Timothy as a Christian from Ephesus who had remined loyal to the author in all troubles (1:16-18; 4:19). Strictly, the references are not to Onesiphorus himself but to his household; whether this implies a temporary absence or the previous death of Onesiphorus is not known. The references have played an important part in discussion of the authorship of this epistle. The usual modern view is to reject the Pauline authorship of the 'Pastoral Epistle' (1 and 2 Timothy, Titus), others have argued that at least the personal notes of the kind outlined above are genuine Pauline fragments, and that the reference to Onesiphorus seeking Paul out in his Roman prison is a valuable piece of evidence toward the life of Paul (2 Tim. 1:17).

P

PAUL is a dominant figure in the New Testament, second only to Jesus himself. Some indeed have claimed that Christianity owes more to Paul than to Jesus, but Paul would indignantly have denied this. Nevertheless, it is clear that his work was of fundamental importance in transforming the nascent church from a small group within Palestinian Judaism to a movement which rapidly came to affect the whole of the Mediterranean world. Paul is unique also in that we have a substantial collection of his writings; other biblical books are either the product of a long period of growth with many authors, or are ascribed to individuals about whom little or nothing else is known. Of no other biblical figure are we enabled to anything like the same extent to obtain a picture of the man by the testimony of his own words. We shall consider first which letters are actually by Paul, then what may be known of his life, and then something of his lasting significance.

Older translations of the Bible ascribe fourteen epistles to Paul, but of these one — Hebrews — is universally agreed to be an anonymous treatise only attributed to Paul from a very late date. Among the remaining thirteen, there is universal agreement that Paul wrote Romans, Galatians and 1 and 2 Corinthians, and investigations by means of computers in recent years have confirmed the common origin of these four letters. The great majority of New Testament scholars would add at least Philippians, 1 Thessalonians and Philemon to this basic list; here the computer evidence is more ambiguous, partly because these letters are so short as to make statistical comparisons difficult. It may be that in one or more of these cases Paul was dependent upon an amanuensis for the actual penning of the letters. With regard to the remaining letters opinion among scholars is more divided; 2 Thessalonians stands somewhat apart from the others, and is difficult to relate in any convincing way to 1 Thessalonians. Colossians and Ephesians are markedly different in style and theological emphases from the undisputed letters; some regard this as a sign of Paul's own development, while others think it more likely that, particularly in the case of Ephesians, a follower of Paul was writing in his master's name in the changing circumstances of the church in the late first century A.D. Finally, the letters to Timothy and to Titus, usually called the Pastoral Epistles, are now generally not regarded as coming from Paul himself. Not only do language and style differ from that of Paul, but also the situation of the recipients seems to reflect a developed church life very different from the agonies and enthusiasms of Paul's lifetime. There may be genuine Pauline fragments embedded in these letters; they are unlikely to be by him as they now stand.

When we turn to consider what may be known of the life of Paul, a basic problem confronts us. There are two sources, which often show disparities among themselves. On the one hand Paul is the leading figure of the second half of the book of Acts, which describes his missionary work largely in terms of three journeys, beginning and ending in Palestine. The last chapters of Acts are devoted to an account of various hearings before Jewish and Roman authorities in Palestine, as a result of which Paul appeals to Caesar and after an exciting sea-voyage reaches Rome, where the book ends with him still at liberty and no indication is given of a formal trial there.

Traditionally this source has been widely used for reconstructions of the life of Paul, but in recent years there has been a strong reaction against this approach. The primary source of our information consists of Paul's own letters, and these should therefore be our basic guideline. Nor is it wise to attempt to 'slot' the Acts stories into the outline reconstructed from the letters; Acts is a later book, with its own understanding of the events of the earliest Christian days, a perspective that at times differs sharply from that of Paul himself. In what follows, the main outlines of Paul's life, as far as we know them, will be traced from Paul's own letters, using as primary evidence the seven letters generally agreed to be from Paul himself. It will be noted by those familiar with the account in Acts that it is very difficult to present such a reconstruction in terms of a specific number of 'missionary journeys'.

Paul on various occasions stresses his strict upbringing in Judaism (2 Cor. 11:22; Phil. 3:5f.), but our detailed knowledge begins with his conversion to Christianity when he had a vision of Jesus (1 Cor. 15:8). In Galatians 1:12-2:14 he spells out what he considers to have been the salient details of his early years as a Christian, but as references to periods of three and fourteen years (Gal. 1:18; 2:1) show, this account covers a considerable period of time. It is therefore likely that some of his activity in what is today Greece had already taken place within the period here covered. For example, the references to persecution and opposition in 1 Thessalonians (2:2), show something of the difficulties under which he laboured. It may well be that the epistle(s) to the Thessalonians are the earliest surviving letter(s) of Paul, and if so, the earliest surviving Christian literature. No absolute dating is possible, but the period around A.D. 50 gives the approximate time. (If 2 Thessalonians was written by Paul, it may have been the earlier to be written; many interpreters think it easier to envisage 1 Thessalonians as a sequel to 2 Thessalonians than *vice versa*).

Though much of Paul's ministry was exercised in what are now Greece and Turkey, he made periodic visits to Jerusalem, which he naturally regarded as in some sense 'headquarters'. But his relations with the Christian leaders there were not always easy, as is shown by Gal. 2:1-10, though it is noteworthy that he spent much energy in organising a large-scale collection for the impoverished Christians of Palestine, and several of his letters refer to this concern. It is, indeed, details of this kind which make his writings genuine letters and not doctrinal treatises. The references to this 'offering for the saints' are especially prominent in 1 and 2 Corinthians (1 Cor. 16:1; 2 Cor. 8:4; 9:1), and it may be that his letters to the church at Corinth followed shortly after those to Thessalonika. Our Bible contains two letters to the Christians in Corinth, but it is clear from them that Paul wrote at least two other letters: 1 Cor.

5:9 refers to a previous letter already dispatched, and 2 Cor. 2:3 and 7:8-12 refer to another letter, clearly written in severe terms which make it scarcely possible to identify it with our 1 Corinthians. Probably our Bible contains no trace of the letter previous to 1 Corinthians (though some scholars have argued that it may have survived as 2 Cor. 6:14-7:1, which fits awkwardly into its present context); the 'severe' letter referred to in 2 Corinthians might be chs. 10-13 of that letter, which display a marked difference in tone from the more eirenic spirit of the earlier chapters. Certainly on these matters cannot be attained, but it is clear that the affairs of the church at Corinth, whose members included people from many walks of life, gave Paul a great deal of concern. 1 Corinthians cannot be compared with Romans as an exposition of Christian doctrine, but it stands out for the remarkable way in which Paul deals with the many practical issues which were exercising the Christians at Corinth: unity and division, marital and sexual relations, the hope of resurrection, and above all the need for charity and love.

Some of Paul's letters were written while he was in prison (the 'captivity epistles'), but we have no means of knowing whether all were written during the same imprisonment. Philippians stands somewhat apart from the other epistles in this group, and so a theory which has gained ground in recent years is that it was written, not from Rome, as were the later captivity epistles, but from an otherwise unrecorded imprisonment, probably at Ephesus in modern Turkey. The frequent journeys back and forth mentioned or implied in Philippians (2:19-28; 4:10-20) would be very difficult to envisage if Paul was being held in distant Rome. Certainty once again is impossible, and we have to reconcile ourselves once again to the fact of ignorance of much of the detail of Paul's life. But, wherever it was written, Philippians brings out a side of Paul's character very different from the Corinthian letters; here he is able to share a deep joy because of the faithfulness of the Christian community to which he writes (1:4-11). But even at Philippi there are traces of dissension and strife (1:15-18), and to warn against this Paul quotes probably from an existing hymn about Jesus, the famous passage setting out the way Christ's humility should be a model for all his followers (2:5-11).

The two other major epistles which are certainly from Paul's own hand are Galatians and Romans. Those who have used Acts as a basis for reconstructing the life of Paul have for the most part regarded Galatians as one of the earliest of his writings; Galatians makes no mention of the Council of Jerusalem described in Acts 15, and, so it is argued, must have been written before that took place. But if the evidence of the epistles themselves provide our starting-point, it is more natural to link Galatians with Romans, as the climax of Paul's literary activity. Both have as their central concern the assertion of the righteousness of God, and the overwhelming requirement of faith if man is to be justified before God. In Galatians these convictions have to be defended vigorously, at times even angrily (Gal. 1-2), against those who asserted that salvation was to be achieved through adherence to the requirements of the Jewish law; in Romans they are developed more fully and reflectively, in a way that has provided the starting-point for new depths of insight into Christian faith in every subsequent age. Both Martin Luther in the sixteenth century and Karl Barth in the twentieth came to their profound understanding of Christianity through wrestling with the Epistle to the Romans.

This already gives some measure of Paul's lasting significance. The New Testament itself already provides illustration at two levels of the adage that imitation is the sincerest form of flattery. On the one hand are those books written in the name of Paul, though probably not coming from his own hand: probably Colossians and Ephesians, almost certainly the Pastoral letters. On the other hand the picture of Paul in Acts has, as at least one of its objects, the setting-forth of an ideal of Christian devotion and service, sanctioned by the words of Jesus himself (Acts 22:6-21), approved by the imperial authorities though not by his own fellow-countrymen (Acts 23), and finally bringing the Gospel to Rome itself (Acts 28). But there can be no doubt that Paul's most profound importance has been at the level of theology, and it is as true today as it has been throughout the history of the church that anyone who wishes to enter into the full understanding of Christian belief about God, man and the world, must be prepared to sit at the feet of Paul and listen to his continuing message.

PETER is a figure whose words and actions occasioned dispute within the lifetime of his master Jesus, and whose role has not ceased to be a controversial one ever since, particularly in connection with the claims of the Papacy. On any showing he is one of the three or four most important figures in earliest Christianity.

His original name was apparently Simon (Mark 1:16), or as it is occasionally found in the New Testament, Symeon, a form closer to the Hebrew original (Acts 15:14). But as a follower of Jesus he came to be known as Peter (and of this name, too, a Semitic equivalent, Cephas, is found, e.g. at 1 Cor. 15:5). Peter and Cephas both mean 'rock', and two different accounts are given attributing this change of name to Jesus himself (Matt. 16:18; John 1:42). Neither

217

the precise circumstances of the change nor the particular reason for it (?rock-like character or appearance) can now be established.

Peter's original trade was clearly that of a fisherman in the lake (or 'sea') of Galilee (Mark 1:16), but the Gospels are characteristically vague about other domestic details, since their main purpose was an apologetic and religious one. So we know that Peter was married (Mark 1:30), but nothing is said about his wife; his father's name is reported as 'Jonah' in Matt. 16:17 and as 'John' in John 1:42; his home appears to be in Capernaum according to Mark 1:21, 29, but Bethsaida according to John 1:44. Again, all the Gospels are agreed that Peter had a brother named Andrew, but whereas the first three Gospels speak of their call by Jesus taking place by the lake of Galilee, with the emphasis very much on Peter (Mark 1:16-20; Matt. 4:18-22; Luke 5:1-11, where Andrew is not even named), the fourth Gospel sets out quite different circumstances, with Andrew's call being given the priority (John 1:35-41). We are reminded that the kind of personal detail which would fascinate a modern reader may not have been preserved very accurately in the earliest Christian communities.

Whatever the precise circumstances of his call, it is certain that Peter abandoned his trade in fishing to become a companion of Jesus in his life as a wandering teacher and preacher in Galilee. He was one of the group of twelve whom Jesus appointed, perhaps on the analogy of the twelve-fold division of Israel according to the Old Testament; he was also one of the 'inner circle' of three chosen to accompany Jesus at particularly solemn moments in his ministry (e.g. the raising of the ruler of the synagogue's daughter, Mark 5:37, or the Transfiguration, Mark 9:2). Indeed, the first three Gospels in particular regularly present Peter as the leader of the disciples, who can sometimes be described as 'Simon and those who were with him' (Mark 1:36).

This prominent position meant that all the human limitations of the disciples tended to be associated with Peter as their spokesman and representative. Thus, at the time of crisis, all the disciples deserted him despite previous protestations of loyalty (Mark 14:31, 50), but it is Peter's denial which is described in full (Mark 14:66-72) and has been embedded in popular tradition. It seems proper, therefore, to see in Peter's weakness and impetuosity the dangers inherent in all following of Jesus rather than a detailed assessment of his personal character.

This point is relevant also for two other features of Peter's role. He is the 'rock' on which the church is to be built (Matt. 16:18), and he is the prime witness to Jesus' resurrection (1 Cor. 15:5). In both cases Peter is in a sense representative, not only of the twelve, but also of what is involved in Christian discipleship at any age. With regard to Peter's status within the church, the more extreme views basing all later papal claims to infallibility upon this verse are now generally abandoned; it is much disputed whether these words, with their picture of a continuing community, are likely to have been spoken by Jesus.

The fullest account of the next part of Peter's career is found in Acts 1-12, where he is the dominant figure in the nascent Christian church, organising the structure of the believing community, preaching boldly, and taking the initiative in proclaiming the Christian message. In the remainder of Acts he is scarcely mentioned, and the only other extended references to him in the New Testament give a different impression, for in Gal. 1:18-2:14 he and Paul are clearly at odds about the appropriate attitude to take toward potential Gentile converts, while in 1 Cor. 1:12 he is the figure around whom a dissident group in Corinth is identified. Some have taken these as signs of a deeper rift within the early Christian community, with Peter and Paul sharply at odds, and Acts written at a later date as an attempt to present an idealised picture of harmony. In fact, though there were no doubt differences, it would be misleading to exaggerate them. Paul recognises Peter's primacy as a witness to the resurrection of Jesus (1 Cor. 15:5), and as the leader of the mission to Jews (Gal. 2:7); his prime concern is not to denigrate Peter, but to ensure that the importance of his own mission should be recognised, and that no impossibly constricting limitations should be imposed.

Later tradition associated Peter with Antioch and particularly with Rome. There is no secure New Testament support for this link, but from the second century onwards it is a strong tradition, which may well have a historical basis. If so, its likely origin is in the persecution of Christians in Rome by Nero in A.D. 64, and the inclusion of Peter among the number of those put to death; search for the burial place of Peter has continued, but it is unlikely that any decisive identification can be made. At a later date, a variety of traditions, such as the famous 'Quo vadis' story of Peter turning back after his initial thought of escape, were woven around the basic traditions, and to separate the historical fact from later accretions is no longer possible.

Not surprisingly, in view of the prominence of Peter, he has come to be associated with various writings. In Acts we have accounts of his speeches, but these will have been composed, according to the custom of the time, by the author, putting into Peter's mouth what should have been said on such occasions. Of the various books associated with Peter, none can with confidence be ascribed to him as author. The strongest case can be made out for 1 Peter, accepted as genuine by some scholars but usually held to be pseudonymous in view of its excellent Greek and its lack of connection with the characteristic Petrine emphases known to us from elsewhere in the New Testament. 2 Peter and the various apocryphal writings attributed to Peter are almost universally regarded as the products of a later age, written in pious memory rather than actual products of his pen. These doubts should not detract from his reputation; rather, the urge to attribute writings to him reflects the significance of the role of one who was believed to have made the great confession in the lifetime of Jesus himself: 'Thou art the Christ' (Mark 8:29).

PHILEMON is the addressee of the shortest of Paul's letters. It appears that he was the master of the runaway slave Onesimus, on whose behalf Paul was pleading. It is curious that so brief a note, for it is little more, should have been preserved at all, and still more that it should have come to be treated as Scripture; one suggestion that has been made is that Onesimus was in fact the person responsible for gathering together Paul's letters, and therefore took special pains to include the letter which referred to himself. However that may be (and it can only be a speculative theory) Philemon remains known to us only as a leading Christian among the community at Colossae, in Asia Minor.

PHILETUS.
See *Hymenaeus.*

PHILIP was a common name in the Greek-speaking world of New Testament times, and four different individuals with this name are mentioned in the New Testament.

Two of them were members of the Herod family. One, mentioned only in Luke 3:1, was the son of Herod the Great and succeeded him (4 B.C.-A.D. 34) as ruler of the area described by Luke as 'Ituraea and Trachonitis', that is, the northern and eastern parts of Palestine. The city of Caesarea Philippi (Mark 8:27) was built by and named after him, but in general the area of his authority was beyond that in which the events described in the Gospels took place. By comparison with most members of the Herod family, his rule is remembered as a beneficent one.

Another son of Herod the Great, by a different wife, was also called Philip according to the Gospel writers (Mark 6:17; Matt. 14:3), but is in other sources always called 'Herod', so that it is not known whether the biblical accounts have confused him with his half-brother, mentioned above, or whether he was also known as Philip. The reference to this Philip is in any case only an incidental one, mentioning him as the previous husband of Herodias (q.v.).

There was a Philip among the group of twelve disciples who accompanied Jesus. In the three synoptic Gospels, he is no more than a name in a list (Matt. 10:3; Mark 3:18; Luke 6:14) and this is also the case with the only reference to him in Acts (1:13). In the fourth Gospel, however, he plays a more prominent part, and as always with traditions confined to this Gospel, there is sharp disagreement among scholars as to the significance of this fact. Some take such references to be evidence of an early, historical tradition underlying the fourth Gospel; others regard the elaborations found there as more akin to the later creation of stories about all the early Christian leaders which was largely the satisfaction of pious curiosity.

The particular traditions relating to Philip are that he came from Bethsaida in Galilee, was one of Jesus' earliest disciples and was instrumental in bringing Nathanael to Jesus (John 1:43-49); that he was the disciple who expressed doubts whether so few loaves and fishes would feed five thousand people (John 6:5-7); that he brought certain 'Greeks' (perhaps proselytes to Judaism) to Jesus, a tradition in connection with which the Greek name Philip may be relevant (John 12:21f.); and that he engaged in the discussion with Jesus at his last discourses (John 14:8f.). Nothing is known of his subsequent life.

The last Philip is mentioned in Acts, where he plays a secondary but important role in the story of the spread of Christianity. He is first heard of as one of the seven appointed in 6:5, apparently to 'serve tables'. But his subsequent career shows him as an evangelist (this title is actually used of him at 21:8), who was expelled from Jerusalem in the persecution after the death of Stephen but who was then involved in two major works of missionary activity (Acts 8). First, he went to Samaria and won many converts, including Simon Magus (vv. 5-13); and then, being guided by the Spirit to go to the desert road he met and baptised an important Ethiopian royal official (vv. 26-39). After that he is described as preaching in the towns of the Mediterranean seaboard (v. 40), and the only later reference has him in the same area at Caesarea, with four daughters who were prophets (Acts 21:8f.).

PHOEBE is named first among the many Christians to whom Paul sends greetings in Rom. 16 — so many, indeed, that many have questioned whether this chapter really forms part of the Epistle to the Romans, a church in a city which Paul had never visited. We cannot therefore be sure that Phoebe, who came from Cenchreae, near Corinth, was necessarily in Rome; the chapter might have been addressed to Christians elsewhere, perhaps at Ephesus. Phoebe is described as a 'deaconess', and it is disputed whether this implies a regular order (so the Revised Standard Version translation) or should be understood in more general terms ('who serves the church' – the Good News Bible).

PONTIUS PILATE has been immortalised in Christian tradition by the phrase in the Apostles' Creed, 'crucified under Pontius Pilate'; he is also one of the few important New Testament characters whose existence and role is clearly demonstrated by non-biblical sources. Nothing is known of his background or career before A.D. 26, when he was put in command of Judaea by the Roman emperor Tiberius. He remained there until A.D. 36, when he was recalled. His exact title as governor was for a long time disputed: traditionally he has been styled 'procurator', but there is evidence, including a contemporary inscription, to suggest that this is anachronistic, being a title introduced only at a later date, and that 'prefect' is correct.

Jesus' ministry all took place during Pilate's rule (Luke 3:1), but since he spent most of it in Galilee, it is unlikely that the two men will have had any direct links. Only once in the New Testament is reference made to an action of Pilate other than his involvement in Jesus' death; in Luke 13:1 reference is made to an otherwise unknown massacre carried out by Pilate apparently at a time of religious festival. This accords well with the reputation which Pilate enjoyed in the eyes of the Jewish historians, who speak of his insensitivity to Jewish religious beliefs, bringing images of the emperor into Jerusalem and allowing his troops to interfere with Jewish ceremonies. It was allegedly as a result of complaints about such behaviour that Pilate was finally recalled. The accounts are clearly not impartial, but the implication can hardly be avoided that his rule showed a mixture of high-handedness and obstinacy.

The accounts of his role in the condemnation of Jesus appear to have been softened, so as to heap an increasing measure of blame on the Jewish leaders. In our earliest account, Mark, Pilate is simply the judge carrying out sentence, with little interest shown in his character. Increasingly the later Gospels shift the blame for the death of Jesus from Pilate to the Jews and their leaders. Matthew ascribes to the Jews the acceptance of blame which has led to so much anti-Semitic feeling in subsequent centuries (Matt. 27:25); both Luke and John emphasise how Pilate found Jesus to be innocent, and only agreed to his death because of the insistence of the Jews (Luke 23;13-25; John 19:12-16). Indeed John pictures Pilate as little more than a puppet, carrying out actions over which he has no control (John

19:11). It will be seen that it is impossible to decide with certainty just how the responsibility for Jesus' death should be apportioned; the fact remains that his death was by crucifixion, a Roman method of punishment, which only Pilate could have authorised.

The Gospels already show traces of legendary accretions, for example, in the story of Pilate's wife and her dream (Matt. 27:19), and this tendency was carried much further in later romances, according to which he was later converted to Christianity and came to be revered as a saint in some parts of the church.

PRISCILLA and Aquila, wife and husband, are mentioned together in all the six New Testament references to them; in 2 Tim. 4:19 the wife's name is given in the shortened form 'Prisca'. It is interesting and unusual that on three occasions the wife is named first, but no certain reason for this can be established; it would be very unsafe to deduce, as has been done, that she was the more learned and even the author of the Epistle to the Hebrews! All we know is that they were tentmakers, expelled from Rome along with other Jews (Acts 18:2), and that they befriended Paul and accompanied him from Corinth to Ephesus (Acts 18:18f.), where they were instrumental in the conversion of Apollos (Acts 18:26). 1 Cor. 16:19 refers to a church in their house at Ephesus, and Romans 16:3f., where Paul sends greetings to them, may also originally have been addressed to Ephesus (see under *Phoebe*).

QUIRINIUS, the legate of the Roman province of Syria, is referred to in classical sources, and is mentioned in Luke's account of the birth of Jesus (Luke 2:2). There are, however, major difficulties in using the account of the census associated with Quirinius as a means of dating Jesus' birth. Quirinius became legate in A.D. 6, whereas Luke 1:4 links the events with the 'days of Herod' who died in 4 B.C. Two other points in Luke's account are surely unhistorical; the statements that the census involved 'all the [Roman] world' (v. 1) and that everyone had to go 'to his own city' (v. 3). The latter point may have been introduced by Luke to overcome the difficulty that Jesus came from Nazareth whereas Jewish expectation was that the Messiah would be born at Bethlehem.

SALOME is the name of one of Jesus' early followers, but, by a curious irony, a 'Salome' who is not named at all has become much better known in later tradition. The named Salome is mentioned in Mark (15:40; 16:1) as one of the Galilaean women who had followed Jesus and helped in ministering to his needs. In Matt. 27:56 "the mother of the sons of Zebedee" is mentioned in a verse parallel to the account in Mark, but is not named; it may be that Salome is meant here.

Much more famous because of the many literary and artistic representations of the event is the daughter of Herodias, whose dancing so pleased Herod that he made extravagant promises of gifts, only to be dismayed by the request for the head of John the Baptist to be brought on a dish (Mark 6:22-25). This girl is unnamed in the New Testament, but subsequent tradition has given her the name Salome.

SAPPHIRA.
See *Ananias.*

SATAN.
See Old Testament section.

SAUL.
See *Paul.*

SCEVA is described as a 'Jewish high priest' in a curious episode in the account of Paul's missionary work in Acts 19:14. The account has been discussed in terms of the reliability of Acts as a historical account. Sceva was certainly not one of the succession of Jewish high priests, but it is possible either that he was a renegade Jew now involved in a pagan cult, or that he was a member of a Jewish priestly (not high priestly) family; wandering exorcists of the type described certainly existed in Judaism.

SILAS, an early Christian, is referred to both in Acts and in several of the epistles. It is now generally agreed that Silas (the form of the name found in Acts) and Silvanus (that found in the epistles) are variants of the same name, and that the intention is to refer to the one individual. Again, there is no reason for doubting that the reader is to understand that the same person is meant both in the Pauline references and in 1 Peter.

The primary references are in the Pauline epistles. In both 1 and 2 Thessalonians Silas is included with Paul and Timothy as co-authors of the letters, but no more detailed information is provided, and later in the letters the first person singular is used as if only Paul were the author. Silvanus was probably an assistant of Paul, associated with him in his correspondence and also in his preaching (2 Cor. 1:19). This picture is filled out by the account in Acts 15-18, which describes Silas as a prophet (15:32), as Paul's chosen companion (15:40-17:14), and as sharing his imprisonment (16:24-40). 1 Peter is unlikely to be by Peter himself, and the reference to Silas there (5:12) is probably an addition wishing to give an extra touch of authenticity. In all this, nothing of Silas' personal character comes through; he is a significant but minor figure.

SIMON, the Greek form of the Hebrew Simeon, is a common New Testament name. Of its nine bearers, one is better known as Peter: see the article on Peter for the relation of the different names by which this disciple was known. The others are listed below.

SIMON was another member of the twelve (Mark 3:18). Mark and Matthew (10:4) call him 'the Cananaean', as if this were a place-name, but Luke (6:15) recognised the true meaning of the Aramaic word, and rendered it as 'the Zealot', that is, one of those who advocated active resistance to Roman rule in Palestine. (The Zealots are only known from a time later than that of Jesus, but there is no reason to doubt that comparable groups were found in Jesus' lifetime.) No other details of this Simon are offered, and it is to go far beyond the evidence to suggest, as has sometimes been done, that Jesus himself took this nationalistic view because of the presence among his adherents of one of its members.

SIMON. A brother of Jesus was called Simon (Mark 6:3; Matt. 13:55). The natural meaning of this reference is that he, and the other brothers listed were actual brothers of Jesus; it was at a much later date that the belief in Mary's perpetual virginity arose.

225

SIMON. The account of the Passion of Jesus begins, in Mark and Matthew, with Jesus having supper in the house of 'Simon the leper' (Mark 14:3; Matt. 26:6). The main point of the story is the act of devotion performed by a woman who in this version of the story is unnamed. But the similarity in details suggests that this story is one found elsewhere in the Gospels in different versions, and so this Simon (otherwise unknown) is likely to be the same as Simon the Pharisee.

SIMON the Pharisee (Luke 7:36-50) also invited Jesus to a meal at which a woman poured ointment upon Jesus as a symbolic action. This story suggests that there may have been closer links between Jesus and the Pharisees than we should expect from other parts of the Gospels, but otherwise supplies no details about Simon.

SIMON of Cyrene is mentioned in all three synoptic Gospels (Mark 15:21; Matt. 27:32; Luke 23:26), as having carried Jesus' cross to the place of the crucifixion; the fourth Gospel, by contrast, speaks of Jesus carrying his own cross (John 19:17), a change in the tradition which both reflects the evangelist's conviction that Jesus was in control of his own destiny, and also serves to rebut the charge that it was Simon, and not Jesus, who was actually crucified. Nothing else is known of this Simon; he was presumably a Jew, from the Jewish community in North Africa, and the mention by Mark of his sons implies that they became Christians and would have been known by Mark's readers.

SIMON, the father of Judas Iscariot, is mentioned only in John (6:71; 13:2, 26), and on each occasion Simon is referred to only as Judas' father, without further personal detail.

SIMON, a tanner, is mentioned in Acts as Peter's host while he was staying at Joppa (Acts 9:43). In view of Peter's involvement in the controversy concerning the status of Gentiles in the early church, the author of Acts may have wished to stress the fact that he stayed with one whose trade was unacceptable to strict Jews, because it involved handling dead bodies.

SIMON MAGUS played a part in the religious history of early Christian centuries out of all proportion to the significance ascribed to him in the New Testament. There he is mentioned only in one story in Acts (8:9-24). Regarded in Samaria as a magician, he was converted and baptised by Philip, but then apparently relapsed by trying to buy the power to work miracles; this earned a rebuke from Peter, and the story ends ambiguously with Simon praying to avoid punishment. It is from this attempt to buy ecclesiastical power that the word 'simony' originates.

It is not possible here to spell out the enormous variety of the literature concerning Simon that developed in succeeding centuries. Second-century Christian writers indulged in vigorous attacks against those who followed Simon's teaching; traditions relating to Simon played an important part in both Jewish and Samaritan thought; and the whole complex is related, unmistakably but imprecisely, within the larger movement of religious thought known as Gnosticism. It is very doubtful whether any of this rich growth of legend had any historical connection with the actual figure of Simon himself, but speculation on this topic will probably never be satisfied.

SOSTHENES is the name of an early Christian mentioned in both 1 Corinthians and Acts, and it is disputed whether the two references are to the same man. In 1 Cor. 1:1 Paul associates Sosthenes with himself in writing his letter, and no further reference to him is found. In Acts 18:17 the inhabitants of Corinth beat Sosthenes, the ruler of the synagogue, without incurring any punishment from the Roman authorities. If a different Sosthenes is referred to here, this will have been a case of anti-Semitic behaviour by a city mob being winked at by the authorities (as so often since); if there is only one Sosthenes, then he must have become a Christian, and the affray would have been caused by Jews taking revenge on one of their own community whom they felt to have deserted them. Certainty is not possible; but if Luke (the author of Acts) knew the letters of Paul and assumed that his readers also did so, he may have intended his reference to have been to a known Christian.

STEPHANAS and his household play an important and slightly ambiguous role in Paul's relations with the church at Corinth, as shown in 1 Corinthians. At the beginning of the letter, he is anxious to play down the part played by individual Christian leaders in setting up the church, to avoid the tendency to divisions apparent among the Corinthian Christians, and so he mentions his links with Stephanas in an almost apologetic way (1 Cor. 1:16). By the end of the epistle, however, he is stressing the importance of Stephanas, who had acted as an intermediary between Paul and the Corinthians and is probably to be seen as an early example of a Christian with a local ministry (1 Cor. 16:15-18).

STEPHEN is the central character of Acts 6-7. His story develops in an unexpected way. At the outset he is one of a group of seven appointed, it would seem, to carry out merely administrative functions in the growing church (Acts 6:1-6). (This group has often, but without adequate evidence, been called 'deacons'.) But there is no record of their acting in this way; instead Stephen is spoken of as doing 'great wonders and signs' (Acts 6:8), just like the apostles, and he is then charged with blasphemy, particularly with being opposed to the temple. Acts 7:2-53 is an elaborate speech in defence, which has the effect of enraging his opponents still more so that they stone him to death, thus making Stephen the first Christian martyr after Jesus himself (Acts 7:54-60). The account of his trial and death is very clearly modelled on that of Jesus.

There is much about the figure of Stephen which remains obscure. It is not clear whether he should be linked with the Hellenists or with the Hebrews mentioned in Acts 6:1, nor whether it is safe to argue from the details of his speech (which in many respects is similar to the speeches attributed to other speakers in Acts) to Stephen's own distinctive standpoint. If this is legitimate, then his speech shows a hostility to the Jerusalem temple very different from the attitude of the apostles (Acts 3:1), and has suggested to some scholars that Stephen may have been of north Israelite, or even Samaritan, origin. Clearly details of this kind were much less important for Luke, the author of Acts, than the way in which he illustrates both the development of the Christian community and its ability to produce those who were willing and able to follow their master even to death.

THADDAEUS appears in some of the lists of the twelve disciples of Jesus (Mark 3:18; Matt. 10:3). Nothing else is known of him, and the uncertainty with regard to his identity can be illustrated by the fact that some manuscripts of Matthew call him 'Lebbaeus' and other traditions concerning the twelve appear to have Thaddaeus' place taken by 'Judas not Iscariot' (q.v.). The twelve no doubt played an important part as witnesses to Jesus' ministry, but recollection of the distinctive role of most of them soon faded in the early church.

THEOPHILUS was the addressee of Luke (1:3) and Acts (1:1), the only non-Christian individual to whom a New Testament writing is dedicated in this way. Who he was is unknown.

Presumably he was an individual, but the name may be a pseudonym (it means 'beloved of God'), and it may be that Luke and Acts were addressed to him as someone in authority, believed to be sympathetic to Christianity, in the hope that the imperial authorities would not be adversely affected by rumours hostile to the church which were being circulated. But this can only be a speculative reconstruction.

THEUDAS is referred to at Acts 5:36, as the leader of an insurrection against Roman authority. The reference is of some importance in establishing the character of the book of Acts, for it is virtually certain that it betrays a dating error by the author. The rebellion of Theudas took place around A.D. 44, but the speech in Acts alluding to it is supposed to have been given several years earlier. It seems clear then that this, like other speeches in the first part of Acts, was an imaginative reconstruction on the part of the author of the book, and this would tie in with the custom of ancient historians. The suggestion that there were *two* rebels named Theudas seems to be an unnecessary complication.

THOMAS, one of the twelve disciples of Jesus, is known chiefly through his portrayal in the fourth Gospel as the one who doubted the fact of Jesus' resurrection; hence the expression 'doubting Thomas'. Characteristically the fourth Gospel has developed personal details, while the other gospels simply include Thomas as one of the twelve with no further elaboration (Mark 3:18; Matt. 10:3; Luke 6:15). In fact the development in the fourth Gospel includes not only his doubt (John 20:24-28), but also his willingness to die with his master (John 11:16). There is continuing dispute whether this kind of elaboration reveals historical sources otherwise unknown, or is simply a late and unhistorical development.

There were many later traditions relating to Thomas. His name means 'twin', a point underlined by calling him 'Thomas Didymus' (John 11:16), and a pious belief developed — still held in some parts of the church — that he was in fact a twin brother of Jesus. Among various later writings attributed to him, the most notable is the 'Gospel of Thomas' discovered in Egypt in the 1940s.

TIBERIUS succeeded his step-father Augustus as Roman emperor and ruled from A.D. 14 to 37. The ministry of Jesus therefore took place during his reign, as is made clear by Luke (3:1), in the elaborate dating scheme with which he begins his account of Jesus' adult life. This is the only direct mention of him in the New Testament; though references to 'Caesar' would strictly speaking

229

apply to him, they are not of personal significance, but are concerned with 'the Caesar' as the symbol of Roman authority.

TIMOTHY played an important part in Paul's apostolic ministry. No fewer than five of Paul's letters (2 Corinthians, Philippians, Colossians, 1 and 2 Thessalonians) associate Timothy with Paul in the first verse, and a number of passages within the letters speak of Timothy's particular work. Thus on various occasions Timothy is sent by Paul to carry out personal tasks on his behalf (1 Thess. 3:1-6; 1 Cor. 4:17; Phil. 2:19). In such a role, his task may not always have been easy, so that 1 Cor. 16:10f. implies that there might be some cause for anxiety, either about Timothy's own capacity or about the Corinthians' treatment of him. In all of this the references are indirect, and do not really enable us to gain any personal picture of Timothy.

Material of a different kind is provided by Acts 16-20, which describes Timothy's involvement in Paul's missionary work. Acts 16 describes him as the child of a Greek father and a Jewish mother, who had not been circumcised until Paul did so — an interesting tradition in view of Paul's insistence, especially in Galatians, that circumcision should not be regarded as necessary.

Finally Timothy is the recipient of two letters ascribed to Paul, but it is likely that these were pseudonymous letters written at a later period in the church's history, and not very probable that personal details about Timothy (e.g. his mother's and grandmother's names, 2 Tim. 1:5) preserve a historical tradition.

TITIUS JUSTUS.
See *Justus*.

TITUS, a colleague of Paul, plays an important part in the various missionary plans described in 2 Corinthians. Disputes concerning the unity of that epistle have prevented any precise reconstruction of Titus's movements, but it is clear that he had a major role to play as an intermediary, bearing Paul's messages to Corinth (2 Cor. 8:6-24) and reporting to Paul on the state of the church there (2 Cor. 7:6-16). Titus also played an important part in the argument of the epistle to the Galatians, which is much concerned with the question whether Gentile converts should be required to undergo the Jewish rite of circumcision. In Gal. 2:1-10 Paul explains that he had not required Titus to be circumcised — at least according to the most common understanding of the text: some manuscripts state that Paul *had* yielded to the demand that Titus be circumcised. (See the text and footnote of the New English Bible.)

The 'epistle to Titus' is clearly presented as being addressed to this same disciple, but it is now generally agreed that the letters to Timothy (which also include a mention of Titus: 2 Tim. 4:10) and Titus are not from Paul himself, but are an attempt to set out Paul's teachings in the light of the development of the church at a later period.

TROPHIMUS, a Gentile companion of Paul (Acts 20:4f.) unwittingly provided the occasion of his arrest according to the Acts of the Apostles, for Jews supposed that Paul had taken him into that part of the temple precincts wherein only Jews were admitted (Acts 21:29). Presumably the Trophimus referred to in the list of names at 2 Tim. 4:19 either was the same person, or, if that list is a later imaginative reconstruction based on the account of Paul in his letters and Acts, is meant to be regarded as the same person.

TYCHICUS is mentioned on five separate occasions as one of Paul's fellow-workers. The Pauline authorship of Colossians is disputed, but if it is by the apostle, then Tychicus will have been a companion of Paul who was allowed by the authorities to bring Paul's letter and personal greetings to the Colossians (Col. 4:7f.). These words are virtually repeated at Ephesians 6:21f., and are usually thought to be an artificial and later addition in that context. The author of the epistles to Timothy and Titus (probably not Paul) either used fragments of a genuine Pauline letter or supplied what he took to be detail of an authentic type by referring to Tychicus (2 Tim. 4:12; Titus 3:12). Finally it is likely that the Tychicus of Acts 20:4 is the same person, and the information supplied there makes it possible that Tychicus came from Ephesus, and was a companion of Paul as he gathered together the collection from the different churches to take to Jerusalem.

ZACCHAEUS is unusual in the fact that it is rare in the synoptic Gospels for those whom Jesus encountered, other than his own immediate disciples, to be named. The fact that Zacchaeus is named, in the incident describing his eagerness to see Jesus and his total commitment when challenged (Luke 19:1-10), together with the note of his shortness of stature, has characteristically divided New Testament scholars: some have seen these points as indicative of a genuine early tradition; others have supposed that this kind of detail, more commonly found in the fourth Gospel, points to a later tradition which developed, partly at least, to satisfy pious curiosity concerning homely details of this kind.

ZEBEDEE plays no personal part in the events described in the Gospels, but his sons, James and John, are frequently referred to by their father's name (e.g. Matt. 26:37), perhaps to avoid confusion with others named James and John. Zebedee himself was a fisherman on the lake of Galilee, based on Capernaum (Mark 16:20). Both his sons and his wife became followers of Jesus, and apparently left home (Matt. 27:55f.), but there is no evidence to indicate that Zebedee himself was influenced by Jesus' message.

ZECHARIAH is an extremely common Old Testament name, and it is in keeping with the character of the beginning of Luke's Gospel, which is full of Old Testament reminiscences, that one of its principal characters should be called Zechariah. The story told of him also has many Old Testament parallels: the faithful couple apparently too old to have a child, and therefore despised in a society in which the gift of children was taken to be a mark of divine favour. Abraham and Sarah, the parents of Samson in Judg. 13, and the parents of Samuel in 1 Sam. 1, all provide similar examples. Unparalleled, however, is the punishment of Zechariah for his failure to accept the divine message (Luke 1:20). After the son, John the Baptist, was born, the story reaches its climax with the song of praise, closely resembling a psalm, attributed to Zechariah, and now usually known as the Benedictus (Luke 1:68-79).

The almost fairy-tale-like character of this story has led to sharp differences of opinion as to whether any historical nucleus can be detected in it. Not the least of the problems is that Zechariah is said to have been of priestly descent (Luke 1:5), whereas Jesus, his kinsman, was of Davidic, Judahite, descent.

P A N N O N I A

D A C I A

I L L Y R I C U M

A D R I A T I C

S E A

THRACE

B L

I T A L Y

MACEDONIA

Byzantium

Rome

Philippi

BITHY

Thessalonica

Troas

Beroea

A

Pergamum

C

Sardis

H

Smyrna

Rhegium

A

Corinth

Athens

Ephesus

Laod

Pe

SICILY

LYC/

Syracuse

PAM

MALTA

CRETE

M E D I T E R R A N E A N

A F R I C A

Cyrene

Alex.

Carthage

C Y R E N A I C A

THE
NEW TESTAMENT
WORLD

0   100   200   300
miles

WFNW